HOLD IT AGAINST ME

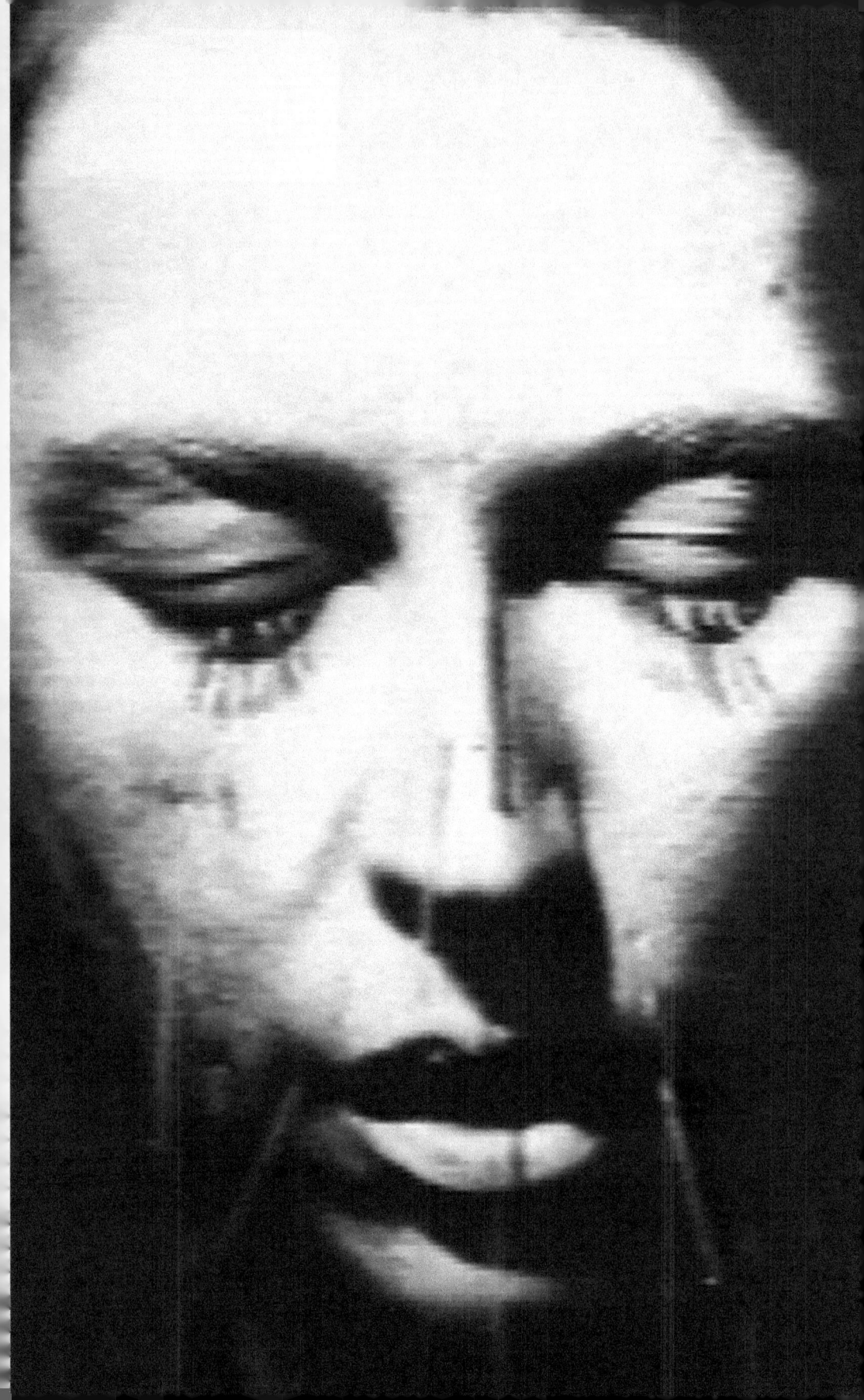

JENNIFER DOYLE

HOLD IT AGAINST ME

difficulty and emotion in contemporary art

Duke University Press *Durham and London* 2013

Designed by Amy Ruth Buchanan
Typeset in Garamond Premier Pro
by Copperline Book Services, Inc.

Frontispiece: Linda Mary Montano,
Mitchell's Death, 1978. Video (black and
white, sound). Edited by David Wagner.
From the archive and courtesy of Linda
Mary Montano.

MM | PUBLICATION OF THIS
BOOK HAS BEEN AIDED
BY A GRANT FROM THE MILLARD MEISS
PUBLICATION FUND OF THE COLLEGE
ART ASSOCIATION.

Library of Congress Cataloging-
in-Publication Data
Doyle, Jennifer.
Hold it against me : difficulty and emotion
in contemporary art / Jennifer Doyle.
p. cm.
Includes bibliographical references
and index.
ISBN 978-0-8223-5302-7 (cloth : alk. paper)
ISBN 978-0-8223-5313-3 (pbk. : alk. paper)
1. Emotions in art. 2. Art, Modern—
21st century—Psychological aspects.
3. Art, Modern—21st century—Themes,
motives. 4. Art criticism. I. Title.
NX650.E46D698 2013
709.05'1—dc23   2012044742

FOR RON.

CONTENTS

At the opening of *Mitchell's Death* (1978), Linda Montano's face appears on the screen as a ghostly blur just barely moving to the sound of her voice. That voice intones a monk-like chant. Montano is reciting the story of the death of her ex-husband from a gunshot wound. When her face comes into focus, we see that it is covered with acupuncture needles (fig. 1). Over the course of twenty-two minutes, Montano shares in a meditative drone the experience of absorbing the fact of Mitchell's death.[1] She takes us through the flow of events: the first phone call, then others, the turning of her mind to their relationship, the decision to fly to Kansas and attend the funeral. The performance is carved from the rhythm of the artist's breath as she pushes the story out and pauses for air. The story is sung with the same rhythm, in the same tone. She rehearses the cycles of thought and speech, the routines of grief. Finally, she describes being overcome by the need to see Mitchell's body, and touch it, to hold him. She sees him at the crematorium, touches his head, hands, and feet. As the story arcs from shock and grief to this scene, the image dissolves back into its ghostly blur.

Visually *Mitchell's Death* is restrained; we see only the artist's face, and it is immobilized. Montano's voice goes on and on; one's attention drifts and flows back. The story is a mantra; it feels as if it has been repeated so often

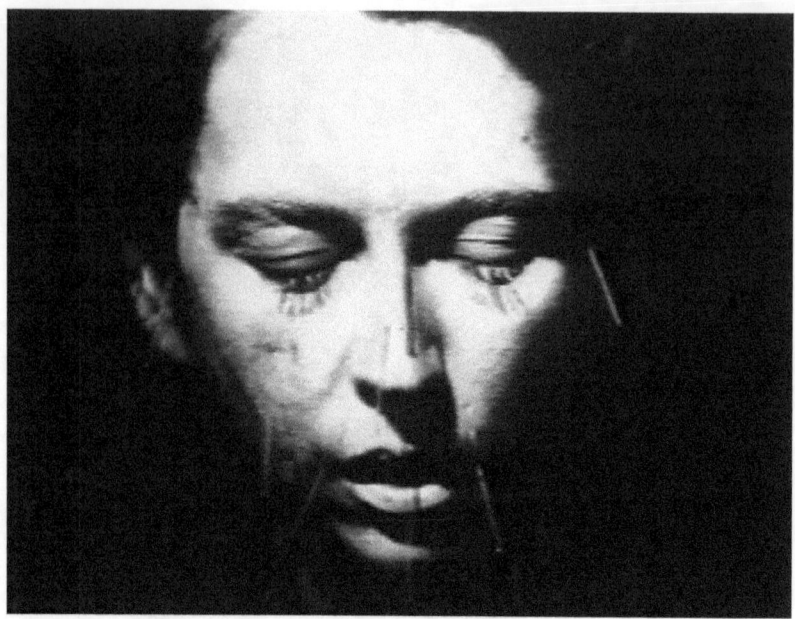

FIGURE 1. Linda Mary Montano, *Mitchell's Death*. 1978. Video (black and white, sound). Edited by David Wagner. Fom the archive and courtesy of Linda Mary Montano.

that its sequence is automatic for the speaker. Over the duration of the performance her voice is unwavering. The needles make her face a curiosity. It takes a little while to get used to the image. They tell us that there is a pain here that needs attention and that the artist performs this story as a healing ritual.

In spite of the difficulty of the image and the drone of her voice, Montano holds our attention. Her incantation radiates feeling as a strange hum. Addressing her decision to chant *Mitchell's Death*, she asks, "Don't singing words go to a more sensitive part of the brain than do spoken words?"[2] This might be true if only for the way her chanted delivery asks her audience to "tune in." To get it at all, you have to open and submit yourself to it.

Mitchell's Death is a difficult work in the sense meant by this book's subtitle. Its difficulty is inseparable from the emotions that the work produces. It is also woven into the form through which those feelings are produced. It is not a work one wants to watch. It has contradictory effects. On its surface it is conservative, offering only an image of the artist's face and the sound of her voice. At first glance, it looks and sounds boring. For those who commit to it, however, *Mitchell's Death* bodies forth the otherworldly texture of intense grief—that feeling of being removed from the world of the living, of feeling like a ghost, of being numb with it, of being lulled by the sound of grief's rhythms. *Mitchell's Death* addresses too the toll grief takes on language—indeed on all expression. In the flow of events that Montano shares with us, in the things spoken over and over again by the artist in the hope that this will be the last time she needs to recite them—or as a way of keeping this experience of loss alive—Mitchell's death emerges as a black hole, an absence that organizes the space around it. When Montano's voice and image fade, they seem to recede into that void.

———————

This book describes the process of learning how to write about work like *Mitchell's Death*, work that feels emotionally sincere or real and that produces a dense field of affect around it even as it seems to dismantle the mechanisms through which emotion is produced and consumed.[3] The artists I work with turn to emotion because this is where ideology does its most devastating work. As Theodor Adorno once observed, "the supreme independence" that we experience as pure feeling, unadulterated passion or joy is "precisely the tool of society."[4] This is where we come to know the contours of our selves, our bodies, our sense of soul—and this zone is always under constant policing and negotiation. The artists that interest me turn to emotion, feelings, and affect as a means not of narcissistic escape but of social engagement.

Over the past decade, I've been trying to write about how these artists take on emotion, as subject and material, especially where such work requires an engaged form of spectatorship. For years I sat with the work of three artists in particular: Ron Athey, Carrie Mae Weems, and David Wojnarowicz. For a long time, I made little progress and was deeply frustrated by the trouble I had writing about the three works to which I was drawn: *Dissociative Sparkle, From Here I Saw What Happened and I Cried,* and *Untitled (Hujar Dead).* All three are rich with affect, but none can be described as expressive in any traditional sense (none, in other words, can be explained as a representation of how the artist feels). All three feel political, but *why* they do is complicated. They are unnerving, depressing, or upsetting; none offers the positive message one associates with political art, and they each (differently) reject the basic geometries of identity and politics that normally ground discussions of art, identity, and politics. They leave us in a strange space: like *Mitchell's Death*, each work pushes the spectator away and draws her in at the same time. And as hard as they are (in subject and in tone), all three are deeply moving (for some, including myself).

That very fact seemed to cause me to stall. My initial attempts to write about these works felt hollow and forced or maudlin. Sometimes the affect of my own writing was at complete odds with the work, adding a level of pathos to something that was actually restrained, or hesitancy where a work was furious or melodramatic. The book began to find its focus only when I started to pay attention to the nature of the difficulty of writing about these works: in each of the works that I was drawn to, difficulty itself was an integral part of its emotional landscape.

Difficulty has long functioned as a keyword in poetics, music criticism, and, to a lesser extent, film studies. Technically, when a literary critic identifies a poem as difficult she makes no value judgment: the word is used to describe the poem's accessibility (not only in terms of comprehension but in terms of pleasure). "Poetic difficulty," writes John Vincent, "serves as a trace of drift or pulsion into the unmeaning, unknowable, and unspeakable. Much of the most exciting modern and contemporary poetry hovers at this edge, its lexical and affective power arising from unmappable, but somehow accessible, journeys out of and back into the known."[5] A poem can be hard to understand—actively so—and still be very good and very moving. When we teach such works, we often begin discussion by asking students not "What does this poem mean?" but "What makes this poem hard to read?" and "Is it hard to understand, hard to enjoy—both?" The answers to these questions might be textual (a density of references), contextual (its rhetoric may seem strange to contemporary readers), narrative (characters with whom one can't relate), or interpretive (the work may in fact resist the effort to make sense of it).

Usually the critic's mandate is to resolve difficulty when we encounter it, to write as if that difficulty doesn't exist for us, even as we produce that difficulty as a noble, productive challenge, worth confronting and working through. Instead of erasing the labor of interpretation and instead of writing as if the critic's aim is to resolve difficulty, in *Queer Lyrics: Difficulty and Closure in American Poetry* Vincent imagines certain kinds of difficulties as deeply pleasurable and important, *especially* where they can't be resolved. Some of the decisions I make in this book were directly modeled after Vincent's writing about these kinds of difficulty and the readers who are drawn to them. *Queer Lyrics* extends and critiques George Steiner's essay "On Difficulty" (1978). Today Steiner's insights are a given in literary criticism. Understanding a poem, he argued, requires sensitivity to the ways that a reader encounters poetic interference or obstacles to understanding. The failure to get a poem is not always taken as the reader's fault but may signal a defining aspect of the work's poetic structure; difficulty may in fact be integral to the work's overall meaning. Steiner offers an analysis of four categories of poetic difficulty: contingent (the challenge posed by what you happen to know or not know), modal (the challenge posed by works produced from within communities whose values and sensibilities are alien to yours, often by virtue of historical shifts in taste and canonicity), tactical (the challenge created by the author who wants you to work to resolve the work's meaning), and ontological (the challenge of works that call into question the very nature of poetic expression). Steiner's categories are useful and provocative rubrics for thinking about difficulty within visual culture (and I discuss them substantially in the notes).[6] But they are not as important to this book as is the place from which Steiner begins: the reader. His typology requires the reader and that reader's desire to make sense of the poem. His essay was part of a movement in literary studies toward understanding the literary text as dependent upon the context of our encounters with it.[7] If I've consigned discussion of Steiner's categories to a long note, it is to make room in this preface for the reader.

Steiner's reader is a remarkably abstract and depersonalized figure. As Vincent rightly observes, his reader is looking for the same thing (understanding), seeking the same pleasures (of knowing), and reading for the same reasons (a sense of mastery over the text). "Steiner celebrates the extreme edge of sense making, but decries and disregards nonsense making. His typology . . . holds when a reader's only desire is the desire for sense, elastically defined but referencing a fantasy of sheer lucidity."[8] The forms of difficulty addressed by Steiner all revolve around the frustration of the desire to understand, and they are ultimately solvable. Vincent asks, "What about other kinds of readers?" Is it possible to imagine readers who *don't* want closure, whose reading practices are not fueled by a penetrative, epistemic drive, moving always toward "deeper" levels of meaning? What about the "perverse" reader who takes pleasure in those aspects of a poem that frustrate, that don't fall in line, *ever*. What about the reader who enjoys the surface of writing? This reader is more attached to what Roland Barthes called "the pleasures of the text" (the fluid creation which is always unfolding in the act of reading) than in reaching any definitive meaning that would bring such a process to a conclusion.[9]

Vincent works with an expanded sense of difficulty; he even makes room in his practice for difficult people, such as the poet Jack Spicer, who drank too much and hated the "poetry establishment" and generally made it very hard to write about his work. He gives us a way to think about such artists without apologizing for their refusal to cooperate with disciplining mechanisms, placing the poet's failures at the center of an ethics of radical refusal. Vincent furthermore takes a strong stand against Steiner's "project of cataloging difficulty." That typology, however provisional, "disregards the fundamentally constitutive vastness and variety of interpretive communities and readerly desires."[10] Maintaining his commitment to the fluid complexity of some forms of difficulty, Vincent decides against packaging his insights into the writing of Spicer, Marianne Moore, and John Ashbery as an accumulation of discrete categories.

Vincent's approach to poetic difficulty leads the way for us, as art critics, to ask what people want from works like *Mitchell's Death* but also indicates the care one must take in order to avoid simplifying difficulty.[11] My aim is not to produce a reader who can point and declare, "The difficulty of this performance belongs to category 4." Nor will this book tell the reader how to identify specific emotions as they appear in works of art. I hesitate to add more negative promises regarding what this book *won't* do, but I also avoid naming, once and for all, the difference between an affect, an emotion, and a feeling. I am not convinced that art defined by its work with affect, emotion, or feeling can be appreciated using a critical language that presumes (even provisionally) that feelings are self-evident, that emotions can be parsed and catalogued, produced and consumed at will. In any case, mastery over the terms *difficulty*, *emotion*, and *affect* won't lead to a better understanding of the individual works I discuss here. Each takes us to a different place, where emotion is a site of unraveling and dispossession. This book uses the terms *difficulty* and *emotion* in order to take up the questions of who is being dispossessed of what, who is being unraveled, how and why.

One of the most significant forms of unraveling addressed by this book is that of the art controversy. We will spend time with the work of three people who have appeared in news headlines as scandalous examples of what artists get away with (Aliza Shvarts, Ron Athey, and David Wojnarowicz). In these cases, their work was presented as universally shocking—not because it is emotionally intense but because the subjects of their works are so politically charged. Art controversy invariably simplifies its object. The announcement that an artwork has become controversial is a promise that we will not be given the chance to talk about its difficulty; discussion of the work will be organized by the controversy it provoked and not by a need to come to grips with the work itself—even as that difficulty may well be the very thing that moved people to outrage.

Work marked as controversial is oversimplified and marginalized not only by journalists and politicians but also by scholars and critics. It is troubling that in the long wake of the culture wars of the late 1980s and early 1990s, we have rarely attempted to explain such work. Even those of us who defend it often do so at the cost of actually confronting the work itself: we tend to defend controversial work by asserting what it is *not*, what it does not do. To

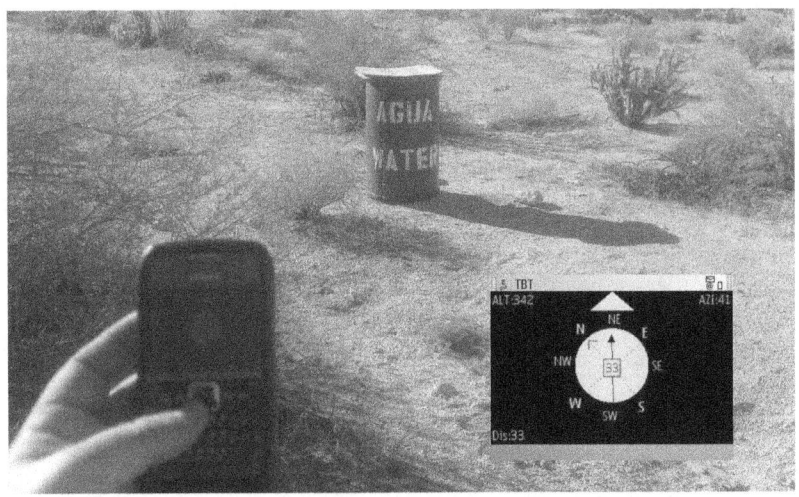

FIGURE 2. Electronic Disturbance Theater / b.a.n.g.lab (Ricardo Domínguez, Brett Stalbaum, Micha Cárdenas, Amy Carroll, and José Najarro), *Transborder Immigrant Tool*. 2011. Courtesy of Electronic Disturbance Theater 2.0 / b.a.n.g.lab.

cite cases I address in this book: responding to the scandal of Aliza Shvarts's performance in 2008, in which she artificially inseminated herself, the few critics who defended her explained that she did not give herself abortions, as was asserted by conservative pundits. In defending the artist against headline accusations, critics and scholars have explained that in *Four Scenes in a Harsh Life* Ron Athey did not expose his audiences to HIV-infected blood, as was asserted by myriad newspapers and by the Republican senator Jesse Helms in his assault on the National Endowment for the Arts in 1994. Art historians and critics have explained that David Wojnarowicz's work is not the pornography the American Family Association represented it to be in 1990. (The artist himself won a lawsuit against the AFA for misrepresenting his work in a pamphlet.) We have more recently defended his anti-Catholic diatribes by asserting the artist's spirituality.[12]

Apologies and denials like this are at best weak defenses of these projects, and in some cases they are complete disavowals of the work's politics. Take, for example, the accusation that Ricardo Dominguez and his b.a.n.g.lab collective produced an artwork designed to help people to cross the Mexico-U.S. border (*Transborder Immigrant Tool*; fig. 2). Those of us defending the project often did so by explaining that the accusation was unfounded and that Dominguez is not a migrant-smuggling "coyote." The artists themselves, however, present *Transborder Immigrant Tool* as a working mobile phone application designed to map water sources for those crossing the border. Ignoring their assertions of its practical application with the apology "It's only art" is not a defense of the work: it is a bad faith capitulation to its critics. The work of defending artists against accusations launched by people who hate the idea of the work (or of the queer, feminist, antiracist, migrant artist) has derailed us into declaring that their work has no real-world impact. Most of our defenses of these practices minimize the challenge of these works and the anger that the work can provoke. But we've been shown again and again that this kind of response to the discourse of controversy does nothing to quell scandal, to calm the nerves of extremists and reactionary politicians. If anything, we bare our throats with the exclamation "But it's only art." I can think of no more effective argument for privatizing the arts than the assertion that an artist never meant to make a difference.

Although b.a.n.g.lab's work is clearly pitched at an anti-immigrant public sphere, shocking conservatives is not the work's aim, nor is it the aim of any of the works discussed in this book. *Four Scenes in a Harsh Life* is about power and desire, pain and pleasure. It has the blood-and-flesh poetics of art practiced in the shadow of the AIDS pandemic. Although the actual performance was misrepresented in the phobic press, the fears spoken by Athey's critics tap into something quite real about his work. Athey's performances are intense not only for those uneasy with the sight (and smell) of blood. They sometimes hover over intensely masochistic scenes and foreground the unnerving intimacy of aggression and desire. And his audiences are drawn to that. Shvarts's untitled project depends on and exploits the deep stigmatization of abortion in even liberal discourse. The artist deliberately left open the possibility that she may have interrupted a pregnancy in her action. How people have responded to the idea of this possibility is a part of the work. In the wake of recent attempts in the United States to defund Planned Parenthood and expand the criminalization of abortion, this aspect of her project has only become more relevant, more politically loaded. Wojnarowicz's work is explicitly concerned with desire, love, and intimacy between men. It is frank in its depictions of a sexual life, and he sometimes used gay pornography as source material. He was quite clear about his hatred for the Catholic Church and suspicious too of institutional discourse on spirituality. (As he put it himself, "I have about as much spirituality as a humpback toad.")[13] Given its prohibition of condom use, one would have trouble arguing against his characterization of the Catholic Church's policies as murderous. Many of the Catholic icons that appear in Wojnarowicz's work are there to signal Church hypocrisy, to question the destruction of spirituality by institutionalized religion, and also to tap into the queer underbelly of Catholic iconography. He worked with images of violence and suffering lifted from the lives of saints, the same archive used by Athey and other queer artists, from Caravaggio to Jean Genet and Pier Paolo Pasolini. Before we can argue successfully for the necessity of work that pushes most people past their comfort zones, we need to acknowledge what that work actually *does*. We need to tune in to how they do this and absorb their methods. That is the lesson I learned from Linda Montano. If we want to hear what this work is about, we need to listen to it more carefully and allow ourselves to be moved.

————

This book places controversial works into an expanded conversation about difficulty, emotion, and identity. There is already room in the art world for acknowledging that certain forms of difficulty are good for us: the illegibility of nonfigurative and nonrepresentational work; the austerity of abstraction and minimalism; the rigor of institution critique. There is a lot of language out there celebrating the silence of John Cage, the sparseness of Donald Judd. The difficulty of a work of art that withholds, that turns its back on the spectator, that eliminates sentiment and romance is so fully absorbed into the sociology of contemporary art that for the fully initiated such works don't feel very hard at all. The difficulty under examination here is quite different: it turns to the viewer, in some cases making him or her into a witness, or even a participant.[14] This can make people uncomfortable in ways that feel distinctly personal.

Finally, a few more words about the structure and content of this book: its arguments unfold cyclically and cumulatively. Its chapters explore the idea of difficulty, ideologies of emotion, and how emotion circulates in and around art in flows that are directed by histories that are simultaneously personal and political. The tone and pace of this book shifts. Readings of individual artworks reflect their affective pitch. The book's opening chapter examines the project's central terms and revolves around an analysis of my own resistance to the idea of *Held*, a one-on-one performance by Adrian Howells. This chapter is followed by three studies of works that offer different roads into a conversation about difficulty and emotion: Aliza Shvarts's *Untitled*, Thomas Eakins's *The Gross Clinic*, and Ron Athey's *Dissociative Sparkle*. Four additional works form the backbone of chapters 3 and 4 and their discussion of the relationship between emotion, identity, and politics: Franko B's *I Miss You*, Nao Bustamante's *Neapolitan*, James Luna's *History of the Luiseño People*, and Carrie Mae Weems's *From Here I Saw What Happened and I Cried*. The affective economy of these works differs significantly from the works in chapter 2: all four are much more explicitly about emotion, but as we move from Franko B to Weems, those emotions will be put under increasing pressure and into more and more overdetermined environments. In these two chapters I regularly step back from discussion of these specific works in order to consider why contemporary art criticism has such a strange attitude regarding work like this, and then develop my points regarding difficulty and emotion, the relationship of emotion to identity, and the way discourses of emotion, identity, and history come together.

Thinking about emotion and art requires thinking about the nature of expression. It also requires thinking about identity as a thing produced through (and dissolved in) emotion. The deeper we get into this subject, the closer we get to issues at the core of art history and the challenge of acknowledging a broader spectrum of viewers, seeking a wider range of experiences than those recognized by traditional articulations of that discipline. The term *history* comes under unique pressure here, especially in Luna's and Weems's works and in the book's concluding discussion of Wojnarowicz's *Untitled (Hujar Dead)*.

My bibliography is strongly informed by other fields: film criticism, feminist philosophy, queer and critical theory, literary and cultural studies. I have tried to write this for the nonacademic reader interested in contemporary art, by which I mean the reader who is not fully saturated with art criticism and theory. For this reason (with a few exceptions) I have moved many of the book's most obviously academic points to notes. The tone and structure of this book closely resembles how I teach this material. Recognizing that the material itself is hard, in the classroom I usually take a soft approach. I give more time to individual works with a dense and what I call "noisy" affective field, encouraging a nonjudgmental attitude in my students as they look at work that challenges their ideas about what art is, as well as their ideas about fundamental social issues. (Nearly all of the work discussed in this book does both.) As a teacher, I also advocate for a rigorous but also generous classroom environment, in which students can ask questions without fear of seeming ignorant or naïve. Expecting students to be familiar with sadomasochistic performance, for example, is both impractical and wrongheaded.

It turns out, however, that some of our students are far more receptive to this work than the average art critic. I've found these supposedly noncosmopolitan students to be open-minded and eager to make connections to the emotional intensity of Wojnarowicz or the political complexity of Weems and especially the music they listen to (which, in the Inland Empire, is a lot of rap, punk, and heavy metal). That contrast—between the interest and openness of some of our students and the jaded disaffection of much art criticism—led me to put terms like *emotion* and *sincerity* at the heart of this book. To insist on them. They may operate in critical parlance as synonyms for the naïve and the simple, but they are the very things that make these works difficult, complicated, hard to talk about, and worth the effort.

ACKNOWLEDGEMENTS

I start by thanking my family: Justina and Bob Cassavell, Jocelyn and Kyle Sell, and my parents, Michael and Jeanne Doyle. This book is the culmination of a process begun in a conversation with my parents about David Wojnarowicz's work.

A large group of friends and colleagues supported me while writing this book: José Muñoz, Ming Yuen S. Ma, Molly McGarry, Heather Lukes, Karen Tongson, Kathleen McHugh, Margherita Sprio, Mandy Merck, George Haggerty, Adrià Julià, Jim Tobias, Michelle Raheja, Traise Yamamoto, John Cairns, Dominic Johnson, Vaginal Davis, Amelia Jones, Theasa Tuohy, Victoria Shannon, Margherita Long, and Torsten Leder. I am lucky to enjoy the support and companionship of so many wonderful people.

The English Department at the University of California, Riverside, is a terrific home for interdisciplinary scholarship. We do more than work together: we advocate for each other. Today we do so as a way to remember our colleagues Greg Bredbeck, Emory Elliott, and Lindon Barrett, while fighting off the wolves of an oligarchy that would strip public education for parts and abandon those we serve.

I am especially grateful to all of the artists who have lent their support to this project: Ron Athey, Franko B, Nao Bustamante, Adrian Howells, James

Luna, Aliza Shvarts, and Carrie Mae Weems. John Vincent's *Queer Lyrics* sat on my desk and was much in use while I wrote this. Lauren Berlant and Gavin Butt pushed this book forward with their rigorous attention to drafts and frank observations about where the writing drifted away from the project's heart. The first complete draft of this book was written in the space of a correspondence with Şenol Şentürk. What is usually an isolating experience was quite the opposite because of this.

I owe a special thanks to Gavin Butt and everyone at Goldsmiths College; much of the book's foundation and structure was generated while I was in residence in the Department of Visual Cultures. It simply would not have been written without the Leverhulme Fellowship that supported this residency. I am also deeply grateful to Hedi El Kholti for the invitation to contribute to *David Wojnarowicz: A Definitive History of Five or Six Years on the Lower East Side*. That essay ("A Thin Line") is the earliest draft of this book's conclusion. Nicholas Baume's invitation to write "Critical Tears: Melodrama and Museums" in support of the Boston Institute of Contemporary Art exhibit *Getting Emotional* was also instrumental in getting this project going. Marc Mayer invited me to contribute a series of blog articles on controversy for Art21's website, and that was the first time I tested using the language of difficulty for thinking about Athey, Weems, and Wojnarowicz. Early versions of this project were written while I was in residence at the Center for Humanities at Grinnell College and at the Center for Ideas and Society at UC Riverside. My fellow residents, Ken Rogers, Joe Childers, and Margherita Long, read tentative drafts of my work on Wojnarowicz and provided much needed support and guidance. Finishing this book while working as the director of Graduate Studies was possible only because our graduate student advisor, Tina Feldmann, is so caring and knowledgeable.

Marvin J. Taylor and the staff at NYU's Fales Special Collections Library made working with David Wojnarowicz's papers maximally productive; the Downtown Collection is an incredible resource, and we are lucky that this material is housed in such a generous environment.

Ciara Ennis, who was then at the California Museum of Photography, Shane Shukis and Tyler Stallings at the Sweeney Art Gallery at UC Riverside, Robert Crouch, Carol Stakenas, and the folks at Los Angeles Contemporary Exhibitions supported curatorial projects that informed the writing of this book. "The Ethics of Presence / You Belong to Me" and "I Feel Different" were funded by the University of California Humanities Research Institute and the Pasadena Art Alliance, respectively. The administrative labor of "You Belong to Me" fell on Laura Lozon's desk at the Center of Ideas and

Society, and she made that complex event work. Lezley Saar, Susan Silton, Niña Yhared (1814), and Monica Duncan contributed beautiful and moody work to "I Feel Different." Ursula Rucker brought her magnificent words and music to "I.E. You Belong to Me," and Julie Tolentino, Heather Cassils, and Zackary Drucker staged unforgettable performative interventions for "You Belong to Me." Julie, Michelle Johnson, and Stosh "Pigpen" Fila helped to produce that event and keep things flowing. I still can't believe we all pulled that off. Shane, I must thank you twice. Thank you.

Renaud, *je l'ai finit sous les platanes, pas trop loin de toi.*

Ron, thank you for sharing your archive and your friendship and for reminding me just why I got into this in the first place. This book is dedicated, with love, to you.

1 INTRODUCING DIFFICULTY

Critics have limits. Our faculties break down when an artwork reminds us of something so painful, or makes us so mad, or is something we like so much we struggle to write about it. Or when we are tired and having a bad day. There are whole genres certain critics just don't get (for Adorno, famously, it was jazz). Critics can be tone deaf; we can miss the pleasures others take, ignore the irritation that others feel. We can be willful and stubborn, blind to the dwindling relevance of those artists we love and indifferent to the emergence of new practices we don't understand. We all have limits that look pretty uncritical from most angles, and we rarely know these limits until we encounter them.

I begin this chapter with a story about hitting my own wall. In the fall of 2007, I booked and then failed to make an appointment for a one-on-one performance encounter with the English artist Adrian Howells. I had also made an appointment that day at a beauty salon for a cut and color, far too close to the timeslot I'd arranged to see Howells's performance. My hair was covered in a mud of dye and wrapped in plastic when I looked at my watch and realized that I needed to be across London in an hour, and it would take at least that to get there. I flipped through magazines, doing the math in my head. Anxiety

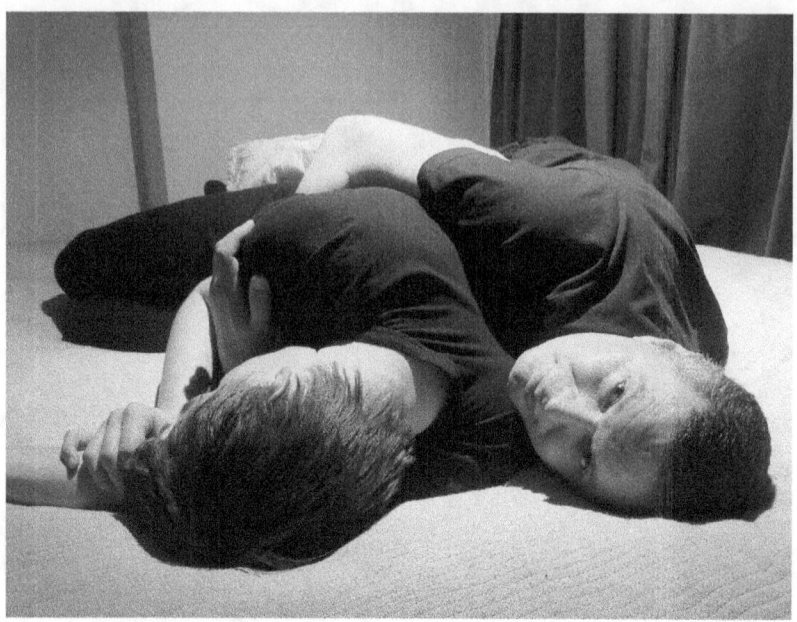

FIGURE 3. Adrian Howells, *Held*. Fierce Festival, Glasgow. 2006.
Courtesy of Adrian Howells.

rose like a tide in my throat as I realized that there was no way I was going to
make it there. I dug the phone out of my purse and called to cancel, without,
however, leaving enough time for another person to take my place.

It was a careless and ordinary mistake. But the nature of Howells's performance and my reaction to missing the appointment suggested that something
more was in play. Howells's work maximizes the possibilities of what he describes as "accelerated intimacy." He has explored the contours of confession
and autobiography in performances that rehearse the most painful and embar-
rassing moments in his history for small audiences, and sometimes audiences
of one. In *Held*, Howells invites his audience into three twenty-minute scenes.
First, they sit at a table, drink tea, and chat. Then they sit together on a couch
in front of the television and hold hands. Last, they go up to a bedroom, lie
down together, and spoon (fig. 3). Participants respond to this performance
differently. Some are ill at ease and on their guard; some make themselves right
at home. One person fell asleep. When Howells stages a performance like this,
he sees perhaps six people in a day. As one might imagine, these appointments
are hard to come by. I felt the full weight of this; by screwing up the appointment, I prevented another person from seeing his work.

Later that day I went to the venue's address to meet friends who had honored their appointments. I held in my hands a small gift of cookies, brought to convey my apologies to the artist. Howells had just finished up for the day when I got there. I wanted to be simply apologetic, but instead I found myself fighting back tears—and, worse, failing to keep them in check. We drank tea and ate the cookies. I was embarrassed and self-conscious that my affect risked expanding into a selfish display of abjection: shame mounted as a kind of counterattack.

Howells was sympathetic and warm. Looking at him through my tears, I felt even worse. My emotionality was well out of proportion to the circumstance. My friends and I walked back to the train station. As I listened to them talk about their experience of *Held*, I tried to come to terms with the fact that I'd subconsciously sabotaged my appointment. I'd been looking forward to it all week, had been careful to make sure I got the timeslot, and then scheduled a pointless event right over it. Clearly the whole idea of *Held* challenged me. Apparently I couldn't inhabit the structure of that encounter without being overwhelmed—by what, though?

I was afraid of what might happen, of how it might make me feel. I think too I was equally put off by its artificiality—not that my own feelings would be inauthentic but that they would be delivered within a temporary architecture of intimacy. What happens at the end of the appointment? I was attracted enough to the idea to schedule the appointment but disturbed enough that I made it impossible for me to honor it. In doing so, I subconsciously preempted the betrayal I expected, for the experience of *Held* would feel either very empty and disappointing or very *full* and disappointing. I had reacted badly to what Jon Cairns describes as the "confusing context of 'staged' intimacy" in which Howells works.[1] His medium is the affective density of the interaction between artist and audience, and even a failure like mine should be understood as part of the work's performative field. By failing to make the appointment, by failing to cancel in time to allow another person to take my place, and then by trekking down there anyway to solicit his forgiveness, I managed to extract the caretaking that Howells offered within the boundaries of *Held* but outside the boundaries of the event. I insisted on getting what I thought the artist had promised me, but on my own terms, and after blowing him off. (Of course, behind this self-analysis are years of therapy. The responsibility to each other's time is one of the first things one works through with an analyst, especially if one has missed an appointment or is habitually late.)

Until that day I had considered myself a seasoned spectator to some of the most challenging forms of performance. When we think about challenging performance art, we generally mean not the domestic normalcy cited by *Held* but what is often described as "extreme" performance involving violence toward the body and sexualized forms of display. Familiar with this kind of work (e.g., the work of Ron Athey, Bob Flanagan, Franko B, Kembra Pfahler, Kira O'Reilly), I had come to assume that there was nothing I couldn't handle. I would say, in fact, that prior to this experience I was cavalier about my own limits and dismissive of others', as if it were a moral failing to be averse to the sight of blood or be uncomfortable with the idea of live performances engaging in acts that look (and sometimes are) sexual. Howells showed me how deluded I'd been: the mere idea of certain kinds of performance provoked in me a defensive need to assert control over my place in the picture. As a spectator to performance art, I might have a high tolerance for blood, nudity, and noise, but I seem to have a lower tolerance for work engaged with more ordinary forms of relational intimacy, for the things that "feel" like life and therefore cut too close.

———————

This book is an experiment in thinking about the difficulty that many of us have with some forms of contemporary art and the centrality of emotion to that kind of difficulty. Emotion can make our experience of art harder, but it also makes that experience more interesting. It may make things harder because the work provokes unpleasant or painful feelings. It may also make things more complicated; an artwork might provoke contradictory feelings, and it may provoke in the viewer feelings that are at odds with the affective culture of its context. Emotions themselves are very complicated. They can be impossible to stabilize. For example, none of the following questions is easy to answer: Does a feeling come from inside the spectator or from the artwork? Does an artwork represent feeling? Whose: the artist's or the viewer's? Does a work make feelings? How?

The setting for our encounters with art can make thinking about our feelings especially confusing. For all the ways that emotion animates the way we talk about art—being "carried away" or "moved" by the beauty of a painting, for example—it can be hard to have intense feelings in museums when those feelings go against social protocol. In an art gallery, anger, tears, arousal, and certain kinds of laughter may appear to signal the disintegration of composure, naïveté, and a lack of class. In such spaces, as much as we are encouraged to be moved by works of art, we are also encouraged to remain cool. One of the primary disciplinary contributions of cultural studies to the study of art and literature is its observation that questions of aesthetic judgment are questions of taste and that they are historically and socially conditioned.[2] They reflect and reproduce the values of a class. What you enjoy, how you enjoy it, and how you express that enjoyment can reveal a lot about who you are and where you come from. For this reason, few places will make people more self-conscious of their reactions than a museum or an art gallery. Museums and art galleries are like schools: they are spaces in which we encounter culture, usually on someone else's terms. Many find themselves at odds with a world in which appearing to be cool and aloof is the mark of sophistication. Many of us feel weird and ill at ease before we even cross a museum's threshold. As Jennifer González writes, "The museum as a whole, as an ideological home, does not welcome us equally."[3]

Thankfully, museums and galleries are not the only grounds upon which we encounter art. Many artists project their work into completely different social spaces, in no small part because they want to avoid the affective protocols of official culture. Festivals, underground music venues, city streets, fields, deserts, and private homes can all be more generous in terms of the range of affects they will accommodate. The mood of such contexts is very important to how we experience works of art, for understanding how those works can develop and how their meanings shift as they migrate from one social context to another. Some artists choose to work from the edges of the social spaces of art-making; as practitioners of challenging art, they know all too well the difficulty such work presents to schools, galleries, and museums and so work happily in alternative venues. As critics, what are our responsibilities toward work that quite literally takes us out of our comfort zone, and toward the audiences who seek out these experiences?

Hard Feelings

I was caught off guard by my reaction to *Held* not only because I am a regular at performance art events that people might characterize as extreme but because I am also an avid consumer of cinematic melodrama (*Stella Dallas* is one of my favorite movies) and nearly all forms of novels that demand emotional investment from their readers (from the sugary *Little Women* to the grim *Germinal*). In general, I love a good weepie like *Now, Voyager*, and I eat up the stark realism of a film like *Matewan*. Perhaps it's the professor in me (always looking for the teachable moment), but my reaction to the idea of *Held* made me reexamine how I thought about the emotionality of such work. Previously I'd approached emotion as something that cuts across mediums; for example, I thought of a sentimental pop song as like a sentimental novel or film, as if sentimentality were a thing in and of itself, which a text might embody and communicate.

The sentimentality deployed within Howells's performances has its own particular challenges. Much of his work has evolved around a feminine persona named Adrienne. In *An Audience with Adrienne* (2007), for example, Adrienne invites people to watch home movies with her and to talk about episodes from her life that participants select from a café-style menu. Audience members may be invited to share their own stories. Reviewing that work for *The Guardian*, Lyn Gardner explains that the "unthreatening realm of the domestic" offers the viewer-participant "a direct conduit to our own childhoods, the episodes we recall with pin-sharp clarity and those we bury somewhere deep inside and try to forget."[4] The coziness of the domestic space is a lure; as any student of sentimental fiction knows, homes are haunted. Howells invites his audience into a queer space of intimacy whose edges are shaped by failure and isolation. (What domestic scene isn't?) *Held* distills the autobiographical exchange of his other projects to the act of simply keeping company.

There is something jarring about the idea of Howells receiving visitors for *Held*, as if this home were a bordello offering not the sexual excitement of the mistress but the grounding companionship of the wife. He may use the innocence of domestic normalcy to frame your encounter with him, but this very slight shift in the most banal scene of intimacy (from that of a romantic couple to that of an artist and his audience; from that of straight romance to queer domesticity) exposes just how loaded, how overdetermined that scene of domestic intimacy is for many of us. Cairns therefore describes the artist as practicing an ambivalent form of intimacy—a fundamentally queer occupation of domestic, personal, feminine, and reproductive scenes in which sites associated with privacy and safety become instead scenes of exposure. Lauren Berlant describes these kinds of spaces as "intimate publics"; Tavia Nyong'o uses the term *extimate* to suggest how they can *fail*, leaving us feeling more alone than ever.[5]

If we expect such a performance to be easy on the spectator, it is because we've already coded these terms (privacy, domesticity, the personal) as well as the feminized labor that defines them (nurturing, supporting, caring) as such. My failure as an audience for Howells forced me to take notice of the contingency of difficulty and consider the place of affect and emotion in a conversation about what makes a work hard for one person and easy for another. Those contingencies pertain not only to the person (and his or her history) but also to that person's conditioning as a viewer, reader, and audience member.

Comparing different forms—novels, music, films, and visual art—one might ask why we are prepared to accept the value of feeling bad when we read a novel, for example, but are less prepared to do so when we go to a museum. Why is it easier for us to watch an upsetting movie than it is to keep company with contemporary art that makes similar emotional demands on us? Why should the idea of attending Howells's performance be more unsettling than sitting through a movie like *Secrets and Lies* (1996) or *Steel Magnolias* (1989)? Most of the works of art I discuss in this book ask far less from their audiences in terms of time and emotional investment than does a feature length-film. (*Held*, for example, is relatively long for performance art, and lasts an hour.) Similarly, why is it easier for many of us to read an upsetting novel than to attend a performance event in which our comfort zone is being challenged? When I read Cormac McCarthy's *The Road* (2006)—a painful postapocalyptic nightmare in which refugees wander a barren planet, surrounded by starvation, rape, and cannibalism—I felt like someone had ripped out a piece of my soul. Typical for the author, its flatly narrated portrait of a world of extreme violence is also a deeply sexist novel in which women figure as dead weight, objects of rape, or emptied-out symbols of salvation. Finishing it was (for me) an emotional chore. *The Road* won the Pulitzer Prize, Oprah selected it for her book club, and it was made into a film starring Viggo Mortensen. As readers and filmgoers, we are, apparently, eager to suffer. Contemporary art presenting its audiences with challenging, urgent, but far less cruel images, on the other hand, tends to provoke moral outrage, even when it asks far less of us than do these other genres. So when I ask, "Why is it harder?," I am referring not only to our individual reactions to the idea of certain kinds of works but also to the social contexts that frame those reactions. Try contrasting the reaction to Chris Ofili's *Holy Virgin Mary* (1997), Ron Athey's *Four Scenes in a Harsh Life* (1994), or David Wojnarowicz's *A Fire in My Belly* (1986–87) with the celebration of McCarthy's novel or the laurels awarded the artists behind difficult films.[6] Think about it: it takes days to read a novel, and a feature-length film like Lars Von Trier's bleak *Dancer in the Dark* (2000) demands far more from its audience than does looking at Ofili's work or watching an Athey performance or a short film by Wojnarowicz. Maggie Nelson describes that director's cruelty as both unforgiving and self-righteous: "Von Trier's cruelty does not lie in any capacity to strip away cant or delusion, but rather in an ability to construct malignant, ultimately conventional fictions that masquerade as parables of profundity, or as protests against the brutalities of the man's world in which we must inevitably live and suffer."[7] Thus this kind of work accrues cultural value not in spite of its cruelty but because of it: it rationalizes the brutality of the status quo. It presents "the way things are" as realism, as insight, when in fact it is pure ideology. If people have reacted to work by Ofili, Athey, and Wojnarowicz as if it represented the absolute limit of the tolerable, it is because that work bucks against those conventional narratives regarding the brutal, the abject, and the obscene.

Institutions struggle to find solid ground on which they might argue for the necessity of art that not only is *about* hard feelings but *produces* them.[8] "More and more," writes Wendy Steiner, "people do not wish art, criticism, and education to present reality as problematic." She also suggests that the Left has not helped itself by presenting art criticism as a deadening of feeling: "An education in contemporary art seems like an arduous training in alienation. Aesthetic maturity is the ability to take contemporary art on the chin."[9] Lucy Lippard expresses sympathy with a similar complaint lodged by Wojnarowicz. Writing about the contrast between the "literalness" of his work and the opacity of the work of his contemporaries, he observes, "There's so much art out there that doesn't read. The information is so oblique that you can't get it unless there's a library next to it. Creating an elite in the art world, in terms of how one gets the joke or can understand the information, is no better than what happens in the larger social structure. You see group shows where there are bits of things that touch you but they are really just a few steps above a blank."[10] In an essay on the artist, Lippard responds, "Too true. In June 1990, I was wandering through a group show called 'Quiet Trauma' at the Milford Gallery in New York, wondering why the traumas were virtually invisible, why so few artists can say what they think; why the fear that it is uncool to show feelings on surface, to explain one's work in the titles or captions, seems so universally internalized." She came across *Untitled (Hujar Dead)* (1988–89), the subject of this book's conclusion, and found it "electrifying in every sense that art can be."[11]

Art criticism has aligned one form of difficulty (in which a work's meaning is not readily available to the viewer) with a regulation of affect (in which opacity, the difficulty of meaning, is packaged as cool, distanced, and anti-emotional). Galleries, museums, and magazines sell this marriage of the impenetrable and the unmovable as Art, as if those of us who go to galleries and museums (or become art historians) are doing so in order to be relieved of the burdens of an emotional life.

Patrolling the Border between Art and Politics

In the United States, those of us who actively seek out the literal and electrifying have had trouble finding a place in the official culture (or history) of contemporary art. It is as if our desires as audience members are alien. Much of this is due to the "NEA wars" of the 1990s, in which Athey and Wojnarowicz figured, alongside Annie Sprinkle, Andreas Serrano, Karen Finley, Robert Mapplethorpe, and Holly Hughes.[12] The moral panic of the decade led to the adoption of an antiobscenity clause in the administration of NEA funding (eventually found unconstitutional) that prohibited the use of federal funding to support work that depicted homosexuality or that might offend religious viewers (for starters).[13] Even as such legislation has been repealed or overturned, it has led to softer forms of censorship in which the expression of specific points of view becomes stunted as institutions hesitate to support challenging work and as artists anticipate censorious attention.[14]

Although the culture wars of the late 1980s and 1990s are not the focus of this book, they inform nearly every dimension of it. The book's title, *Hold It Against Me*, is meant to invoke that context. The culture wars have produced an ocean of hard feelings in their wake (artists who feel abandoned, curators who feel betrayed, museum directors who fear their own patrons, journalists who know no other story about art than scandal). After 9/11 and in the midst of a global economic crisis, the situation for artists in the United States has worsened. If things were tight in the 1990s, at the start of the new millennium the relationship between certain forms of art-making and art institutions has been militarized. That last word might seem a bit extreme to some readers, but perhaps not to Ricardo Dominguez. He is an electronic artist, a founding member of Electronic Disturbance Theater, and a tenured professor at University of California, San Diego. In 2010 Dominguez and his collaborators at b.a.n.g.lab came under investigation for criminal charges related to his work on "virtual sit-ins" (legal forms of electronic protest). He was also accused of misusing university resources in the development of b.a.n.g.lab's *Transborder Immigrant Tool*, a mobile phone application designed to guide people crossing the Mexico-U.S. border to water caches. (Thousands have died of dehydration in making this journey.) The application also offers lines of poetry inspired by the desert's landscape. Members of the U.S. Congress petitioned the University of California to investigate the artist for violating Section 274(a) of the Immigration and Nationality Act, for, in their words, "encouraging aliens to illegally enter the United States."[15] In a Fox News broadcast in September 2010, the notoriously conservative Glenn Beck cast

Dominguez's work in terms of "terror" and "reeducation" as he launched into a broad attack on public education. "You can teach whatever you want, but not with damned tax dollars," he complained. "There are a lot of universities that are just as dangerous with indoctrination of our children as these terror groups are in Iran or North Korea."

Beck went on to sneer at a statement in which Dominguez identified the *Transborder Immigrant Tool* with an American tradition of hospitality. The artist has described the mobile phone application as a kind of personal Statue of Liberty—a guiding presence keeping company with the migrant as he or she crosses the desert (a "geopoetic device"). The *Transborder Immigrant Tool* is meant to move people in quite specific directions. (In June 2011 the artist Marlène Ramírez-Cancio walked with a phone equipped with the program from the United States into Tijuana, Mexico, through a tunnel.) Beck took for granted that his viewers would find Dominguez's gooey language regarding American hospitality repulsive. For me, this was the most interesting aspect of Beck's tirade, for here he was responding to the work's strange emotional texture, something scarcely acknowledged in press reports of the project. According to *Sustenance*, an experimental theater piece written by members of the b.a.n.g.lab collective, the *Transborder Immigrant Tool* was partly inspired by the story of a popular Argentine saint, La Difunta Correa, who died attempting to cross a desert in search of her husband. When her body was discovered, her infant son was found alive and suckling at her breast. The b.a.n.g.lab artists write of the mother's experience of the "letdown," in which her body responds to her infant's cry by producing milk. They ask, "What if we made the desert into such a body? . . . Imagine caching water in the Mexican-U.S. borderlands' 'season of dying' as a comparable act of spontaneous release—not as a political statement (or not only that) but as a corporeal reflex, as an intuitive ethical gestus to insist, 'not on my watch.'"[16] The indoctrination to which Beck refers is (among other things) an explicitly feminist education in the politics of bodies, feeling, and boundaries. The material the artists have produced around this project has contradictory emotional textures: the references to La Difunta are maudlin, the reference to the Statue of Liberty and the project's acronym (*TIT*) are sharp and weird. The acronym alone is enough to signal the dark sense of humor that cuts across b.a.n.g.lab's discourse: the collective parodies the liberal sentiment that is normally mobilized in attacks against art's "uselessness," the gentle argument that the beauty of the work of art makes the world a better place. The documents that describe the application toggle between hard tech and soft feeling, providing charts and maps explaining the technology and a pastoral language regarding desert beauty and doing good in the world. The *Transborder Immigrant Tool* hysterically embodies Art's conflict with itself: the desire that it have the value of a science—that its impact on the world be something we can measure and demonstrate—and the desire that art make us all feel better (about ourselves and the world) by actually redressing social inequity (but not really). An object that really did do all of these things might indeed be criminal. Or revolutionary.

Even as the collective solicits right-wing hysteria and parodies liberal discourse on art, the project is sincere and the subject is deadly serious. It was serious enough to provoke national headlines and multiple investigations. The *Transborder Immigrant Tool* was projected into a conflict zone. Its authors are as much new media activists as artists. (Dominguez's work can't be thought of as one or the other; it should be treated as both.) The work here is not limited to the object; it includes public discourse about that object and the interventions of the artists themselves in the media. (The artists continue to index the application's use and public discourse about it and about the border.) While I don't want to minimize the impact of the University of California's attempt to discipline the artist or the awfulness of being subject to an FBI investigation (eventually dropped), b.a.n.g.lab's project was ultimately nourished by media attention. The project itself was designed to fold those battles into its content. Many artists whose work becomes controversial intend no such thing. Controversy's impact on artists who are not media activists is more often than not corrosive and unrecoverable.

The performance artist Guillermo Gómez-Peña has written a compelling description of the psychic toll of such policing, be the artist a target of such controversy or a bystander. The problem is less the outrage these projects generate in extremists like Beck than the isolation imposed on controversial artists as they become inconvenient to institutions ill-prepared to defend their work and uninterested in capitalizing on the kinds of conversations that these works initiate:

> One of the chilling by-products of censorship is that eventually artists begin to accept it as inevitable—*normal*, even. One of our performance projects, titled *Mapa Corpo* (2004), was rejected by a dozen U.S. museums and universities when they learned the nature of the central image: a nude body covered with 40 acupuncture needles, each bearing a small flag of one of the "coalition forces." Audience members were invited "to decolonize the body/map of the performer" by extracting a needle/flag. After so many rejections (some explicit, others euphemistic, such as those citing

"health concerns") we decided to just perform the piece in other countries, such as the U.K., Canada, Mexico and Brazil. . . . As a result, *Mapa Corpo* went virtually unnoticed in the U.S. The question for us performance artists is, How much of the new terms and borders of permissiveness and/or prohibition, the new (implied or enforced) censorship, the euphemistic disclaimers, are we willing to accept?

It's truly a very heavy question for all of us. Performance artists can put on clothes again, no biggie. Female artists can "tape their nipples" (as my colleagues in Pocha have been asked to do so many times). We can delete certain texts, erase entire scenes, tone down our "outrageous behavior," and eventually, when we least expect it, we will have lost our voices and our souls. If we choose to comply over and over again, eventually a tiny crystal (our dignity?) will shatter inside our chests. We will carry the pain silently wherever we go, and it will worsen each time we face yet another warning or humiliating interrogation. One day we will wake to find we have become broken humans, without even realizing it.[17]

Some of the country's most influential artists quite rightly feel abandoned as institutions have buckled under political pressure not to offend. That is hardly a surprise. But it is a surprise that art criticism has failed to provide those institutions with a compelling argument for the value of this kind of work. If we can argue for the value and necessity of minimalism's black cube, surely we can argue for the value of the *Transborder Immigrant Tool* or *Mapa Corpo*. On many levels, these works are in fact more accessible to audiences than minimalist sculpture—but this, for some critics, is exactly its problem. The legislative marks against federal support of overtly political art has been echoed by art critics who dismiss overtly political work as naïve, literalist forms of propaganda disengaged from aesthetics and art history. For such critics, when this kind of work turns to the social, it turns away from art itself. This is the affectively deadened landscape to which Lippard and Wojnarowicz gesture. Emotion, especially when coupled with a legible politics, appears as critically indigestible matter, a roadblock to "serious" criticism.[18] (How this has happened is discussed in more detail in chapter 3.)

Much of the work I discuss has been deployed in both popular and academic criticism to mark the outer limits of the acceptable. An *ARTnews* article thus asks of Aliza Shvarts's performance, "How far is too far?" and "When does art cross the line from avant-garde to unacceptable?"[19] That is basically all that the author asks of a work that dared to engage the subject of abortion. What the work actually did, what it offers to feminist performance or to queer discourse on reproduction and the body, was ignored in favor of a review of "shock art." That sort of writing erases the differences between controversial practices by lumping them together in a catalogue of insult to taste and quality, as if all insults (or even all work about abortion) were alike. A genuine discussion of how diverse art practices actually work is sacrificed in favor of a sensationalist story about shock. This book aims to move past the tabloid-style headlines that limit critical engagement with hard art to the question asked of the *Transborder Immigrant Tool*: "Is it art, or is it a crime?"

We see more when we shift our attention from the controversy that surrounds artists making politically confrontational work to focus instead on what that work is taking on, using *its* terms to understand the nature of its intervention. At first this may seem counterintuitive; on the surface, it makes sense to look at scandalized reaction to a work as a way of understanding how it challenges the viewing public. And we can't leave the reception of these works completely out of the conversation. But when we allow our thinking to be oriented by the terms and values of controversy, we take our cues about the work from people who have not seen the work or who have seen it and have rejected it with the force of a violent allergy. That conversation suppresses the existence of the work's core audience: the people who actively seek it out, who follow the artist's career and give themselves over to the work's processes. When we take a defensive position, we tell a story about controversy and the art world or controversy and a homophobic, racist, or sexist public sphere. But the work itself often isn't actually about the art world, and while this kind work is often about racism, sexism, or homophobia, it is not aimed at the racists, sexists, and homophobes: it is directed at the people who struggle against these discourses of power and hate. Controversy's undertow draws us away from the work, away from its community and its politics, and has us all talking about museums, galleries, and fundamentalists.

Of course, most of the artists who end up in the midst of such stories do intend to challenge their audiences. Even when an artist does not explicitly set out to make the audience feel uncomfortable, upset, and vulnerable, he or she may set out to challenge expectations and structures of feeling. This kind of work might make us angry or leave us unsure of how to react, confused about our own emotions and the place of those feelings in relation to the work itself. The audience's limits figure explicitly in such work, and clearly we need to think carefully about how these limits ought to inform our critical practices. The defensive critical posture we adopt in the face of controversy fails us because it does not give us room to acknowledge how much failure, refusal, and rejection inform the poetics of the works in question. It assumes that a work of art is either accepted or rejected by its audience. Recent contributions to visual studies suggest less binaristic, less absolutist models for narrating the unfolding of our experiences with art. Irit Rogoff's writing on "looking away," for example, turns our attention to the fluidity of the nature of engagement with art. She asks, "Can looking away be understood not necessarily as an act of resistance to, but rather as an alternative form of, taking part in culture? The diverting of attention from that which is meant to compel it, i.e. the actual work on display, can at times free up a recognition that other manifestations are taking place that are often difficult to read, and which may be as significant as the designated objects on display."[20] The decision to look away, Rogoff writes, can also be a decision to look *around*—to experience the contiguity of art with the social spaces that surround it. Rogoff calls for "expanding the parameters of what constitutes engagement with art." In art criticism, even as terms like *conversation*, *participation*, and *relationality* have moved to the center of discourse, "we rarely question . . . what constitutes the listening, hearing, or seeing in and of itself," and so our perspectives can be blind to the larger social and political resonance of the practices of artists and their publics.[21] Developing a deeper awareness of the space around artworks and expanding our sense of what it means to be present to art goes hand in hand with critical responsibility to the dynamics of representation and participation in the public sphere.

Active and passive constructions of viewership are inadequate to the dynamic practices of many contemporary artists. They are also inadequate to the fleshy complexity of viewership and audience. In making her argument for the generative properties of the desire to look away, Rogoff destabilizes the binary opposition of the work of art itself and its material, social, and historical contexts. This opposition has structured especially contemporary art criticism and art history, in that scholars who write about historical and social contexts are often accused of abandoning the work of art. Rogoff's strategic decision to refuse that zero-sum logic of choice (in which one either talks about the work itself or looks away, to its politics) is important to this book because much of the work I discuss is not structured by that opposition. One actually *must* look away, and look around. Take the emotional field of *Held*, for example. What is the art work? Is *Held* the encounter between the artist and his visitor? If so, where does that encounter begin and end? The conversation I had with my friends as we walked home from *Held* was created by an event that had happened hours earlier and at different times for each of them. The sense of connection between Howells's viewers, as well as the distance between his audience members (none of whom has the same experience), should count as one of the work's most lasting effects. The works of art I discuss here all exploit the watery nature of emotion; this is the primary reason it can be hard (or pointless) to stabilize their boundaries as works of art. Performance art offers a particularly rich context for exploring questions regarding the presence of emotion, audience, and event. This is one reason so much of the work I discuss belongs to this (loosely defined) medium. Performance artists are also uniquely vulnerable to the discourse of controversy; this is a big reason behind my decision to privilege performance-based work. (More than half of the works I discuss are performance-based.) That said, object-based works can also raise these questions regarding the boundaries of the work of art and the limits of criticism, and their affective fields can be just as dense as that of live action.

Vocabulary Shift: From Controversy to Difficulty

Many of the artists most frequently identified as controversial and shocking—such as Jeff Koons, Vanessa Beecroft, and Santiago Sierra—don't make work that is actually all that *difficult*. Some controversial artists are, in fact, quite popular with curators and with the art press.[22] How difficult can Beecroft's work be, really, when even as we complain about its exploitative structures, reproductions of her work grace the covers of art magazines? Critical hand-wringing over the ethical and taste issues raised by the scandalous practices of gallery darlings like Koons and Sierra is a bit of a bad faith exercise. Writers *love* artists like these because they give us something around which we can rally: the expansion of the field of art-making, the defense of a sense of taste, the politicization of the space of art consumption, the literalization of the exploitative dynamics of art as luxury product.

If frequently exhibited and commercially viable work marks the outer limits of our conversations about art, what do we do with work so challenging to convention that it receives little or no institutional support—work that in most contexts is stubbornly unfundable, uncollectable, and impossible to curate for fear of offending politicians and donors? What do we do with artists indifferent to galleries and their cultures and to mainstream taste and values? What do we have to say about artists who aren't making art about Art but about the Mexico-U.S. border, about intimacy and exposure, or in response to a culture of hate and fear?

This is why I find *difficult* a more productive critical term than either *controversial* or *obscene*. Ron Athey is a particularly good example of an artist whose work responds well to this shift in vocabulary. He has been tagged as controversial and obscene in a reception history that has made it almost impossible to access the actual nature of his performances. He has been making art since 1981 and is frequently cited as one of the most influential performance artists working today. He is credited with being one of a small group of artists who have defined *body art*, performance based on the artist's use of his or her own body. He has a substantial international following, and his performances are well attended by passionately supportive audiences. Yet contemporary art critics rarely acknowledge his work.[23] Part of the problem is a general disengagement on the part of many art critics and scholars from the artistic communities within which Athey works. Reviewing Athey's place in performance scholarship, Dominic Johnson writes, "To broach the relations between Athey and varied and often uncategorisable exiles in the hinterlands of cultural practice—such as Genesis P-Orridge, Kembra Pfahler or Johanna Went—is to ask, implicitly, why so little scholarship exists about their achievements. Such questioning also tests the strict yet unstated limits that the academy has drawn around its archive of possible referents. A relatively small coterie of accepted historical precedents have been more or less canonized in the official histories of performance after 1960."[24] In other words, Athey's work is hard for critics to engage because it isn't primarily in dialogue with a specific academic canon. His work may cite Pier Paolo Pasolini, Jean Genet, Pierre Molinier, and Francis Bacon, but its genealogy also includes death rock, disco, S&M culture, punk, radical theater, and Pentecostal ritual. Athey's performances developed from S&M tableaux staged at Los Angeles's Club Fuck! and moved into theater and gallery spaces—without, however leaving behind either the ethos or the audience of his club roots.

Underground artists are underground precisely because they work off the disciplinary grid, spatially and conceptually. This is a choice artists will make and revisit throughout the arc of their development, as they continue to work outside commercial spaces or decide to find a way into them. The fact that Athey isn't art history's darling makes perfect sense: he has not sought a name within art's official spaces and has often described himself as an outsider in relation to the art world. That said, the challenges he faces as an artist are not entirely of his own design; in the 1990s and at the height of the AIDS panic, a cloud of homophobic discourse formed around him and he became an accidental emblem for the kind of art that ought never receive public support (or indeed exist). He was marked as a heretic.

Athey's work can provoke discomfort in people who hear about it, and a lot of what people in the art world hear continues to be shaped by Jesse Helms's denunciation of the artist from the floor of the U.S. Senate in 1994.

The biggest story in the American art world in that decade was the "politicization" of public funding of arts and the conservative Right's attack on the work of out gay artists. The AIDS panic was enlisted in the service of arguments against the support of art that seemed to risk exposing audiences to queer content—as if to look at explicit images of queer sex (or, more accurately, any frank work by queer artists) were to risk contact with the virus that causes AIDS. Kateri Butler describes the nature of the Helms NEA controversy in an article about Athey's work and experiences:

> A poster boy for bullshit. That's how Ron describes his part in the aftermath of a 1994 performance of *Four Scenes in a Harsh Life* at the Walker Art Center in Minneapolis. Catapulted into the heart of the culture wars. Denounced from the floor of the U.S. Senate. Blacklisted by the art world. All over the Human Printing Press scene—in which Ron cut the back of Darryl Carlton (a.k.a. Divinity Fudge) and made impressions of the wound on paper towels, which were then sent by a clothesline pulley out over the audience [figs. 4–5]. It was erroneously reported, by a writer who had not attended the performance, that the audience had been exposed to HIV-positive blood (Ron has lived with HIV for the past 20 years; Carlton is not positive). And with that, the religious right was off and fulminating, and the media dutifully fanning the flames. Because $150 from the National Endowment for the Arts had been used in support of the performance via the Walker Art Center, Ron found himself defending a concept—public funding—that he didn't really even understand, never having then or to this day applied for a public grant in the United States.[25]

This controversy continues to shape people's ideas about not only Athey but also performance artists in general. The truly intense indicator of how difficult his work is: he is almost never included in public representations of controversial art. People opt for the "NEA Four" (Karen Finley, Robert Mapplethorpe, Andreas Serrano, and Holly Hughes), who took their fight against the Helms amendment to the U.S. Supreme Court.

Athey's work has never been integrated into the museum and gallery circuit. He has never applied for federal funding in the United States. The performance in question was not staged at the Walker Center but at Patrick's Cabaret, a queer bar and performance venue. It was cosponsored by the Walker Center as an "off-campus" event supporting the Minneapolis/St. Paul Lesbian, Gay, Bisexual and Transgender Film Festival. The controversy was over less than two hundred dollars of NEA funding used by the Walker Center to produce the event—this is as indirect a relationship between an artist

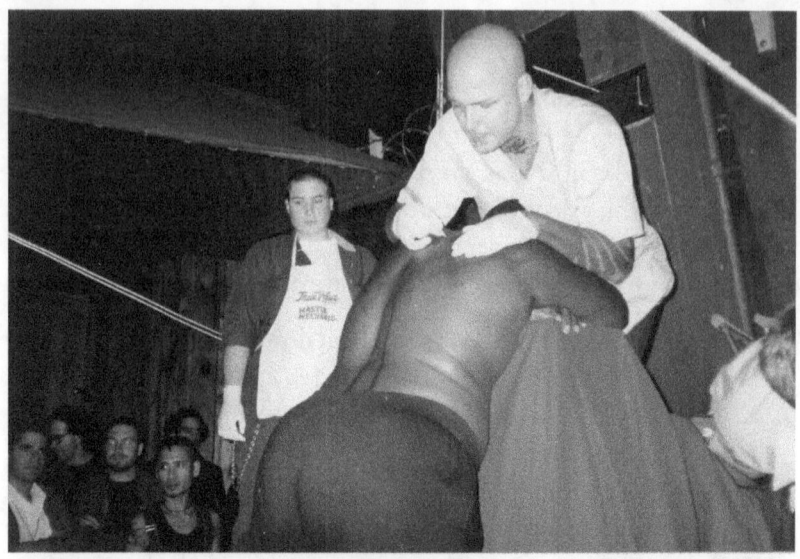

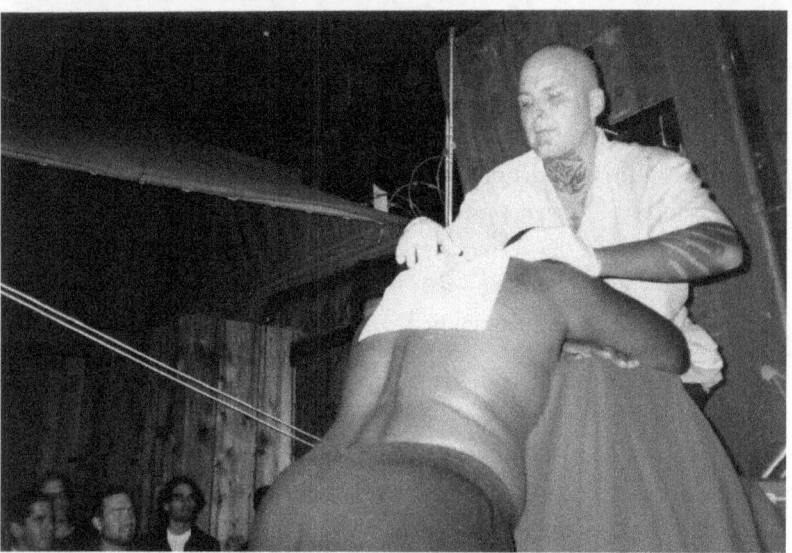

FIGURES 4–5. Ron Athey and Darryl Carlton / Divinity Fudge perform at
The Faultline in Los Angeles. Ca. 1994–96. Photographer unknown.
Courtesy of Ron Athey.

and a grant as one can imagine.[26] Even given the fact that Athey's relationship to public arts funding couldn't be less obscure than this, the controversy over that extremely tenuous relationship is a part of the history of the dismantling of arts funding in the United States. For me, the impact of that event serves as a reminder: such attacks on public support of the arts are not about what federal funding actually does but what people imagine it *might* do, who and what it *could* support. The genuine difficulty of Athey's work has been amplified by the absence of a disciplinary discourse on its value, and that has been aggravated by the fact that U.S. institutions are wary of going near it.[27] All of this has meant that very few critics in the United States have seen any of his performances.

––––––––––

Before looking more closely at Athey's work, I want to put the reaction to it in perspective. A lot of people get nervous about blood (giving it, the sight of it, coming into contact with it). When someone is bleeding as part of a performance, there are of course steps one takes to minimize risk of exposure. Lack of familiarity with those protocols makes the idea of blood in performance even more intimidating. Someone who is familiar with those protocols (a health care worker, for example) might find blood-based performance work less upsetting than someone who has never tended to the vulnerable body. Or someone might be more unnerved for having done so.

We can find other performance contexts in which people risk contact with each other's blood and in which the risk of injury is far more real than it is in performance art: sports, for example. Basketball players who get cut in a game have to step out and be bandaged up before they can take the court again. Not all sports even bother with this level of first aid. Athletes understand that the risk of injury is a part of the game. American football is undergoing a crisis of conscience, as the public grows aware of something players have known for decades: the sport kills its star players. Concussions are frequent; after a hard tackle, obviously stunned players adjust their helmet and get back into the game. These athletes suffer crippling joint pains before they are forty and Alzheimer-like brain disorders that can take hold of their body before they are out of their twenties. Nevertheless football games fill stadiums and are broadcast on television; even more incredibly, children are encouraged to play the sport. As controversial as boxing can be, no one has yet succeeded in shutting down "the sweet science." The idea of shutting down the sport spectacle would strike fans as bizarre, but the controversy produced around art should strike people as even crazier, because in contrast to sports, in art one basically risks nothing *but feeling*. The point here is that it takes relatively little to denaturalize the fear and anxiety that attends to certain contemporary art practices. This raises the question, Why haven't we been able to do so more effectively?

The demands that Athey's work actually makes on us, the challenges posed to programmers and audience members, are not as extreme as we tend to think. Blood and sex may be the subjects of the controversy around Athey's work, but neither, taken in isolation, makes the work difficult for his audiences. People are anxious about what is going to happen at an Athey performance—not to him, but to *them*. Athey developed his signature blood-work pieces in the midst of the AIDS crisis. The protocols of safer sex as well as the medical handling of the sick body are sometimes as much a part of his performances as are sadomasochistic practices. And the two are deeply related in his work.

The fact that his work confronts us with our limits regarding things like blood and fear of contamination is not incidental to either its poetics or its meaning. But the enduring difficulty of Athey's work is more closely tied to the way that it mixes pleasure and pain—and does so in spectacles that speak to larger social experiences of belonging and alienation, care and abandonment, hope and despair. The work is hard because it forces us to keep company with vulnerability, intimacy, and desire. In other words, the things that make Athey's performances hard for some people are not all that different from the things that make Adrian Howells's seemingly tame performances hard for others. They are not that different from what is hard about Linda Montano's performance video, *Mitchell's Death*. These are the things that, in fact, make *life* hard. They are productive and important kinds of difficulty—not because they expand our ideas of what constitutes Art but because they speak to quite fundamental aspects of being a social subject.

The controversy that surrounds Athey's work is engineered to keep us from thinking about and working through these aspects of its difficulty. Attention to a work's controversy actually suppresses attention to a work's difficulty. This axiom offers a good explanation for how an artist like Athey can operate as a bogeyman in the art world and yet at the same time not inspire much writing (and why, when we do approach his work, we find ourselves taking on whole disciplines). It also allows us to acknowledge that there are different kinds of difficulty and that some forms of difficulty are harder to acknowledge than others. The ideological work of art world controversy happens in the translation of difficulty into scandal, the secret of which is constructed as always already known, relieving the critic of the need to discuss it.

Difficulty's Audience

To repeat some of the key points made so far: The difficulty of the artworks discussed in this book is tied to their emotional and identificatory geometries. That difficulty has been flattened by traditional critical practices. Because this kind of work is shaped by a comingling of narrative, feelings, and politics it can appear to some critics as naïve and propagandistic, especially when race and gender are on the table. Hal Foster, for example, writes that some artists "treat conditions like desire or disease as sites for work. In this way they work *horizontally*, in a synchronic movement from social issue to issue, from political debate to debate, more than *vertically*, in a diachronic engagement with the disciplinary forms of a given genre or medium." For Foster, these "discourse-specific practices" often seek out a relationship with "the other" and risk an overidentification with the subject "othered" by the discourse these artists engage, in a collapse of critical distance. Foster worries that in such work (often autobiographical and overtly political) "an ideal practice might be projected onto the field of the other, which is then asked to reflect it as if it were not only authentically indigenous but innovatively political."[28] Critics interested in this work suffer from "ethnographer envy," he argues, meaning that they indulge a fantasy of proximity with the other. Joining a growing crowd of dissenters (Amelia Jones, Kobena Mercer, Jane Blocker, Jennifer Gonzalez, Darby English) and using the work of James Luna, Nao Bustamante, and Carrie Mae Weems, I argue that the literalism attributed by some art historians and critics to certain kinds of work (engaged with questions of history, identity, and identification and almost always by artists of color, feminists, and queer artists) reflects a critical limit, and not a limit to the work itself. In fact that desire to read artists as having "ethnographer envy," as so many relics and theoretical primitives, is anticipated and refused in the work of the artists I discuss here. That fact is barely recognized in mainstream art criticism, which tends to reject work once it detects the presence of an identity and a discernible politics.[29] As I suggested in my preface, to get at how this particular category of work challenges us, we must turn away from art criticism and mine other disciplines for insight. We need to stage a different kind of conversation.

Certain forms of difficulty hook up with feelings, mood, and affect. The closest analogue for some of the instances of difficulty discussed in this book will be found in conversations about the relationship of noise and music. Punk and metal are challenging musical forms for people who are put off by music they experience as noise or by the aggressive texture of the music's environment. The social and historical contexts for the music can be impossible for these listeners to avoid, much as they might want to.[30] Following the lead of Jacques Attali, music scholars have come to consider the shifting line between music and noise as a productive line of critical inquiry into the social and political meaning of sound within aural culture. Attali describes the relationship between music and noise as a dialectical working-through of discipline and genre: "Music responds to the terror of noise, recreating differences between sounds and repressing the tragic dimension of lasting dissonance—just as sacrifice responds to the terror of violence. Music has been, from its origin, a simulacrum of the monopolization of the power to kill, a simulacrum of ritual murder. A necessary attribute of power, it has the same form power has: something emitted from the singular center of an imposed, purely syntactic discourse, a discourse capable of making its audience conscious of a commonality—but also of turning the audience against it."[31] The antidisciplinary noise in music announces new social possibilities, revolutionary communal formations, as well as their regulation and institutionalization. The noise in and around music appears as interference, as an interruption of a signal—an incursion on harmony and order. The affective density of the works discussed in this book may be understood as one way of working with noise, in which case affect appears as an interference, as a rupture in which the viewer is thrown back onto, into a disoriented self. That noise feels like the other side of art.

This kind of work often also defies judgment. The most shocking work is destined to fail when tested against the art critical mandate to evaluate. When you are shocked by art, you usually don't think, Wow, that's great art! but What *was* that? Noisy works, in other words, often have a foundationally difficult relationship to genre and discipline. They appear to be at odds with Art, or they contain within them elements that seem to come from the "outside."[32] In an essay on Attali's work, Susan McClarey points to the association of noise with specific bodies: "Many of the principal figures in these new styles come from groups traditionally marginalized, who are defined by the mainstream as noise anyway, and who thus have been in particularly good positions to observe the oppressive nature of the reigning order. . . . All are people who managed not to be silenced by the institutional framework, who are dedicated to injecting back into music the noise of the body, of the visual, of emotions and of gender."[33] The appearance of work from marginalized communities can produce an affective environment that from the outside feels like static. Such work confronts the listener with a saturated, affectively overdetermined experience that she might experience as an act of aggression. In visual art, bringing "the noise of the body" into one's work presents a multisensory, concrete challenge to the basic protocols by which art is identified as such.

Traditionally, when critics identify an artwork as difficult, it is because a full understanding of its importance requires specific training in the art historical developments that precede it in order to recognize the work's dialogue with art history and with museum culture. Art's difficulty in those instances grows from its engagement with genre, with its material context.[34] The difficulty of noisy works belongs to a different order. Critical efforts to access this dimension of artistic practices make some art historians nervous precisely because such work requires a turn against the discipline (a "looking away"), at least until that discipline is reconfigured (in which case, this noise will transform itself again).

Difficulty can be internal or external to specific works—and in many cases you can't separate the two. Neither *Held* nor the *Transborder Immigrant Tool* can be fully understood independent of their material and social contexts. The relationship between form, content, and context in the works discussed in the following chapters is particularly complex. A work's difficulty might be institutional (in the material history of its development, and suppression and the absence of an apparatus or network invested in supporting it either with an exhibition or in critical treatment); it might be historical (in that the work's site of intervention is not Art as institution and discipline but History); and it might also be affective (in which the spectator is confronted with and enlisted in a powerful and often disturbing set of emotions). Undergirding all of those forms of difficulty, however, is the complexity of emotion itself as a phenomenon shaped by history and discipline.

The following chapter offers three case studies of works whose difficulty requires an analysis of their affective economies and three different examples of how a work's difficulty impacts its interface with discourse on art and art institutions. Aliza Shvarts's untitled (and unfinished) work is hard because the topic, discourse on abortion, is so fraught. It is also difficult because the artist completely withholds the personal, the emotional component of the process from the work. As we will see, this is a particularly challenging move because it forces everyone around Shvarts to provide the work's emotional content. Produced by the artist while a student, the work was interrupted by school authorities. It is worth considering here why Yale took the stand that it did, for the case offers a very condensed example of how, even in an ostensibly liberal environment, brutal gender politics bear down on the feminist artist who would dare go near this particular subject.

I've included a brief discussion of Thomas Eakins's *The Gross Clinic* as a kind of counterpoint; this nineteenth-century painting of a surgery is notoriously difficult for viewers, for obvious reasons. It is a theater of cruelty that aligns violence to the body with the acquisition of knowledge and the display of power. But it also maps a geometry of affect (figures appear bored, fascinated, focused, and horrified), and its own career as a once scandalous work that has become canonical demonstrates how a work's difficulty might be managed by disciplinary structures that rationalize its challenge, even presenting the most intolerable aspects of the work as "good for us." Athey's *Dissociative Sparkle* looks a lot like *The Gross Clinic*. I've juxtaposed a discussion of these two works in order to defamiliarize the shock many people experience in looking at photographs of Athey's performances. Both works explore the vulnerability of the body displayed to spectators. But where Eakins's painting is cruel (and uncontroversial), Athey's durational performance is not (and is nevertheless very controversial). The aim of moving from one to the other is to encourage readers to think about the distinction between the physical vulnerability staged within a hierarchical scene of patriarchal power and physical vulnerability staged within a feminist and queer social space. Athey's audience is not asked to look at the artist's body but to keep company with it and to sit with their feelings about doing so. For many, that experience is revelatory.

Before moving on to the next chapter, I want to share two images from Athey's archive. In one, Stosh "Pigpen" Fila sits in front of the crowd at The Faultline in Los Angeles watching the show before stepping onto the stage to perform his part as a queer St. Sebastian, as he had done in Minneapolis (fig. 6). The Faultline is not a theater but a bar, and here it's packed with a standing crowd of men and women. In club performances, performers often mingle with the crowd before and after their contribution to the evening's program. The crowd is often pressed up against the stage—which is usually more like a platform. That night, Pigpen, head crowned by spinal needles (already in place in this photograph), played the part of St. Sebastian. But in this image he has not yet taken the stage. Everyone seems completely engrossed by what might well have been the very scene that was the source of the controversy in 1994: Athey cutting into Divinity Fudge's back. Julie Tolentino

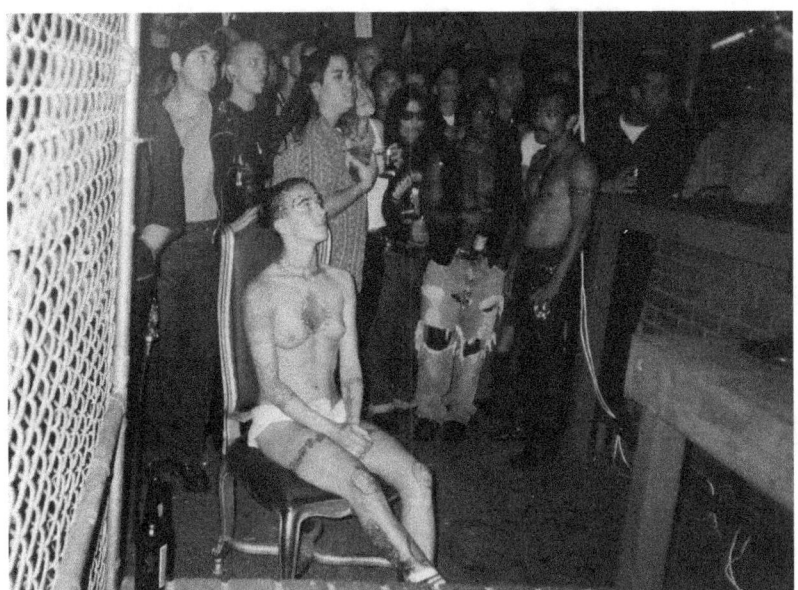

FIGURE 6. Stosh Fila ("Pigpen"), watching the performance before taking the stage at The Faultline, Los Angeles. Ca. 1994–96. Photographer unknown. Courtesy of Ron Athey.

(who worked closely with Athey's company and produced the Walker event) explains, "The blood lines as I recall for [the Minneapolis] performance were crafted more like a tone of a 'pre-show' . . . a kind of tempo hand-hold, as in setting a tempo. . . . The dense part of that show was certainly later" (and Pigpen was at the center of it).[35]

The controversy about that night in Minneapolis has put a malicious fiction in the public mind, in which such performances are reputedly staged as an act of aggression against the audience. (Perhaps this is why in the artist's archive I can find pictures of almost every performance but that one.)[36] That controversy has also nearly obliterated the queer architecture of the performance, leaving us with that one image of Athey standing over Divinity's scarred back instead of the even more complex geometries of gender, sex, and race which structured that evening's performances. The event was shaped by the strong presences of Tolentino, Pigpen, and Divinity Fudge. On the menu that night: "Bloodletting, branding, piercing, cutting, purging, exhaustive dancing and gender bending."[37] The performance had contradictory moods. As Athey promised in the night's program, "Most of my pieces deal with actual physical and emotional trauma. What's new in this piece is

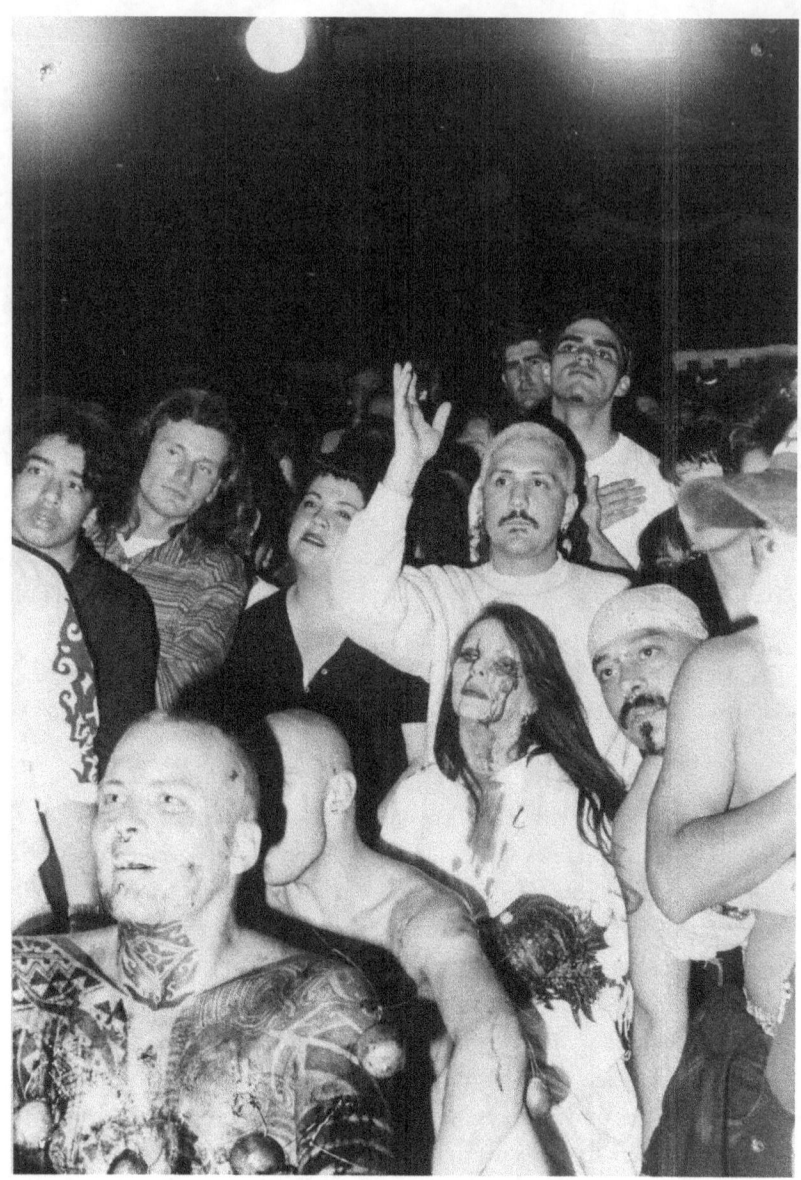

FIGURE 7. Audience at Sin-a-matic in Los Angeles. Ca. 1994.
Photographer unknown. Courtesy of Ron Athey.

that every scene has a healing." He freely admitted, however, that whereas the performance might be "cathartic" for some, it might hold for others "a certain sideshow appeal." Some might even find it "burlesque."[38] These different investments and reactions were not mutually exclusive. There was a lot more room for the diversity of that Minneapolis audience's feelings than the NEA controversy allowed us to see or acknowledge.

In another photograph in the artist's archive, the entire crowd is riveted (fig. 7). It could be a rival meeting; one person holds his hand over his heart, another raises his as in a "Hallelujah." The crowd is packed in tight, leaning around each other to see the show. They seem oblivious to the spectacles immediately in front of them: Duchess deSade, a musician and performer, is dressed as a virginal Goth. She looks bloodied. In front of her is Athey, in his tattooed glory. Limes have been sewn into his skin like Christmas ornaments. He's not alone, as the man sitting behind him is similarly decorated; you can see one lime dangling from the skin above his elbow. Nevertheless it's the audience's collective rapture that dominates the image.

Using words like *hard*, *challenging*, and *difficult* to describe the work in this book is slightly misleading; it suggests, for example, that audiences at Athey's performances are uncomfortable, freaked out, and miserable. But generally speaking, that is not the case. This audience's attention is being held, but not by Athey or the bloody Duchess. The crowd has moved on to the next act. They are watching an Easter Pageant mock crucifixion featuring Pigpen at the Los Angeles club Sin-a-matic (ca. 1994).

A friend who was in the audience pictured here described that night as her first time in a place "like that." She'd been in gay bars, but the clubs where Athey performs are not part of the lesbian and gay mainstream. They are queer venues that welcome genderfuck of all sorts. As my friend watched Richard White sew the limes into Athey's skin, she thought, "Is this really happening?" Another friend who was also at Sin-a-matic that night remembers that it changed her life even though at the sight of so much blood she (like quite a few other audience members) passed out.[39]

The people in this picture sought out that experience. They knew what they were getting into, even if they didn't know exactly what was going to happen. Athey and company are giving them something that they want. Or something that they think they might want.

The thing about something "like that" is, in the space of the performance, you adjust and accommodate to what's happening and also to the flexibility of your own desire. If you can't, you look away or you leave.

These are portraits of the people who stayed.

2 THREE CASE STUDIES IN DIFFICULTY AND THE PROBLEM OF AFFECT

A Blank: Aliza Shvarts, *Untitled* (2008)

A friend, a deeply committed feminist scholar, asks me what I am working on. "Abortion," I email her. "Yuck," she writes back. She was kidding—but only partly. I know what she means. I am tired of the topic before I start. If I found myself put off by the idea of writing about abortion before I'd even written a word it was because I'd given myself over to the deadening effects of the rhetoric that polices and contains our relationships to the topic. This is a very specific form of difficulty: certain subjects are completely overdetermined as sites of intense conflict in public discourse. Artists who dare to engage them risk not only the critical flattening of their work (in which discussion of the work itself is subsumed by willful misreading guided by the well-worn grooves of discourse on the subject) but censorship and worse. In the United States (but not only there), abortion is easily one of those subjects. It is in fact hard to think of a more difficult subject in American art than abortion. (And this only gets more true as time goes by.) Today American artists broach the topic rarely and carefully.[1]

In 2008 a Yale University art student ventured into this territory and wound up the subject of international headlines. Hers is an unusual case. Aliza Shvarts's work provoked a very intense emotional reaction from both mass media and art critics, but the work itself completely withholds from us any access to the artist's feelings. And that fact lies at the heart of its scandal. From the start, the controversy orbited around a perceived problem in her affect, although no one, really, had any access to it. Once the student thesis project became a scandal, the artist refused to make any public statement about the work.

Jeannie Ludlow observes that there is a hierarchy within feminist discourse about abortion, with a premium placed on "trauma-tized" abortion stories, in which the ordinariness of abortion is eclipsed by politically expedient narratives about unwanted pregnancies brought on by sexual violence and abuse. The implicit demand that "abortion be the exception, and not a normal part of women's lives" pushes the extreme suffering of victims of rape and abuse into the public sphere and throws a blanket of silence, shame, and anxiety over nearly every other kind of unwanted pregnancy as they become stigmatized as personal failures. "Because they are presented so frequently, these circumstances [rape and abuse, medically dangerous pregnancies] have become reinscribed as the 'appropriate reasons' to have an abortion, and they render all other reasons for aborting questionable at best, and frivolous at worst."[2] One of the many nasty effects of this form of narrative policing is the stigmatization of the agency of the vast majority of women who choose to have abortions; the choice becomes a disorder of will and desire. Ironically, we become more comfortable with abortion stories in which the pregnant woman is herself more like a child than an adult, a helpless victim of circumstance.[3]

In 2007–8, for her thesis project as a fine arts student, Shvarts set out on a "yearlong performance of repeated self-induced miscarriages." She artificially inseminated herself over the course of nine months and took herbal abortifacients at the same point in her menstrual cycle in order to facilitate menstruation or miscarriage (in the case she successfully impregnated herself; there is no documentation of this). Her expressed plan had been to produce a narrative about the experience as well as an installation of documentation of the performance.[4] An element of uncertainty figures in her conceptualization and enactment of the process. Because she never took a pregnancy test, there is no record of her having successfully fertilized an egg, of having been pregnant, or of having aborted an embryo. The biological possibility of pregnancy was left open in order to foreground the ideological investments in legal and medical management of the female artist's body as the most reliable framework for reading the truth of the piece.[5] (For reasons that will become clear later in the chapter, there is no proof that any of the events she describes ever took place.) The truth of the piece resides in how one chooses to interpret Shvarts's account of what she did; this quickly becomes identical to how one *feels* about what she did.[6] In an essay on the controversy provoked by the work, Shvarts writes, "To miscarry, to carry wrongly—that is what I did. Indeed, the entire work was configured to create a physical act so ambiguous and inconclusive that the language applied to it could never be completely felicitous, drawing attention to the force of language itself: the reality of the pregnancy, both for myself and for the audience, was always a matter of reading."[7] *The Drudge Report* picked up a *Yale Daily News* article about her ongoing project. Soon afterward, it became a national controversy. The story was broadcast on U.S. national networks and made headlines in the *New York Times* and the *Chicago Tribune*. Daily scandal sheets in London plugged the story into their roundup of attention-grabbing headlines. Several Facebook sites were devoted to hate campaigns against Shvarts; newspapers across the country received scores of letters and emails responding to their coverage of the story; the artist received untold amounts of hate email; and in the art world it became an occasion to grandstand about the state of performance art. Few cultural critics even came close to standing up for the work.[8]

Surprisingly, given its support of the distribution of "the morning-after pill" without a prescription and the facilitation of abortion on demand for the students who rely on its health services (though you won't find the word *abortion* anywhere on its website), Yale University did not stand behind Shvarts's work. Campus officials responded by distancing themselves. They reframed the entire action as "fictional." The student was, in their view, "never pregnant" and had "never miscarried." University publicists claimed, "The entire project is an art piece, a creative fiction designed to draw attention to the ambiguity surrounding form and function of a woman's body." According to them, the artist's statements to the contrary were also fictional and part of the performance. "Had these acts been real," explained the university spokesperson Helena Klasky, "they would have violated basic ethical standards and raised serious mental and physical health concerns." Campus administrators then took a very unusual step and threatened to prevent the work's display unless the artist would "confess in writing that the exhibition is a work of fiction."[9] Robert Storr, the director of the 2007 Venice Biennale and dean of Yale's art school, reiterated the institution's representation of Shvarts as unbalanced: "If I had known about this, I would not have permitted it to go forward. This is not an acceptable project in a community where the consequences go beyond the individual who initiates the project and may even endanger that individual."[10] Shvarts refused to sign a disclaimer about her descriptions of the action and was barred from presenting any aspect of it in the final thesis show. The project remains untitled and unexhibited; it exists only in the stories told about it, including this one. Shvarts decided to remain silent throughout the controversy and approaches the project as ongoing; the content of the performance has expanded to include nearly all reaction to it.[11]

At the height of the controversy, "Was Aliza Shvarts ever pregnant?" became the central question. The project's most virulent critics (who were offended by the idea of abortion, or by the idea that the whole thing was a hoax, or by both) were obsessed with it. Newspapers consulted fertility doctors to get the odds on the effectiveness of the self-insemination process she described. The question theatricalized a defining part of the lives of heterosexually active women students who do not use contraception (or who experience failure): the monthly uncertainty, conversations with roommates about parsley and sage tea, the search for signs of pregnancy or period, and the circumstances that produce a sense of relief, a feeling of escape, twinges of regret or shame, or a sense of loss. For Shvarts, the question of whether or not she was ever pregnant was not the work's point: the point was to explore the discursive field surrounding sex and reproduction—and, in particular, to draw attention to the strange status of the female body. On this point, the work returns to old issues within feminist theory and art-making, to the entanglement of authorship with reproductive discourse, the assertion of patriarchal authority as a means of disabling epistemological models grounded in feminine forms of relationality (including the artist's experience of her own body), and the hysteria produced when a woman throws a wrench into the gear works of reproductive discourse.[12]

Shvarts provoked a moralizing disgust grounded in a collective sense of ownership over the artist's body. People responded to the scandal as though the artist had mutinied: anti-abortionists condemned her as a reproductive citizen who willfully turned biology against destiny; feminists were made uneasy by her realization of the right wing's claims that abortion on demand leads to women aborting at will, recklessly, pointlessly, and for fun. A spokesperson for NARAL Pro-Choice America, for example, described the project as "offensive and insensitive to women who have suffered the heartbreak of miscarriage."[13] The feminist website Jezebel tagged her an "avant-garde asshole."

On its face, Shvarts's project explores the discursive field through which the female body is produced and read as a reproductive body. She hardly needed to exhibit in the student thesis show to realize the full impact of this dimension of the project. In fact the interruption of the project by Yale's interdiction brings the work to its most compelling formal conclusion. The project raises a more interesting issue, however, when it draws attention to the fact that access to abortion is an effect of entitlement; a college student attending one of the most expensive universities on earth can afford to toy with this, because as long as she is a member of that community she has access to a significant amount of resources supporting the decision to abort. Indeed it would be far more scandalous for a Yale undergraduate student to see a pregnancy through and have a baby than it would be for her to have an abortion. None of *that* was raised in the moral panic produced by the idea of this performance—or rather, it was, insofar as blogs, editorials, and comments posted in response to stories about the action dismissed Shvarts as a "spoiled brat."

It is as a conceptual exploration of sexual entitlement that Shvarts's work takes on its most powerful political charge. Grandstanding about her project, dismissing it as the work of an overprivileged art student masks much more complex and darker social truths about gender, class, and reproduction. From the indignation of right-wing pundits (who accuse her of subordinating potential life to the pursuit of an idea—or worse, her own career) to the paternalistic self-righteousness of Yale's administration (who worry about the artist's mental and physical health) and liberals (who condemn the action as a "bad" representation of the issue), we bear witness to the political difficulty of identifying abortion as necessary to the practice of sexual freedom.

Shvarts's story produces the interruption of fertilization and pregnancy as not the negation of sexuality but as part of the practice of a sexual life. The story moves abortion into exactly the domain aggressively silenced by the liberal discourse that suppresses the ordinariness of interrupted pregnancies in favor of the traumatic unwanted pregnancy. This was borne out not only in the reception of Shvarts's project by mainstream media journalism but within the arts community. In an admissions interview with a highly regarded art school (noted for both its theoretical sophistication and the support of experimental work), faculty pressed Shvarts on the "Yale project," asking her if she "felt sorry [for] what [she'd] done to Yale," if she had regrets, and what she felt about the project and why she'd done it. Shvarts recalls feeling that the admissions committee kept returning to this set of questions as if she "would eventually feel the appropriate things."[14] She also suspected that the campus wanted reassurance that she would not undertake such a project again. Given than the project involved nothing more than the production of the *idea* that she *might* have been pregnant at some point during a nine-month period, it is hard to imagine how an artist might go about making such a guarantee.

The controversy provoked by the idea of her project surfaces the production of sex as an affective disciplining of the reproductive body. This is where the controversial nature of the work intersects with its difficulty, for abortion discourse is shaped by both a guideline regarding how one is supposed to feel about the topic and a disavowal of the incoherence within our notions of the body and the subject. At the heart of this project is the complexity of the reproductive body as an object of juridical, medical, and political discourse. In her analysis of ways that nation-states reproduce power, authority, and their borders in and through the regulation of family, Jacqueline Stevens writes, "It is not that some people give birth and others do not that leads directly to gender roles. Rather, gender is what occurs through very specific rules a political society develops as it reproduces itself. The marked mother, subject to the institution of men taking her for the purpose of having children (matrimony), affects all who grow up as potential mothers. Perhaps these effects are what we perceive as sex."[15]

The attempt to free the body from this discursive regime can thus appear as criminal, queer, and, in fact, as an attack on sex itself. This makes Shvarts's removal of sex from her project particularly provocative and, I would argue, disturbing for both her anti-abortion and pro-choice critics. Shvarts evacuated all traces of romance, love, and desire from the work. In doing so, she centered the work in her body and its processes; furthermore she asserted full control over the representation of those processes. This brought the project into direct conflict with the thornier issues in abortion discourse.

As Penelope Deutschler has argued in her work on legal discourse about abortion, the liberalization of access to abortion in the 1970s in countries like France, the United States, England, and Australia reflects not a decriminalization of abortion but an "affirmation of abortion's illegality except in certain circumstances."[16] The criminalization of abortion, Deutschler points out, is embedded in the very wording of *Roe v. Wade*, the Supreme Court case that opened up access to abortion in the United States: "A woman's right to terminate her pregnancy is not absolute, and may to some extent be limited by the state's legitimate interests in safeguarding women's health, in maintaining proper medical standards, and in protecting potential human life."[17] Legislation and regulation of access through obligatory parental consent, counseling about alternatives (such as adoption), and state-mandated bureaucratic approval (requiring medical confirmation that the pregnancy is damaging to the woman's mental health, for example) confirm this strange truth. Legally and conceptually, abortion remains in a category of criminalized acts for which the law makes (fewer and fewer) exceptions. In this discursive universe, it is always a source of shame and apology. The scandal produced by Shvarts's conceptual project underscores the fact that within contemporary discourse on abortion it is always in some sense "wrong"; it is always bad, and even in liberal settings women may abort only when given permission by the apparatus and are spared condemnation only when they manifest the proper degree of shame and regret.[18] That institutions are deeply invested in the reproductive body isn't news. The organization of that policing of not the only body but the "idea," the presentation, the context and affect is worth examining more closely, however, for it is here that we see the political dimensions of Shvarts's project most clearly.

Let's compare the scope of this controversy to another scandal related to body art, performance, and pedagogy. On its surface, Shvarts's project and the uproar left in its wake bear a striking similarity to problems created several years earlier by Joseph Deutch, an MFA student at the University of California, Los Angeles. In a course on extreme performance taught by Ron Athey in 2006, Deutch brought what looked like a real gun to the class, told students that it was loaded, and then—amazingly—appeared to play Russian roulette with himself.[19] No one was hurt, but, understandably, some students in the class became very upset, and Deutch had to answer to an angry campus administration that reprimanded him for not thinking about the consequences of his action on fellow students, on the course instructor, and on the department itself. Regardless of what one thinks about *that* piece, one must marvel at the nearly identical positions adopted by both programs, which have long been associated with the vanguard of contemporary art: UCLA stated that the student's action was, again, fictional, that the gun was not real, and that it was never loaded. (The gun was not produced for the university, and we don't actually know whether it was real or fake, but the students in the seminar believed that it was real.) University administrators also worried about the student's mental health and recommended counseling. Unlike Yale's administration, however, at no point did UCLA insist that the student's performance be excluded from material used to evaluate his work in the seminar. In fact Chris Burden—infamous for having shot himself, crawled through glass, and nailed himself to a Volkswagen in early performances—then head of the Art Department, resigned at least partly in protest of the university's generosity toward the student, who was allowed to continue his studies.[20] Incredibly, at the UCLA student conduct hearing regarding the incident, Deutch's defense team grilled Athey about the Minneapolis controversy and tried to suggest that his performance history (which has never involved guns) was somehow to blame for the incident. While the story eventually made its way into the media and generated very heated debates within the department, it did not create a scandal of nearly the order induced by Shvarts's piece. At no point was Deutch the focal point of Facebook hate campaigns (such as they are).

I do not have an easy answer as to why this is. The different degrees of scandal partly reflect the different structures of the universities. Yale, as a private institution, can act more unpredictably and secretively than can the University of California, which is public. Normally, private universities will work hard to keep their students out of the headlines. Yale served up its student on a silver platter, disavowing any relationship to her work by preventing her from submitting it. Whether or not one believes Shvarts's story, and whether or not she was ever pregnant, she broke no rules, laws, or Yale's code of student conduct. The controversy surrounding her untitled, unfinished, and unexhibited project and the university's need to assert some disciplinary control over her reveal the absolute difficulty of integrating abortion into the field of art, even if the artist does so only discursively. In the intensity of the controversy provoked by artists who work with sex and against the reproductive matrix, we see the particular limits of art discourse when it comes to thinking intelligently about the hard feelings that are produced when artists call us out on our sex politics.

Part of the problem here is the literalism of much phobic response to feminist and queer body art. As Jane Blocker explains in her book on this subject, artists who work with the sexual body—and especially artists who reference flesh and blood in their work—are subjected to a literal interpretation that functions as "an effective strategy of marginalization." Examining critical reception of the feminist project *Womanhouse* (1972) and Judy Chicago's installation *Menstruation Bathroom* (1972), a white bathroom stocked with toiletries and bloodied sanitary napkins and tampons overflowing from a large waste bucket, Blocker explains that such work complicates the distinctions between the figurative and the literal and the tendency to represent the former as "more noble": "What troubles [critics] most is the prospect that [such] work could be both 'literal' and 'a statement' at the same time." She suggests that "the female and the queer" are both defined against and precluded from the figurative "because they are not seen to be performing at all."[21] Moral panic about queer art practices are almost universally shaped by this—thus the attempt to censor Robert Mapplethorpe's photographs for fear that looking at them might make viewers gay, and the willful misrepresentation of Ron Athey's performances as exposing audience members to HIV. We see this, Blocker reminds us, in the categorical resistance to feminist art that works with flesh—to the reactions of critics who see in feminist art the literal body, who see a metonymical intrusion of the artist's flesh into their critical space. That reaction, though, misses the ways such artists deploy the literal body against the trope of the metaphorical to politicize processes of figuration, the dynamics of representation itself. This perfectly describes the reception of Shvarts's conceptual performance as the conversation devolved into discussions of the likelihood that she would have gotten pregnant by using the methods she described.

The difficulty of integrating (for example) piercing, sadomasochistic gestures, and the abortive into art discourse does not seem surprising—until we consider the things that we *do* accept in art: Santiago Sierra's exploitative use of day laborers to perform menial tasks, Vanessa Beecroft's regressive displays of nude women, Andreas Serrano's and Teresa Margolles's work with the bodies of the dead, Zhang Huan's use of human ashes. All of these practices are controversial, but they also have extensive exhibition histories and significant places in critical discourse about the politics of art. All are, in fact, blue chip gallery artists with very successful careers. The difficulty of talking about Shvarts's project reveals not only the discursive field surrounding the reproductive body (this is its most obvious element) but the deep policing from every corner of narrative and affect when it comes to the representation of abortion as an ordinary aspect of sexual life. Mirroring the ideology that requires that sex be defined through reproduction, art engaged with the topic of abortion is supposed to be *productive*. As critics, we are more prepared to defend feminist art projects that educate people about abortion or that help women gain access to abortion. The abortive body, in other words, is easiest to handle when configured as a helpless woman. Staging a conversation about the reproductiveness of the female artist's body is an entirely different matter.

———————

Shvarts has shed no light on her feelings about the project or the controversy it generated. Her deliberate silence mirrors the erasure of the female body from representations of abortion; the photographs of the fetus in utero, for example, treat the pregnant woman as an amorphous background. The relationship between the pregnant woman and the fetus has been increasingly depicted as an antagonistic war of conflicting interests. "Fetal personhood," writes Carol Stabile in an essay on fetal imaging, "depend[s] upon the erasure of female bodies and the reduction of women to passive, reproductive machines." She points out that even the term *fetal imaging* renders the woman's body invisible in the service of a larger discourse on reproduction that renders her disposable. Humanism here is a zero-sum game. Stabile explains,

"Whatever rights 'women' may have had within the legal system . . . are dramatically being reversed in the so-called interests of an amorphous subject: the fetus, or as advocates of IVF (*in vitro* fertilization) technologies as well as anti-abortion factions put it, 'the early human being.'"[22] Valerie Hartouni writes, "For a genuine and complex story of abortion to be heard, the speech that would render women speechless must be interrupted. . . . This entails . . . interrupting 'the visual discourse of fetal autonomy'—reembodying the disembodied fetal form or resituating the gestating fetus in a uterus and the uterus in a body, thereby re-membering what is otherwise dis-membered and, as such, truly in a perilous state."[23]

In the United States, the law takes action against what is increasingly represented as the hostile environment of the pregnant woman's body, in which fetal interests are at war with the mother's desires, with her appetites, with her illnesses, with her vices. In fact the anti-abortion movement has started borrowing from the language of abolition in making its case, casting the mother's body as a slaveholding state from which the fetal person must be liberated. The rhetorical violence of abortion politics nearly always hinges on the personification of the fetus and the depersonification of the body of which the fetus is a part. The idea of the fetus as "a future person" divorces the future embodied by the fetus from the present embodied by the woman; her present is recast as the future's abject past. Within mainstream discourse on reproduction, in other words, the body standing in the way of reproduction, futurity, and life itself is quite specifically that of the abortive woman. Liberal feminist discourse on abortion has done little better to address the "problem" posed by the abortive subject—and there is a good reason for this. Anchoring a pro-choice political position without grounding that argument in a notion of individual rights is hard. But the stakes are high, for, where pregnancy is concerned, the legal maneuvers around who has what rights over what body have become increasingly bizarre in their erasure of the pregnant women's voice. This is not to drift from the question of art. Parental rights have come to be articulated in the courtroom as questions of authorship, as in the resolution of one U.S. court case in which a surrogate mother sued for parental rights over the child she carried to term, and lost; the court found that the "idea" for the child belonged to the genetic parents who had hired her to carry the baby.[24] Here concepts like life, personhood, and family are grounded not in the gestating body but in the acquisitive desires and material privilege of the domestic subjects empowered enough to engineer the transformation of that idea into a pregnancy. In this case, the pregnant woman becomes little more than a hothouse with an inconvenient sense of attachment.

Mary Poovey, in her polemic "The Abortion Question and the Death of Man," identifies "coherence" as a crucial problem in discourse on abortion: the more we insist on the difference between the mother and the fetus, the more we give in to this zero-sum logic. She argues that the subject of abortion intervenes in humanist discourse because the very state of pregnancy defies the demand to cohere in the form of a unitary subject. Drawing from Judith Butler's writing on the regulatory practices of gender, Poovey writes, "Coherence . . . is a property that belongs to our ideas about gender and to many of the institutionalizations of those ideas. [It is] *not* a property of the human subject."[25] Coherence develops according to one's cooperation with those institutions, according to one's successful interpellation by those ideological systems. Subjective coherence is a discursive effect. (To oversimplify this point: the more I write "I" and write as if this described a stable persona, and the more I resist the urge to contradict myself, the more you take this use of the first-person pronoun to refer to the author of this book. This collaboration creates the conditions of possibility for the production of authorial coherence.) The fictive nature of subjective coherence, of the idea that we are bounded, autonomous individuals whose liberty is expressed independent of other people and our environment, is belied by pregnancy and abortion. For you actually can't have it both ways: you can't treat the fetus and the mother as persons in this way without making pregnancy itself into a war of position. "In the mouths of antiabortionists," Poovey writes, "'choice,' 'privacy,' and 'rights' invert effortlessly into their opposites, precisely because, regardless of who uses them, these terms belong to a single set of metaphysical assumptions." The metaphysics of substance that currently underwrites legal advocacy for the liberalization of access to abortion is, Poovey argues, "an inadequate basis for all the arguments thus far advanced for the right to legal abortions." She explains, "The individualism implied by the metaphysics of substance is a dead end appeal for supporting abortion on demand for two reasons: first, because the appeal to individual rights *in the absence of* an interrogation of the metaphysical assumptions behind the idea of rights leads almost inevitably to a proliferation of those considered to have rights—in other words, to a defense of fetal personhood; second, because appeals to this metaphysics obscures that both the metaphysics and legal persons are always imbricated in the system of social relations, which, given the existence of social differences, are also inevitably politicized."[26]

Feminist political arguments for abortion must, Poovey argues, move away from a discourse of individual rights and from the notions of privacy and embodied personhood that currently ground liberal and conservative stands on abortion. Such a politics "would emphasize not the ways in which subjects are isolatable, autonomous, centered individuals, but the ways in which each person has conflicting interests and complex ties to other, apparently autonomous individuals with similar (and different) needs and interests."[27] Some of the most powerful critiques of liberal humanism come from this area of feminist scholarship.

It may feel like I've drifted far from Shvarts's project, but this rehearsal of the complexity of the topic of abortion is necessary to understanding the work. If we do not look beyond the feelings people have about the work, we miss the very concrete challenge that pregnancy, reproduction, and the decision not to reproduce pose to our ways of thinking about the self and others. That is Shvarts's topic, and it is the best context for understanding her refusal to speak about the performance. By withdrawing her personal story from the public, she created a situation that forced into view an ideological alignment between those who appear to be political opposites, and she also exposed the investments of a range of institutional systems in her body as both a creative and a reproductive organism. Shvarts's work is hard because her project cannot be understood by critical tactics seeking to gain mastery over the text by learning, once and for all, what "really" happened and how she felt about it.

In withdrawing herself so totally from public discourse on the work, she also raises the possibility that she felt nothing. And this makes the rest of us do all the feeling instead.

Theater of Cruelty: Thomas Eakins, *The Gross Clinic* (1875)

Although this book is centered on contemporary art, the dynamics I am describing, in which the challenge of certain works is entwined with their emotional economy, is not exclusive to the present. In turning to the past we gain some traction on how the difficulty of some works has been managed, revalued, and absorbed into art history. Thomas Eakins's *The Gross Clinic* (1875) is perhaps the most unlikely candidate in the whole of American art history to emerge as an emblem of civic pride (fig. 8). It is large, dark, and gory. The painting's dramatic effects are generated by the horrifying juxtaposition of the patient's body—naked, vulnerable, sliced open—against the calm, reasoned, patriarchal authority displayed by Dr. Gross. Blood glistens on his scalpel. His assistants pry open the flesh of the nameless person on the table. The wound yawns open, like a mouth. The surgical theater is crowded; the surgical table is surrounded. The atmosphere is claustrophobic, nightmarish. At the center of the drama, Dr. Gross and his students use their surgical

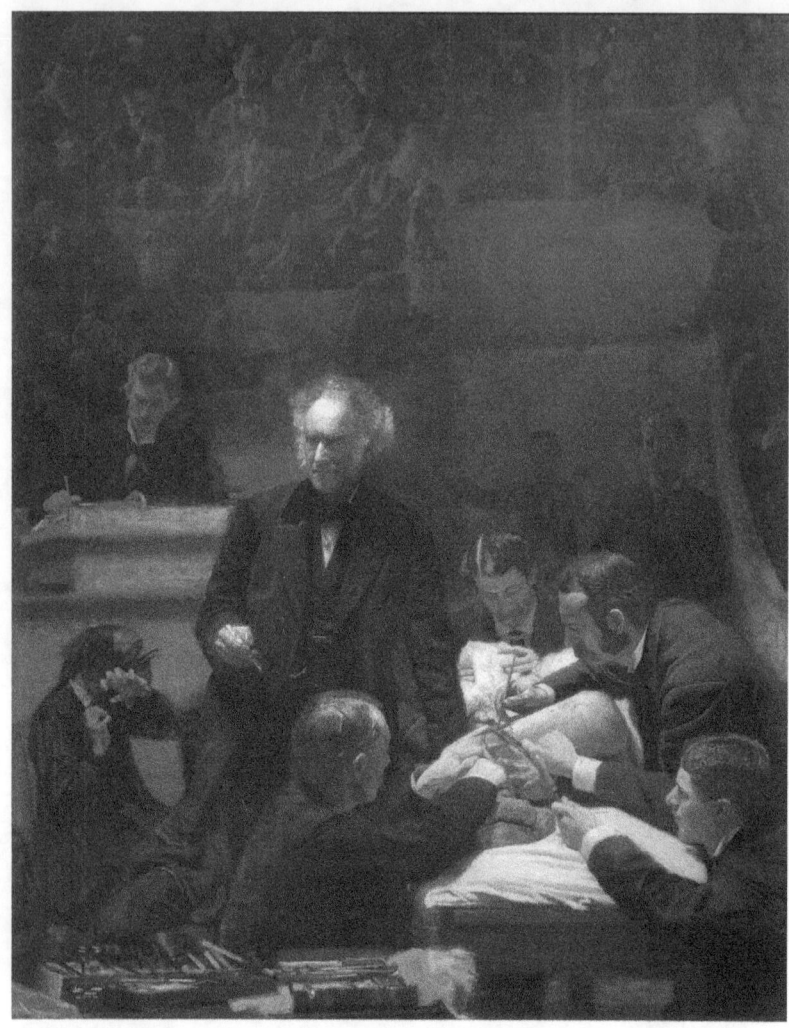

FIGURE 8. Thomas Eakins, *Portrait of Dr. Samuel Gross (The Gross Clinic)*. 1875. Oil on canvas, 8 ft. × 6 ft., 6 in. Philadelphia Museum of Art: Gift of the Alumni Association to Jefferson Medical College in 1878 and purchased by the Pennsylvania Academy of the Fine Arts and the Philadelphia Museum of Art in 2007 with the generous support of more than 3,600 donors, 2007.

tools to pry open and peer into the patient's flesh with a cold curiosity. They are masters of their emotion and masters of the body. The difficulty of *The Gross Clinic* is one of proximity and invasion: medical hands that have no feeling cut into the body with their instruments; that body is presented to us as an object of scrutiny and interest, the anesthetized body whose own incapacity for feeling gives permission to those who crowd around it to do as they will. The painting juxtaposes an extraordinary vulnerability with extraordinary power. As if in reaction to this, the lone woman in the surgical theater is overcome with horror. The painting's emotional drama is concentrated in her gesture: hands thrown over her eyes, body twisting away from the frightening wound at the center of everyone's attention. As I have pointed out elsewhere in my writing about this painting, in the distance between the cold, rational demeanor of Dr. Gross and his students (many of whom appear to be bored) and the nearly hysterical woman we have an indication of how important emotion is to this painting and to the discourse of art historical seriousness that develops out of its integration into the canon.[28] The painting isn't merely difficult; it is about difficulty and about mastering one's limits as a viewer. These limits are represented as emotional and are marked as feminine in the figure of a woman so overcome with feeling that she turns away from the action. The fact that from her vantage point she can't see the cut, the gaping wound, or the blood underscores her function as a surrogate for the spectator unable to meet painting's challenge—and heightens too our sense that she is less an embodiment of the problem of seeing than an embodiment of the problem of feeling.[29] *The Gross Clinic* imagines that conquering emotion is good for you, as if looking at the work without feeling will make you stronger.[30]

Sort of. Yes, the painting seems to celebrate Dr. Gross as heroic patriarch, master of his emotional universe, but it also quite clearly presents us with a complex and disturbing image of castrating violence. Yes, Dr. Gross cuts into the body to heal it, but the *painting* gives us that cut for other reasons. It seems to take the occasion of the serious portrait of the rational man of science in order to present us with the image of a traumatic cut into the body, the image of a body completely vulnerable and powerless. His mastery is expressed as the clinical practice of violence.

In a reflection of its difficulty, *The Gross Clinic* has a strange disciplinary location. Eakins himself is far from an uncontroversial figure. As has been well documented, he alienated friends and family with his social bullying and sexually provocative and often abusive behavior.[31] He was a social pariah, blamed for his niece's suicide, and forced out of his teaching position at the Pennsylvania Academy of Fine Arts by the rumors surrounding this and other events. He was a very difficult person who painted some very difficult paintings. And *The Gross Clinic* is arguably his *most* challenging work. Until recently the painting never enjoyed much by way of celebrity outside the circle of scholars, conservationists, and critics who work on this period in American art history.[32] Eakins's rowers, for example, are much easier to love. The cover image for the catalogue accompanying the Philadelphia Museum of Art's Eakins exhibition (2001) featured the rather peaceful *Starting Out after the Rail* (1874), in which a man is sitting at rest in a rowboat on the Schuylkill River. Newspaper reviews of the exhibit featured images from this series, even though *The Gross Clinic* is generally accepted as his first major work and his masterpiece.[33]

Nevertheless *The Gross Clinic* took the spotlight in 2006 when Alice Walton (heir to the Walmart fortune) tried to buy it from Philadelphia's Jefferson Medical College, which had housed the painting since the 1870s.[34] It was this event that pushed Eakins's masterpiece into the public arena. Samuel Gross taught at the school, which, as it happens, is right around the corner from the Pennsylvania Academy of Fine Arts, where Eakins taught. The painting had never been on the market; local art institutions tried several times to purchase it but had been turned down. The college gave Philadelphia institutions forty-five days to raise the money to buy the painting, else it planned to allow Walton to purchase it. The price was $68 million, a record for an American artwork from this period. Incredibly, local institutions met the deadline, and it is now jointly owned by the Philadelphia Museum of Art and the Pennsylvania Academy of Fine Art. With these events Eakins has reemerged in the public arena as a painter of note.

The two institutions anchored their campaign in an argument for the special place of this painting in Philadelphia's cultural history. In terms of its status in art history, it is the most significant artwork produced by a Philadelphia painter and one of the most important paintings by an American artist of any period. These arts institutions enlisted the city's mayor, state and national senators, and the governor of Pennsylvania in their efforts to keep the painting in Philadelphia. Most of these politicians, like most Philadelphians and even a lot of art historians, had never seen the painting before. *The Gross Clinic* was then housed in a den-like salon in a private gallery at the medical college.[35] The story of Walton's offer and the city's campaign to fight it off made headlines across the country and dominated local papers for a season. Visitors poured into the college's salon and guards were stationed around the painting.

One year later, the painting's fate settled, I went to the Pennsylvania Academy of Fine Arts to moderate a discussion with scholars about our work on the artist. *The Gross Clinic* was displayed in a large, well-lit gallery on the floor above us. Checking into our rooms in Philadelphia hotels, many of us were amazed to find the painting staring at us from the front page of the ubiquitous local city guide. Welcome to Philadelphia! Home of brotherly love and surgical gore!

For me, one of the most interesting aspects of *The Gross Clinic*'s difficulty is how it remains unresolved, even as the painting is accepted as an undisputed masterpiece. A lot of the works that we associate with artistic innovation are difficult, but that difficulty usually resolves itself over time as we, in a sense, catch up with its intervention. *Guernica* (1937), Picasso's monumental painting addressing the bombing of the Basque town during the Spanish Civil War, is, in many respects, easier. At least there the figures are stylized, the violence displaced onto form, as if war demanded a reorganization of how we see. We are spared realism's brutal literalism; the painting points toward a traumatic event that exceeds technologies of representation. *Guernica* doesn't try to deceive us into thinking it is meant to be a realistic portrait of the massacre. Instead it attempts to give us a sense of the effects of trauma on the painter's eye, on, in fact, the subjectivity of war's witnesses. Its formal elements seem to cooperate with its content, at least on the surface; it is as if a historical wound has made itself felt on the artist's vision. *The Gross Clinic*, on the other hand, pulls the viewer in different directions at once. It feels in conflict with itself. The painting presents itself as a portrait of a surgeon at work, but the emotional register of the painting is too intense and dispersed across too many figures for the painting to read as "about" Dr. Gross. It is sadistic, hysterical, and suffocating. Its subject matter is at odds with the viewer's comfort zone—and not only that of the nineteenth-century spectator.[36] It hardly represents a welcoming image by twenty-first-century standards either. Somehow the violence of the wound—or rather, the violence of Eakins's representation of the wound—spins out across the canvas, exceeding what the painting would seem to require. This is what makes the painting in and of itself *wounding*. Its first critics saw the painting as brutal and excessive, and they were right. It is.

None of this, however, figured in the controversy stirred up in 2006 by the sale of the painting, except to signal how much Eakins was ahead of his time. The appropriateness of *The Gross Clinic*'s form, tone, and content is no longer considered scandalous. Time and decades of aggressive management of the controversy surrounding Eakins by curators and critics have won the artist something like the protected status in criticism that the mayor very nearly won for the painting itself in law. His status is the direct result of the personal investment of a community of people with the institutional authority to generate a context within which its difficulty might be understood.[37]

Let me explain: Eakins never enjoyed what one might call success. He never made a living from his work. Some of his portraits, in fact, were lost because the friends and family who sat for him couldn't bear to hang his notoriously unflattering images above the mantle, and so they stuck them in the attic, behind the couch, or under the bed. Even some of those close to him, even some of those who helped support him were ambivalent about his work. So, as one might imagine, while he was alive critical reception of his painting was not great. He mastered the art of the rejected commission. He was far from anonymous and he had ardent admirers, but he was also far from accepted. As one learns more about Eakins as a person, one can imagine that some of this was because he was constitutionally incapable of what we'd call networking: over time, fewer and fewer of his colleagues were disposed to do him any favors. He could be an aggressive asshole or a ferociously loyal friend. Recent biographies suggest that he continued painting out of the same stubborn defiance that shaped his bad behavior.

After his death in 1916, the circle formed by Susan Eakins (his wife), devoted friends, and former students laid the foundation for decades of myth making. Slowly the Eakins story was rewritten: he was a man ahead of his time, he was a maverick, a distinctly American artist whose achievements came from hard work and opposition to the restrictive European traditions that had dominated painting in the nineteenth century. He was America's first great painter, and, in his mix of bravado, machismo, and workman-like devotion to his art, his legend offered the template for what continues to be defining characteristics of the figure of the male American artist.[38] Eakins's visibility and the newly awarded emblematic status of *The Gross Clinic* as a painting that represents Philadelphia's cultural achievements are the direct result of a campaign of people who shared a devotion to the artist. The architectural foundation of critical discourse on Eakins is, in other words, the direct result of the affection of people who knew him and believed in his work and of their relationship to art institutions empowered to generate and reproduce a discourse on the value of that work.

Somewhere along the line, the difficulty of the painting was overtaken by discourse on its importance. The violence of the image has been absorbed into a story about the image's seriousness. For example, Eakins's art historical identity as a realist painter—as, in fact, the father of realism in American painting—is grounded in a story about his commitment to a mathematical precision and a scientific approach to the body. *The Gross Clinic* appears to imagine art as a technical practice that opposes the sentimental traditions that dominated popular nineteenth-century American culture and continues to shape American culture to this day. This has had good and bad effects: the identification of Eakins with professionalism and science has helped articulate a field of scholarship, but it also set up an unofficial code of conduct by which a community of scholars agreed to keep quiet about a range of topics (e.g., the scandals of his personal relationships with women students and the overt homoeroticism of much of his work). Those of us writing about controversial topics—such as Eakins's complex sexual behavior, the increasing importance of his work over the course of the twentieth century to the visual articulation of a homoerotic vocabulary, the androgyny of some of his paintings of women, and the uneasy juxtaposition of his realist vision with scenes of sexualized violence—have largely (and happily) worked on the margins of the field.

It is not uncommon for the scandal of works to fade over time. Manet's *Olympia* (1863), Goya's *The Third of May 1808* (1814), Duchamp's *Nude Descending a Staircase* (1912) and *Fountain* (1917) all made people angry once and long ago ceased to do so.[39] In order to understand and appreciate these works, one must understand their historical contexts. Works like *Fountain*, or Warhol's paintings of Campbell's soup cans, were at one time difficult for their viewers because they were hard to accept as art. But now they are relatively harmless—meaning they don't upset people as they once did because their revolutionary turns (toward the ready-made, the assertion of the institutional framework of exhibition as that which makes art recognizable as such) have been absorbed into contemporary art discourse and practice.

The Gross Clinic's difficulty is not like that of these other works. Eakins's work never enjoyed the kind of institutional framework that ironically comes with membership to an oppositional movement like the avant-gardism of the early twentieth century.[40] An avant-garde artist like Duchamp scandalized people with his urinals and bottle-racks but was also recognized for revolutionizing and expanding our understanding of the category of art; in the latter half of the century he had become fully canonical.[41] Unlike those kinds of works, which make people scratch their heads over what can be counted as a painting or a sculpture, *The Gross Clinic*'s difficulty can't be explained by its relationship to institutional articulations of what counts as art. If it was exiled to the medical portion of the Philadelphia Centennial exposition, this is not because people didn't see it as a painting; it is because they thought the subject matter was shocking. It has enormous complexity. But it does not dissolve in paint in the way that Manet's and Goya's canvases sometimes do. Its fidelity is to the representational and narrative project.[42]

By asserting that the difficulty of this painting remains even as it becomes well known and accepted as a masterpiece, I do not mean to suggest that the difficulty it presents is timeless or universal, but rather that the institutional apparatus that surrounds the painting (museums, scholars, and critics, city and state government and university officials) has given us a way to accept its difficulty: the assumption is that the painting's difficulty is good for us. That framework shapes how we see it and shapes how we feel about what we see. For me, this has also served to mask the contemporariness of this painting and its strong resemblance to some of the most controversial artworks of our own period.

The realism of *The Gross Clinic* is bound up in the management of the body's vulnerability and in the rendering of that management as a deeply gendered struggle over feeling and affect. The painting's realism is grounded in a conquering of affect—not of affect itself, but of one affective category in particular: sentimentality, embodied by that cringing woman. The high seriousness of the painting—mirrored by the posture of its nominal subject, the rational man of science, the surgeon Samuel Gross—is articulated against and through vulnerable bodies with troubling relationships to gender: the patient displayed *a tergo*, anonymous, unconscious, and bleeding from a vaginal wound on the thigh; and the maternal, feminized body that feels too much. It was this woman's presence that most scandalized the painting's nineteenth-century audiences; one contemporary reviewer described her as "horror in the shape of a woman." (That phrase has stuck with me since I first read it a dozen years ago.) She added a "melodramatic" presence; she seemed literally out of place, there only to amplify the horror of the cut, which, however, she can't see—not because her hands cover her eyes but because the cut is displayed so aggressively toward *us*, the viewers of the painting. The dramatics of her posture, the theatricality of her pose draws attention to that of the surgeon's, for his restraint is no less a theatrical production than the female hysteria against which it is defined. As we move between the major points of identification offered by the painting, our eyes circle that cut: not a wound the surgeon heals but a wound the surgeon *creates* within the framework of healing. The difficulty of the painting is bodied forth by the bloody wound on the patient's thigh, by the hysterical female who won't look it, by the rational man who has created it. It rests in the story created by that cut; it rests in the story that produces that cut.

Eakins aligns our drive to know the painting, to decode and identify its various elements with the act of cutting into the body, with the production of knowledge, of scientific discourse through the subjection of the body to the knife. This painting flirts with and exploits the difference between contingent and more intractable forms of difficulty. Eakins doesn't call into question what a painting *is* as much as he calls into question what a painting *does*. We are confronted with an epistemological challenge aimed directly at us: it seems to ask us why we are there, and what it is that we want from it. It asks us to consider exactly what we want to know and how far we are willing to go for it. This is an artwork in which "ethical and aesthetic moments become inseparable."[43]

Disciplinary models for the art historical development of painting leave little room for thinking about the difficulty of a work like *The Gross Clinic*. The comparativist in me sees the difference between Eakins's practice and that of modernist painters like Cezanne as analogous with the difference between writers like Henry James and, say, Baudelaire or Gertrude Stein. James obsessively graphed entangled geometries of psychological perspective into his prose; many of his most interesting novels were total failures commercially, and the difficulty of his writing has hardly diminished over time. He was stubborn and complicated, utterly devoted to a writing practice that challenges his readers even as it also delights them. James's writing, however, is narrative; Stein's is experimental, working at the outer limits of narrative structures in much the same way that Picasso mined the frontiers of figurative painting. But whereas in literary studies the differences between James and Stein are not seen as evolutionary (in which James's writing would be cast as more simple, more transparent, more naïve than other brands of literary modernism), and whereas in literary studies, if you work on Stein or Baudelaire you probably know a lot about James and vice versa, in art history, Eakins is positioned on the other side of modernism's diluvian break. You would, for example, be unlikely to encounter Eakins and Cezanne or Picasso in the same art history class. In art history, modernism operates as a profound disciplinary boundary: the modernist painter's turn against narrative, against the figure works at least on the level of curriculum as a total break.

This has served to mask the difficulty and interestingness of Eakins's work (and that of other canonical American painters from this period as well, such as Winslow Homer). This is to say that the ways we understand visual art are deeply informed by the critical premium placed on the challenges specific to modernist art—challenges to the viewer's sense of the pictorial plane, to the question of what a painting is, what sculpture is, what art is (all ontological forms of difficulty, which revolve around what Art "is"), and, most important for the kinds of problems I am describing here, challenges to the presence of narrative in painting. Art historical modernism is in no small part defined by the refusal of narrative—by the attempt to purge all things that feel novelistic or fictive from the two-dimensional plane. There is an implicit agreement that an artist like Eakins, who works within a narrative structure (painting recognizable figures in particular settings, suggesting specific biographies, myths, etc.), is less sophisticated about the way representation works, less specifically visual (in that the painting seems to want us to see *through* it), and less interesting to critics thinking about formal issues in visual art.

This is partly because the difficulty of this kind of artwork has little to do with its relationship to the discursive world of Art—to art museums, art criticism, and the art market. The difficulty of work like *The Gross Clinic* is produced through its engagement with the challenges of social being itself, something these works take up in the narratives they spin and in the way they absorb their audiences into those narratives. Diarmuid Costello and Dominic Willsdon describe such practices as interested in the rhetorical function of art insofar as they exhibit "a concern with *how* the mode or manner in which the work treats its content, and the point of view from which it is addressed, disposes its viewers to see the world."[44] And so contemporary political theory has as much to offer an analysis of the difficulty of *The Gross Clinic* as does art history. Take Judith Butler's writing about "the social vulnerability of the body": "Each of us is constituted politically in part by virtue of the social vulnerability of our bodies—as site of desire and physical vulnerability, as a site of a publicity at once assertive and exposed. Loss and vulnerability seem to follow from our being socially constituted bodies, attached to others, at risk of losing those attachments, exposed to others, at risk of violence by virtue of that exposure."[45] The political management of the "social vulnerability of our bodies" provides the mise-en-scène for most of the works I describe in this book, including Shvarts's project. *The Gross Clinic* works as a portrait of social vulnerability in its terrible juxtaposition of power and subjection, but also—and more disturbingly—in the way that it stages the formation of social networks around the body's subjection to power. When we narrate the painting's power in terms of its accuracy, or when we treat the portrait as a straightforward celebration of Gross's scientific accomplishments, we diminish its difficulty as a statement about the violence that often accompanies the project of knowledge production—especially when that knowledge is wrested from the body. Within the institutional framework given us by Eakins, the "proper" point of identification for this work is not the body under the knife, nor is it the woman who can't look. It is not even the surgeon and his colleagues. This painting places us with the spectators in the dark, nearly invisible, who are learning from this spectacle. They mirror our position en masse. And when we look at the painting through their eyes, we participate in the violation it depicts.

Surveying those students, I wonder what they feel, or indeed if they feel anything. Their disinterest (be it the disinterest of clinical attention or the sleepy disaffection of the bored student) contrasts profoundly with the maternal figure of investment, a woman so overcome with sympathetic pain that her body appears to withdraw from the whole scene, as a reflex. *The Gross Clinic* imagines thinking and feeling as incommensurate; the two are cleaved from each other. Emotion appears on this canvas as a feminine spirit unleashed by a surgical wound.

Touchy Subject: Ron Athey, *Incorruptible Flesh: Dissociative Sparkle* (2006)

The Gross Clinic is a helpful counterpoint for thinking about the difficulty of Ron Athey's work. *Incorruptible Flesh: Dissociative Sparkle* was performed at Artist's Space in New York on 1 May 2006 (figs. 9–10; plate 1). In the juxtaposition of *The Gross Clinic* and this solo performance, we see a shared interest in the social vulnerability of the body, but their dynamics couldn't be more different. In his work, Athey lies on his back on a metal table made from scaffolding. (It looks like an elevated lawn chair.) His body rests against the fat metal rods of his platform for six hours. Built into the table is a pivoting rod, onto which Athey attached a baseball bat, upon which he has impaled himself. He is naked and covered in bronzing lotion and Vaseline. Hooks pierce multiple points in his face and are attached to leather strings to pull his skin back, turning his face into a painful (but also comic) mask. His scrotum is filled with fluid—turning his genitals into a watery, pink, feminine mass.[46] In her writing on the artist, Amelia Jones observes that Athey explores in his performances an "ethics of embodiment" that begins with the "dehabituation of the body," loosening the male body in particular from the codes of the patriarchal norm to insist on its permeability, its pliability, its fragility. Mary Richards similarly describes Athey as an antiphallic artist who re-presents his body as penetrable, leaking, and vulnerable.[47] And, truly, in this performance Athey is greased up, engorged, and violated.

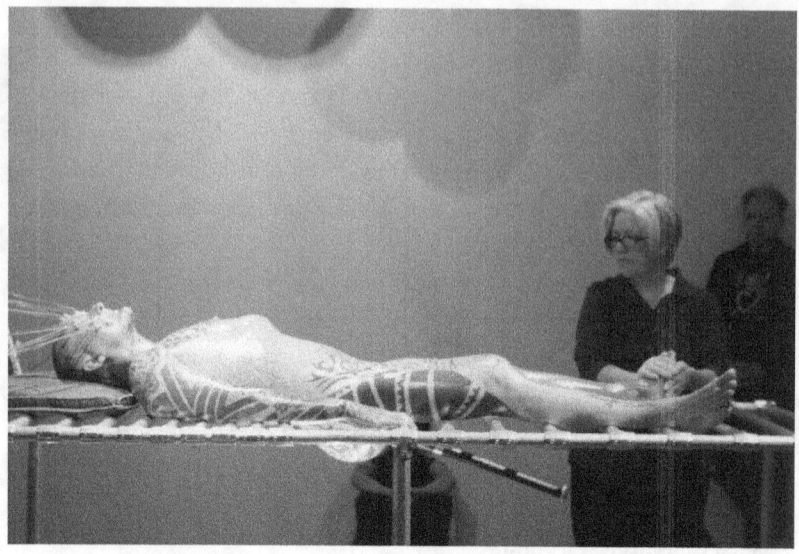

FIGURE 9. Ron Athey, *Incorruptible Flesh: Dissociative Sparkle*. Artist's Space, New York City. 2006. Photo by Julia Portwood Hipp. Courtesy of Ron Athey.

On entering the space, spectators are told by a gallery attendant that they are welcome to put on gloves and touch Athey, using Vaseline as a lubricant. In the center of the white gallery is the artist on his table, lit from underneath by lights covered with red gels. Clusters of disco balls hang from the ceiling above him, sending sparkles of light across the brightly lit gallery. This is the only thing that he has to look at. In fact the hooks pull his skin back so that his eyes are forced open—he can *only* stare up at the ceiling, without blinking. I was present for the duration of the event, administering teardrops to Athey's eyes, attending to him as a supervisory presence.

For this performance, the audience largely stood at a distance from Athey, leaning against the gallery walls, watching the occasional person put on gloves and approach his body. In spite of the fact that the gender balance of the audience was just about equal, most of the people who accepted the invitation to touch the artist were women. In fact, from my own observations I would say that nearly all of the women who attended the show put on the gloves, whereas only a fraction of the men accepted this invitation.

The real show in this performance is not Athey's body but the spectacularization of our communal relationship to it. For Francesca Alfano Miglietti, Athey's performances explore "the complicated, subtle, disconcert-

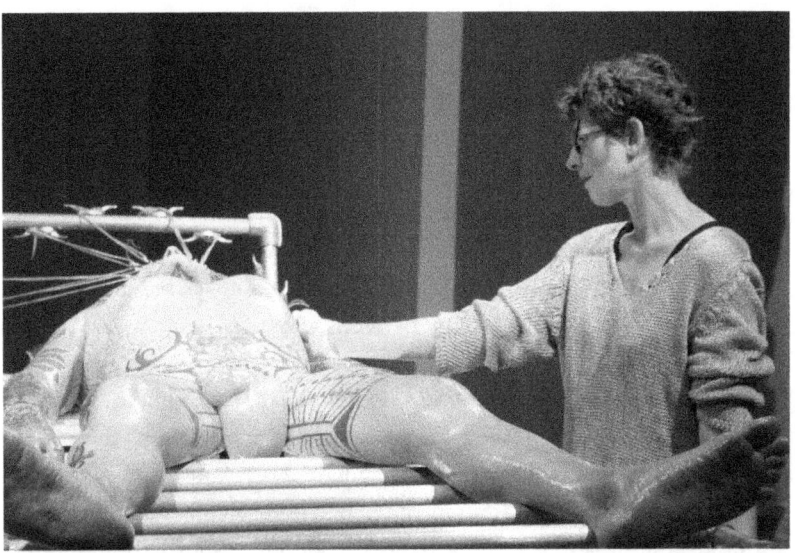

FIGURE 10. Ron Athey, *Incorruptible Flesh: Dissociative Sparkle*. Artist's Space, New York City. 2006. Photo by Julia Portwood Hipp. Courtesy of Ron Athey.

ing, learned, warm behavior with which we become visible to the eyes of another."[48] This is true of *Incorruptible Flesh: Dissociative Sparkle*, but that circuit is not formed between the performer and his audience, and it is not a happy scene in which one is recognized and made whole in a meaningful exchange of glances. Athey may be visible to his audience, but in this work that audience is not visible to him. His connection with the audience is short-circuited by the fact that he can't see them; approaching the table you realize that it is relatively high, and with his face tied to the bed's frame, his vision is limited to the space directly above and in front of him. This foregrounds the spectacular nature of the relationship of the toucher to the touched, not as a site of communication but as an image produced for others. Athey's state of being (penetrated and prone) is fully visible, but his feelings (I imagine hallucinogenic discomfort and pain, meditative boredom) are removed from his audience. (Without an exchange of looks, our sense of how he is holding up is only an empathic guess.) On this point there is a harmony between the position of Athey's body in this work and that of the patient in Eakins's painting. In both instances, we are given startling access to the body. The body is presented aggressively to the viewer, and yet our access to it is strictly regulated. In both, sexualized violence and corporeality are associated with a defacing; both works dramatically refuse to provide the face as a visual focal point for the viewer.[49] Both works address a latent social violence toward the body, furthermore, and link that violent defacing of the body with sex.[50]

Eakins's painting aligns mastery over the body with violence to it, exiling feeling to the painting's margins; pain is displaced from the unconscious body that can't feel to the hysterical woman who can't *not* feel. The violence of that painting is ongoing. The mise-en-scène of Athey's performance is a violent and homophobic universe in which the damage has already been done. The suspension of his body between a disco ball and a baseball bat suggest the relays of fear and desire that link gay and straight, queer and phobic masculinity. But *Incorruptible Flesh: Dissociative Sparkle* doesn't represent gay bashing. A violent gesture is summoned and transformed by this tableau vivant, conjured and recast as erotic, sadomasochistic fantasy.

We enter the room and are confronted by a body accommodating itself to an impossible situation. Approaching Athey's pinned-down, immobilized, bloated, impaled, naked body, we expect something dramatic. But the encounter is strangely anticlimactic: the touch produces no intelligence, no epistemic shift. This is no magical encounter—or, it wasn't for me. Over the duration of the performance, our relationship to Athey's spectacle settled, as we reconciled ourselves to his state and began to participate in a collective maintenance of his body. Although at first glance his work appears to promise some kind of intimacy with that body, as Jane Blocker writes, we are often thrown back instead onto "the body's capacity for producing a sense of 'never knowing.'"[51] At least, never knowing in the sense meant by Eakins's painting. For there is a world of feeling in Athey's action and in our relationship to it, but keeping company with that will not give us a sense of mastery over the event.

This is the opposite of *The Gross Clinic*'s narrative, in which the body is the occasion for the production of knowledge—or, more nearly, reading *The Gross Clinic* through *Dissociative Sparkle*, the surgical theater is crowded with instruments and handlers who manage the "never knowingness" of the body with a sadistic theatricalization of the production of knowledge. The feeling of the body under the knife is buried; it erupts somewhere else as an element at complete odds with the social structure that is the painting's ostensible subject. *Dissociative Sparkle* seems to drop us inside the narrative frame of *The Gross Clinic* and ask us to position ourselves within its drama. Are you a watcher? Are you a handler? A supervisor? A nurse? Do you need to look away? The performance calls out the circuits of desire and pleasure that course through scenes of power and subjection. He gives us his body as *a* body, under bright lights, face pinned into a permanent grimace, his flesh and skin stubborn and elastic, immobile but sensate. The performance is visibly *sexual*, but its relationship to sexual pleasure is painful and distended. The discomfort of the body before us becomes our discomfort and forces our attention elsewhere: our hands roam across Athey's body if only because we don't quite know what else we are supposed to do with ourselves. The strangest thing about this performance was not the spectacle of Athey's body but the uncertain collective movement of his audience toward it, toward him.

My experience of the performance was modulated by my caretaking function. Every ten minutes or so, he needed saline drops administered to his eyes. It took me a while to acknowledge how much this became a part of the performance; if nothing else, it offered a cue to the audience regarding how to handle his body. On this point, I was drafted into a soft version of a role that recurs in many of his works—an attendant, often female (which may be Athey in drag), whose actions can, as Lydia Lunch has observed, "illustrate the cruel and impersonal nature of supposed 'caregivers.'"[52] If I was looking after his eyes, it was to maintain the line between the bearable and the unbearable, not to cure but to extend a tortured position. Lunch's observations regarding the ambiguities that shape how one attends to the wounded body in Athey's works are important. In that instance, she was addressing "Nurse's Penance," a section of Athey's performance, *Martyrs and Saints* (1992; figs. 11–12). As Richards describes it:

> It begins in a hospital setting suffused with uncomfortably bright light. There are a number of "sick" performers on stage. Some are on gurneys, some in wheelchairs, all are in states of physical abjection having been cut from black body bags. Here, Athey and his co-performers enact the pain and humiliation of the exposed and abject body by using grotesquely caricatured and brutal nurses to carry out publicly, physically degrading and intrusive examinations. It would seem that the nurses attend to patients in this abrupt manner because it is only by maintaining a psychological distance from events that they are able to mentally survive the horror. That is, the nurses suffer too or do "penance" through their necessary dealings with the sick.[53]

Martyrs and Saints was produced in perhaps one of the hardest years of the AIDS crisis in relation to its impact on the queer scenes of which Athey was a part. He wrote "A Nurse's Penance" the day after David Wojnarowicz died of AIDS, as he considered what the "penance" might be for a caretaker unable to prevent her charge's death.[54] That same year he also wrote an obitu-

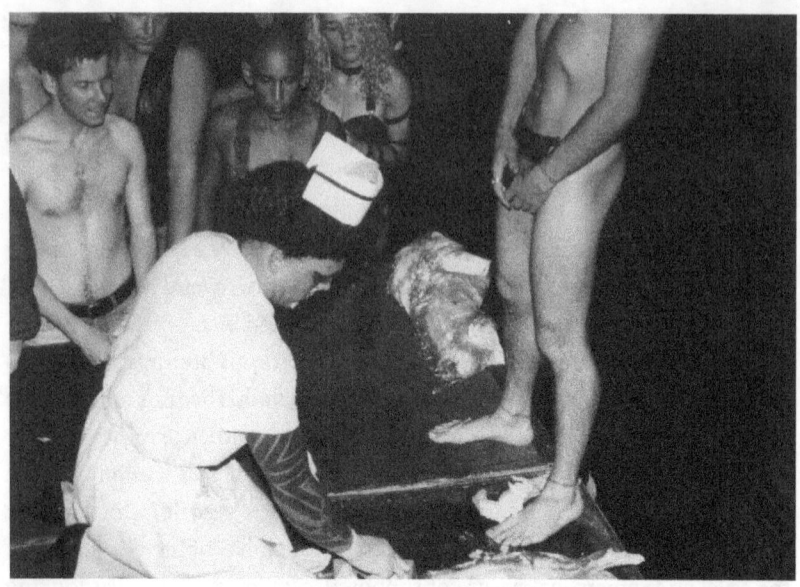

FIGURE 11. Ron Athey, "Nurse's Penance." Club Fuck!, Los Angeles. 1992.
Photographer unknown. Courtesy of Ron Athey.

ary for his friend and collaborator Cliff Diller (cofounder of Club Fuck!,
one of the spaces in which Athey developed his performance practice). He
recalled Diller's affection for the "strong women" who tended to him on his
deathbed: "Archetypal goddesses and wood nymphs, skinheads and punks . . .
spoonfed meals, massaged and shaved and talked and prayed and confirmed
their love." By this point, they were all familiar with the routine. "We are the
visitor and the sick bed," he writes in Diller's obituary. "We live it."[55] That last
statement was made in reference to his and Diller's participation in Karen
Finley's project *Memento Mori* (1992) at the Los Angeles Museum of Contemporary Art (MOCA). Finley's installation was divided into two rooms,
"The Women's Room" and "The Memorial Room." The latter included rows
of hospital beds, some of which held patients attended to by their friends,
others of which stood empty. Diller and Athey volunteered to participate in
that part of the installation. He writes, "We sat in MOCA half naked, relaxed
and had heart-to-heart talks while people gawked at us."[56] They read out
loud to each other from Wojnarowicz's *Memories That Smell Like Gasoline*.
Cliff Diller died on 20 October 1992. *Martyrs and Saints* was performed on
11 November at Los Angeles Contemporary Exhibitions. Stosh "Pigpen" Fila
recalled, "[Cliff and Ron] had written a piece and they were going to perform

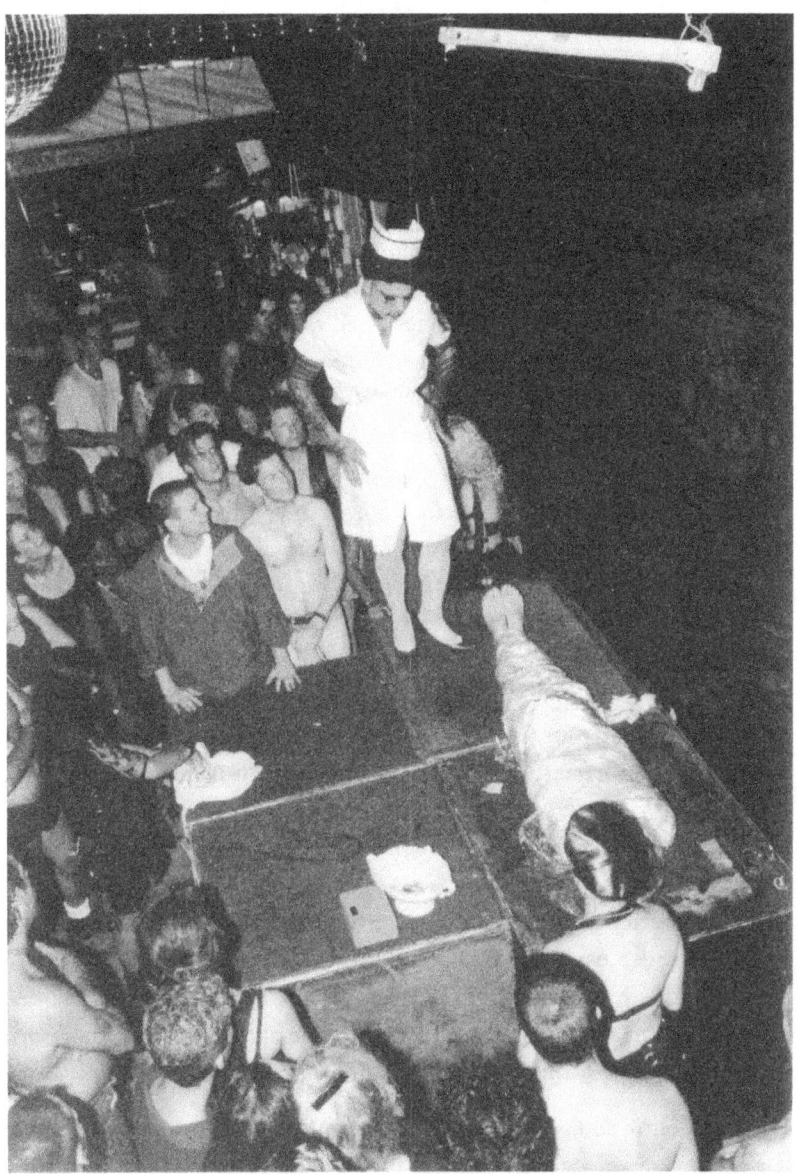

FIGURE 12. Ron Athey, "Nurse's Penance." Club Fuck!, Los Angeles. 1992.
Photographer unknown. Courtesy of Ron Athey.

together at LACE. Cliff got really ill the last two months before it was supposed to go on and Ron was going [to the hospital] every day. All of us were going almost every day to take care of Cliff, and then all of the sudden Cliff wasn't with us anymore." For Pigpen, performing in that event was a way of grieving, a "way of getting a piece of Cliff and Ron into my body, or on my body."[57] The exploration of the relationship between hurting and healing, between one's own pain and the pain of others, between pain and pleasure is a near constant in Athey's work, and it resonates with the art practices of at least a generation of artists who were forced to rapidly assimilate the deaths of friends, lovers, mentors, and idols.

Incorruptible Flesh: Dissociative Sparkle draws Athey's audience into an active relation to a scene that had previously been staged for them. This work is an extension of *Incorruptible Flesh (A Work in Progress)*, Athey's collaboration in 1996 with the artist Lawrence Steger. When the work was commissioned by the Center for Contemporary Art in Glasgow, both artists were HIV-positive and Steger was sick. *Incorruptible Flesh* is composed of a series of costumed tableaux that suggest a story about beauty, sickness and decay, care and corrosion. The work makes visual references to psychic surgery (as practiced in the Philippines), faith healing, and grieving rituals. Steger died in 1999. The Center for Contemporary Art asked Athey to revisit the work on the tenth anniversary of its performance. Implicit in that invitation is a demand that the artist confront Steger's absence.

Athey's name is often invoked in conversation about "art about AIDS," and yet what that means in relation to his work tends not to move beyond the assumption that because he is HIV-positive and because he often works with blood his work must be "about AIDS." Athey was diagnosed as HIV-positive in 1986, and he has outlived a shocking number of friends and collaborators. He addresses this issue in an interview with one of his recent collaborators, the scholar and performance artist Dominic Johnson. Athey explains:

> AIDS destroyed my world, so, how to go forward? And how to reckon with my own sickness? I still feel at odds with planning for the future. I was diagnosed HIV-positive in 1986—a death sentence until the three-therapy cocktail. [By the mid-1990s] I had already lived ten years of that sentence, and had been through the deaths of too many friends. (Having been an IV drug-user, and being gay, I had a particularly high number of sick friends.) And idols I never met also died: the death of David Wojnarowicz devastated me. I wrote down a line, "The Best are Already Dead," and felt this for some time. This heaviness triggered what I call the "dis-

sociative sparkle," which for me was manifested firstly in the grandiosity of the *Torture Trilogy* [*Martyrs and Saints, Four Scenes in a Harsh Life, Deliverance*]. In those three works, all the players (sick men, caregivers) recede into the paintings of Christian martyrology: my appropriation of esoterica and definitions of healing simultaneously heightened and became grim.[58]

Audience members seeking in his work something like a literal story about AIDS, however, are challenged. Many elements of *Incorruptible Flesh: Dissociative Sparkle* are direct citations of the earlier performance (the engorged genitals, the glitter ball, his pose). When asked to return to his collaboration with Steger, Athey chose to stage an extension of the last image from *Incorruptible Flesh (A Work in Progress)* as a meditation on this "heaviness" and "dissociative sparkle." That performance ended with Athey displayed on a plank, "his anointed body glistening," his genitals "Venus"-like, as Steger intoned words of "enlightenment and release," as one reviewer described it.[59] So when Athey places himself on the table in this six-hour performance he extends this last image and opens up the question of how one revisits a collaborative work after the death of one's collaborator—a work that furthermore had explicitly anticipated sickness, caring, and death in its visual vocabulary and framing.

When we enter the space of this performance, we encounter Athey waiting in a state that melancholically asserts Steger's absence. He creates a gap not so that we will fill it but so that we will share it.[60] But this should not be taken to mean that the tone of the performance was grief-stricken. If some members of the audience approached Athey's body with gravitas, others were more playful, and still others—really, a majority—were waiting, bored, and slightly uncomfortable because there were no chairs. Friends leaned against the walls chatting, gossiping, and bitching. By the end of the evening, the mood of the room had changed again, into a playful, perverse sense of togetherness. After the six hours were up, we untied his straps and he dismounted to laughter and friendly applause.

It is strange how different the moods of Athey's performances are from the larger affective cloud that distinguishes his reputation. His name is virtually synonymous with difficulty. In the artist's words, "How do I get interpreted? As a monster."[61] This fact surfaced at a conference in 2006 on "the aesthetics of risk" at the Research Institute at the Getty Museum in Los Angeles. The organizers advertised the conference with a portrait of the artist taken by photographer Catherine Opie (see plate 2). In this image, the artist stands in a majestic brown velvet robe that once belonged to the late artist Leigh Bowery. His shaved head is covered in needles that form a medical crown of thorns. His eyes are half-closed as if in a trance. The portrait is deliberately conservative. He looks regal; the portrait's composition borrows from the spare compositional strategy of paintings like John Singer Sargent's *Madame X* (1884) or Goya's *Cardinal Luis Maria de Borbón y Vallabriga* (1798–1800). The image refers to his performances: Athey wore Bowery's robe in "The Holy Eunuch" section of *Incorruptible Flesh (A Work in Progress)*, for example, and the crown of spinal needles appears in the "Suicide/Tattoo Salvation" chapter of *Four Scenes in a Harsh Life*.

The "aesthetic of risk" informing this image is not Opie's work alone. The heart of this image is the vasovagal intensity of Athey's performances. Opie's careful approach to the defining gestures of Athey's performances manages the viewer's reaction to the needles piercing his skin. Her series of portraits of the artist and his company (commissioned by The Estate Project for artists with AIDS) are the most beautiful and least sensationalist representations of their work. The photographs were made using the world's largest instant camera ("Moby C," in New York City), which was originally used to take life-size photographs of paintings. The unique scale, the intensity of their detail and color lend the photographs an aura of rarity and importance. They are as close to painting as photography can get.[62] Opie's photographs of queer subcultural figures use recognizable conventions of portraiture to set off the outsider status of her subjects. On this point, she shares much with Robert Mapplethorpe, who treated his "risky" subjects with the same rigorous attention to form and composition that he directed toward flowers. The risk associated with Mapplethorpe's and Opie's work grows from their identification with and commitment to queer subjects, as gay and lesbian artists. The risk they took in identifying themselves with their sexual communities was substantial, but it was less precisely aesthetic than it was professional. They certainly challenged notions of aesthetic value by treating socially abject figures as objects of beauty (Mapplethorpe's S&M models; Opie's gender outlaws). But the risk was in the substantial impact that their identification with the gay and lesbian S&M community might (and would) have on the reception and visibility of both artists' work. One might observe, however, that Mapplethorpe and Opie hedged their bets by also making work that fit neatly within the official language of the art world: Mapplethorpe's still lifes and Opie's bleak but gorgeous portraits of freeways allow their work to enter the marketplace without necessarily permanently associating the articulation of their careers with their identities as gay and lesbian artists, or with the identities and practices of those whom they take as their subjects at other moments. Their works exhibit very strategic relationships to risk in their practices as artists.[63]

That said, the "aesthetics of risk" is most dramatically bodied forth by the photograph's subject, Ron Athey.[64] The photograph is a portrait of the artist within his practice; it is a collaborative image produced for the camera much in the same way that Athey's performances produce an image for his audiences. This is a difficult image not only because it features piercing but because, as a photograph that cites a moment from a performance, we don't really know how to look at it or where to place it as a work of art. It has the disciplinary complexity of portraits of performance artists engaged in the performative gesture. Were it not for the aggressive aestheticization of the photograph itself (not only in terms of its composition but in terms of its technical richness), one might label it not a portrait but performance documentation.

The Getty event featured a conversation with Opie but excluded Athey himself from the discussion. Informally deciding to use Opie's portrait as a point of entry into a conversation about risk places Athey's performance practice and its reception history at a careful remove. More problematically, the narrowing of its attribution (treating Opie as the lone author of the work) simplifies the story of the relationship between the two artists: Opie worked with Athey in his early performances as a member of his company, and these images take on new meaning when we see them as a culmination of their shared experiences of the Los Angeles queer club scene in the 1980s and 1990s, and also as a declaration of the evolution of that experience into art practices. When the conference organizers used this image to advertise their event, they drew from Athey's performances—or, more nearly, from the unofficial mythology that surrounds them—to illustrate the phrase "the aesthetics of risk." But at the same time, they didn't want to get themselves mixed up with the baggage that comes with Athey himself, and so they accessed that idea of risk by using Opie's photography as, in essence, a prophylactic. In fact one could say that Athey's work becomes visible to the contemporary art establishment through art controversy, or through the circulation of Opie's photography. As it is used in the Getty program's title, the word *aesthetics* largely signals the creation of that prophylactic barrier between Athey's performance practice and Opie's photographs of it.[65]

Buried in the image's use as an emblem of the relationship between art and risk is the story of the artist's checkered reception history. As discussed in this book's introduction, Athey's work figured prominently in the NEA wars of the 1990s. This was the direct result of a homophobic, AIDS-panicked misrepresentation of the risk involved in attending one of his performances. When his image is deployed to represent the "aesthetics of risk," those doing so tap not only into the viewer's reaction to Athey's strange skullcap but into the reputation that has limited critical discussion of his work since the mid-1990s. Unlike Opie and Mapplethorpe, Athey has never sought the protective umbrella of a commercial career, and since 1994 he has rarely performed in the United States. He was not asked to participate in the Getty's event, and his image was used in their posters and on their website without his permission. (It was removed when the ethics of this use was questioned.) It is just a flyer for a small academic conference held at a research center high on a hill above the mansions of Brentwood in Los Angeles. But the incident has stuck with me, for the halls of such institutions are at a real remove from the spaces in which Athey performs. Although it did host public conversations about the AIDS crisis in the 1990s, the Getty Museum has no institutional commitment to queer underground fetish clubs or the art practices that grew out of them. Athey's performances nevertheless represent *something* to the people organizing the event, else why use that image, with its compound references to queer club work through Opie, Athey, and the homage to Leigh Bowery? Watching that unfold—getting the announcement, thinking that Athey would be on the program, and then learning he wasn't, and also seeing that the entire subject was dropped by the conference organizers (who I know as smart, politically engaged, and interesting scholars)—I felt it was important that someone try to figure out an answer to this question and try to talk about what exactly it is we think we risk by attending one of Athey's performances.

If I felt responsibility to these questions, it was because at the time I was struggling to write about his work. In 2005, frustrated by the lack of art criticism on Athey, I tried pitching a review of his and Juliana Snapper's opera, *Judas Cradle*, to *Artforum*. (The opera was staged in Los Angeles at the Red-Cat performance space in the Roy and Edna Disney Hall.) Given that it was Athey's first major performance in the United States in ten years, I thought the event merited some attention. *Artforum* turned it down, offering the excuse that since it wasn't in a commercial gallery, such a review would not fit within the magazine's review structure. The *Los Angeles Times* sent a theater critic to the same performance. She saw *Judas Cradle* twice, but she felt unable to write about what she saw. I am sympathetic. I later had a chance to write a review essay about the performance for the academic journal *GLQ* and just couldn't find an angle to frame an essay. The full-length opera was staged over four days to a full or nearly full house and wasn't reviewed in a single newspaper or art magazine in the United States. Of course, this happens to artists a lot, for various reasons. This problem in an artist's reception history can be self-perpetuating. With little critical discourse on the artist and with little gallery or museum presence, there is little incentive for people who write about contemporary art to address his or her work. You can't summarize the critical line on that artist and then create space for your own perspective because there is no ongoing conversation about the artist's work into which you may project your own voice. In such instances it can take a lot of work to figure out how to orient your reading.

It's fair to say that this book expresses my commitment to doing just that. Athey is a friend, and so I've long wanted to write about his practice. I find it challenging and often deeply moving, but I've struggled. His work is hard in nearly every sense one might imagine. Often staged outside commercial gallery spaces, it is unsupported by the writing that frames those spaces (reviews in art magazines and catalogue essays). The NEA wars of the 1990s in which politicians invoked Athey's name and sensationalized portraits of his practice to scandalize the public have left U.S. museums keeping their distance, even as they embrace artists like Paul McCarthy or Matthew Barney, whose work is arguably just as "scandalous" but whose reputation, whose institutional worth, is less directly impacted by the AIDS crisis and the homophobic discourse that has shaped the reception of work by HIV-positive artists. Of course, the work of these more institutionally visible artists is object-oriented and structurally different in terms of the challenges that it poses to the viewer. Most crucially, as Blocker explains, Athey's work has been read literally and as an affirmation of critical fear. "The literal," she writes, "is a strategic trope" that works to contain anxieties provoked by especially feminine uses and presentations of the body: the slimy, the penetrated, the prone, the sexualized. From a patriarchal and defensive perspective, the "female and the queer" body is "not seen to be performing at all." And so whereas Barney's work provokes his fans to decode, to read it in terms of a grand, slightly paranoid sexual mythology, Athey's, which can be no less ornate, no less researched, no less operatic (and is in fact cited by Barney as a source for his image-making), is read literally as whatever the critic thinks he sees. Such artists become for the phobic critic "the very essence of filth and pollution."[66]

This problem lies at the heart of the Minneapolis controversy. In 1994 Athey was invited by the Walker Center to perform at Patrick's Cabaret in support of the Minneapolis/St. Paul Lesbian, Gay, Bisexual and Trans-gender Film Festival. *Excerpted Rites of Transformation* included "Working Class Hell" ("a condensed version" of *Four Scenes in a Harsh Life*), "Addiction / Suicide Attempt / Crown of Thorns" (from *Martyrs and Saints*), "Pieta's Rebirth: Washed in the Blood of the Lamb," and "Reinterpretation of False Prophecies / Dagger Wedding" (fig. 13). The controversy centered on the opening scene, in which Athey cuts into Darryl Carlton's back, pats the wounds with paper, and hangs the paper on a clothesline. That the controversy centered on this action is surprising, because nearly everything that follows it is actually *bloodier*. But unlike the rest of the evening's performance, that scene from *Four Scenes* was staged between men, and thus it suited the Right's homophobic campaign. The *Minneapolis Herald Tribune*'s art critic wrote a story about the performance that grossly misrepresented the event. Mary Abbe (who had not seen the event) described audience members fleeing the space after having been exposed to HIV-infected blood. This apocryphal story was picked up by the Associated Press wire service, and it made national headlines, sparking a controversy over the approximately $150 of federal funding indirectly used by the Walker Center to support this off-site event. Athey stood accused not only of "spreading" sexual perversion (the usual charge applied to gay artists) but of putting audiences at risk of coming into contact with contaminated blood. He became the favorite example in a successful attack against federal funding for politically legible, challenging work.[67] This is in spite of the fact that Athey's work had never been supported by public funding. That Senator Jesse Helms would use Athey to illustrate a sermon regarding federal funding of perversion is one of many of this incident's many strange ironies (see fig. 14). But it hardly matters. Blocker writes, "The contradictions of the literal body are especially profound in the era of AIDS and the culture of blood panic. The now infamous performance staged by Ron Athey at the Walker Art Center in 1994 offers bewildering examples of both literalism as artistic technique and the selectively applied literalist interpretation of those techniques."[68] There is a psychotic dimension to that literalist reading. It was Athey's body that animated the homophobic rhetoric of the right-wing senator hell-bent on dismantling public funding of the arts. But if his mere body could do that, it was because people ascribed a supernatural power to that body to initiate the collapse of civilization (see plates 3–4).

A flat-footed literalism informs even liberal responses to the artist's work. Take the following article about *Incorruptible Flesh: Dissociative Sparkle*, written by Andrew Hultkrans for *Artforum*'s website Scene and Heard:

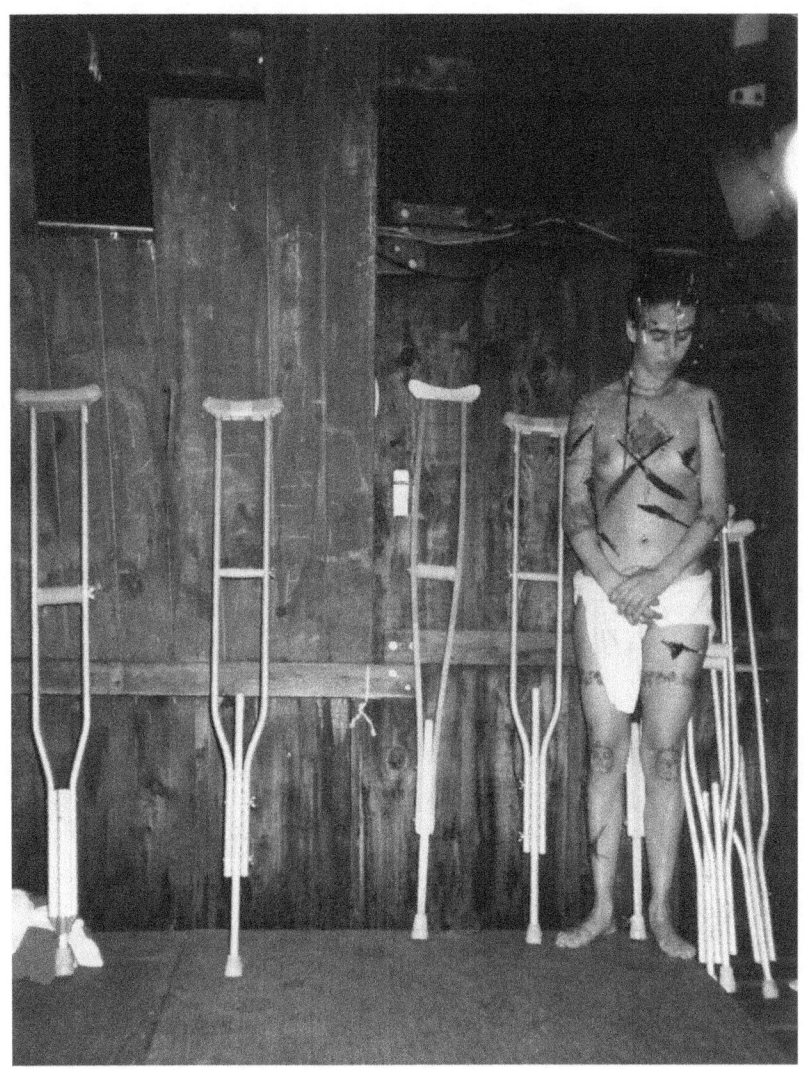

FIGURE 13. Ron Athey and Company. Stosh Fila as St. Sebastian.
The Faultline, Los Angeles. Ca. 1994–96. Photographer unknown.
Courtesy of Ron Athey.

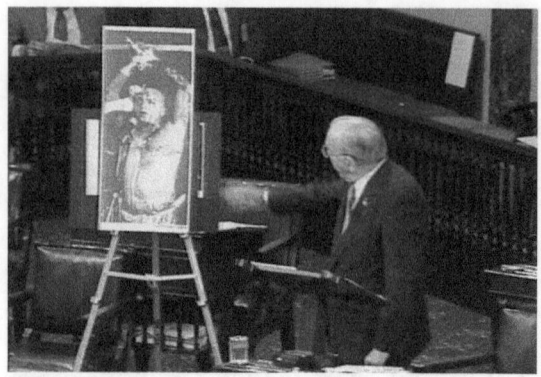

FIGURE 14. C-SPAN
broadcast of Jesse
Helms lecturing on Ron
Athey's practice from
the floor of the U.S.
Senate. 1994. Courtesy
of Cyril Kuhn.

Other than the era's then-emerging scourge of AIDS—through which
Athey found his artistic muse and message as an HIV-positive gay performer—domestic and geopolitical stakes today are much higher than
they were in the late '80s and early '90s. Leaving Artists Space and catch-
ing the tail end of the immigrant march—a far more relevant statement of
identity politics—I couldn't help but conclude that Athey's performance
was solipsistic and, ultimately, empty. That the most thought-provoking
aspect of the piece was the slow drip—probably unintentional—from
the exposed grip-end of the bat onto the floor was dispiriting. Yes, it was
diverting for a moment to wonder whether the fluid was sweat, melted
Vaseline, or anal leakage, but this hardly advanced my understanding of
or sympathy with living with HIV. . . .

On my way out, I was caught off-guard in the elevator when a middle-
aged woman asked me what I thought of the performance. . . . I mumbled
something about "admiring him, as I certainly couldn't do that," but I felt
like a liar. NYU's press sheet claims that Athey subjects himself to "physical,
cultural, and psychological challenges as a means to transform the conditions of the present," yet there he lay entombed in a sparsely attended gallery in SoHo, four hours to go, while millions of "illegal" workers marched
across the country, actively trying to change one of the all-too-real conditions of the present. Obviously, art isn't required to be politically relevant
and this isn't a Marxist critique, but hey, if the bat fits.[69]

I cite this hostile article at length because it was the only attention given to
Incorruptible Flesh: Dissociative Sparkle by an art publication (it appeared in
what is in essence the magazine's society column), and because it is too easy
to blame the Far Right for the way that Athey's work has been marked. The

diatribe is typical of the confusion that Athey's work provokes from the traditional critic of contemporary art (nearly all substantive writing on the artist comes from feminist and queer scholars in theater or performance studies): the expectation is that the work is political and that that political meaning will be obvious. The expectation is that it is somehow literally about AIDS and homosexuality because Athey is gay and HIV-positive. When Blocker writes about the deployment of the "literal body" in the reception of performance and by artists themselves, she does not mean "some essential category that, as an artifact of nature, is purer than the body as cultural product"; she means the body invoked in phobic discourse like that used by Hultkrans. It is "the unnamed counterpart of the logic of the ideal body, the symbolic body, the hoped-for body" (the aesthetic body, or the body in the aesthetic field), and it is conjured as a means for transferring the process of social abjection figured in the work *directly* onto the body of the artist (and his audience), using the artist's identity as the vehicle by which that delivery is made.[70] (As we will see in the following chapter, this is also true for some critical interaction with work about race made by artists of color.) The momentum of that kind of literal thinking is perhaps why Hultkrans couldn't resist the rhetorical satisfaction of ending his diatribe with the bash "if the bat fits."

Yes, Athey's work is about HIV and AIDS. But, again, what does such a statement mean?

Athey explains that the most challenging thing about this piece is neither the bat nor hooks piercing his skin. It is the physical discomfort of lying flat on his back for six hours, on an intensely uncomfortable bed of bars. The spectators who accepted the invitation to touch the artist seemed to intuit this—massaging his limbs, reaching under his back, lifting some of his weight off the bars where they could. It seems likely that what makes his performance something he can endure is this relief. It is no accident that Hultkrans invokes a "middle-aged woman" as the spectator against whom he defines himself on his way out. The touch on display was consistently nurturing, maternal, and sentimental (even when that touch was offered by men).[71] Such nursing is as unusual in an art gallery, at least the kind imagined by Hultkrans, as was the presence of a woman in the surgical theaters painted by Eakins. Furthermore, for some of us, seeing women looking after Athey was not only a reiteration of the feminization of nursing and care but a reminder of the numbers of women impacted by AIDS, as the pandemic turned women in queer circles into caretakers and AIDS activists.[72] Athey has worked with a small army of attentive butches, queer women, and transgendered people since the early 1990s (such as Stosh Fila [Pigpen], who appeared in the Minneapolis performance, and Julie Tolentino, who produced it). Even solo works like *Self Obliteration Solo* or *Dissociative Sparkle* often include supportive labor. Queer women sweep in, just below the focus of attention, to take care of things—to pick up "sharps," adjust straps, keep things running smoothly.

Asked about the frequent presence of female figures in his work, Athey turns to martyrology; images of female saints tend to show them enduring mutilating violence alone. They suffer in isolation. A male saint, however, is likely to be pictured in the arms of the women who will nurse his wounds or bury him.[73] His work explores and complicates this aspect of masculine performance, its absolute dependence on the (often affective) labor of women. This might also explain why most of his works invert the dynamics of the definitional feminist performances that explore the sadistic dynamics of power in relation to an isolated, passive female body. For example, in her performances of *Cut Piece* (1964–65) Yoko Ono sits next to a pair of scissors that audience members may use to cut off pieces of her clothing. *Cut Piece* solicits aggression from its audience. As audience members lean in to cut away at her clothes, one can feel Ono bristle. Maggie Nelson writes eloquently of the work's cruel poetics:

> For the first several minutes of her 1965 performance of this piece at Carnegie Hall, most of the audience members were content with a playful snip. But it isn't long before an aggressive young man comes along and sets to some more serious cutting. As he works on dismantling her, Ono twitches, seemingly struggling to maintain her composure. The pleasure the man takes in snipping through her bra straps feels childish—a small, dim cruelty. Yet the whole point of the piece is that Ono has invited this violation. She didn't lay out a feather or a jar of cream; she laid out a pair of scissors and named the piece *Cut Piece*.[74]

Nelson moves on to describe the poetics of cruelty explored by Marina Abramović in *Rhythm O* (1974). Here the artist famously stood passively next to a table holding seventy-two objects, including a gun, a bullet, a saw, a whip, paint, knives, and matches. Abramović's audience was invited to use any of these items, and by the end of the six-hour performance, she was stripped of her clothes, "she had been cut, painted, cleaned, crowned with thorns, and had a loaded gun pressed against her head."[75] Audience members intervened and brought an end to the performance. Nelson rightfully points out how effectively both of these works disrupt the presumptions made regarding the beautiful woman—that beauty places her on a pedestal where she is protected. These performances instead reveal a latent collective impulse of violence toward that body. Discourse on beauty pulses with a promise of violation.

The dynamics of *Incorruptible Flesh: Dissociative Sparkle* are different from those foundational feminist interventions. When we enter the gallery Athey is already there on display, like a living corpse. He is a passive object to our attention, and our relationship to his body is scripted. He is accompanied by an attendant who implicitly models what one is supposed to do: wait and look after him. One way of keeping company mirrors the other. It starts from a different place, and thus works a different set of social instincts. In this interaction, we encounter the challenges of the public culture that Butler calls for in *Precarious Life*, one configured by something other than the claim for bodily integrity: "If I am struggling for autonomy, do I not need to be struggling for something else as well, a conception of myself as invariably in community, impressed upon by others, impinging upon them as well, and in ways that are not fully in my control or predictable?"[76] Ono and Abramović surface a latent communal hostility—a phobic and violent social instinct against the (female) body. Their performances are much closer to the threat embedded in Eakins's painting, in which the spectator becomes a participant in an imaginary prodding, probing, cutting, wounding.

Shvarts responds to the discursive violence and affective overload that surrounds the abortive body by evacuating that body entirely from the performance. Athey not only exaggerates the social vulnerability of his body; he overtly eroticizes it. It's not mystical. It's a carnal refusal to turn one's eye to the heavens, an insistence on both the magic and the banality of flesh. It's what the body becomes under the disco ball's "dissociative sparkle," the weird and funny appeal of pearls pulled from his ass, or the reveal of wounded flesh: the ordinariness of touch and the frank brutality of the nurse.

He physically pushes his body right up against the female: the bloated, watery, and soft genitals, the penetrated core, everything wet, soft, sparkly, and bleeding—it is more than antiphallic. In this performance, Athey's body is a dichotomous embodiment of the violated body. When he extends to his audience an invitation to touch him, he not only draws out the spectator's relationship to that penetrated body; he confronts our desire to disavow it. Making the work *harder* is the fact that, as a sadomasochistic performance, the entire scene is framed as an expression of desire and longing.

Incorruptible Flesh: Dissociative Sparkle is not about AIDS in any traditional sense of that word *about*, and it is not exactly about remembering Steger, nor does the work memorialize him. It doesn't tell this story; rather it absorbs us into the story's structure. Athey chooses not to make a work about

Steger's death but to work from the final pose of his last performance with Steger. And there he waits for him. There he waits for his own death, already lying in state. We rehearse this relationship of the past to the future together. It is here that the work is haunted most explicitly by its history. Such a performance is not a political act in the same way that a protest march is, but it is no less, and no less powerfully, an act of determined political defiance.

3 | THINKING FEELING

criticism and emotion

What Happened to Feeling?

One of the challenges of writing about this work is the way it forces us to take our feelings into account. We must do so whether we are writing about obviously challenging work like Athey's and Shvarts's, or gentler practices of intimacy, like that of Adrian Howells. This can make the practice of criticism itself feel like trying to stand on shifting sands, for how we feel about a work of art changes, and our own experiences never match perfectly with those of other people. Knowing how we feel is hard enough. Capturing that in writing? Trying to stabilize that experience, to fix it as a photograph captures movement? Writing about Athey's work, I am acutely aware of the aspects of the experience of it that get away from me. So I try, mainly, to give the reader a sense of what happened and where and how those memories of the event travel.

Emotion is no small subject in art history and art criticism. But, as is the case with any discipline, how emotion figures into the field is shaped by traditions of thought. Feelings happen in art on multiple levels: as a subject represented in or by specific works, as something produced in us by those works of art, and as something we experience as expressed by the artist. We are used to thinking about artists as people who feel things intensely, who

even feel things *more* than the rest of us. The artist's emotionality is traditionally transformed into a symbol, an allegory for something much larger—for
some universal, transcendent truth. This is a romantic notion in every sense
of that word. It describes our ongoing cultural fascination with the artist as a
special type of person, and it also describes Romanticism's broad legacy. The
Byronic image of the artist as wild child survives in rock-and-roll icons, on
our movie screens, and in our attraction to the drama of "bad boys" like Paul
McCarthy, Jean-Michel Basquiat, Matthew Barney, and Dash Snow (to name
four very different art world personalities). This romance with the artist's
emotionality lives on, even though in the wake of postmodernist suspicion
of such paradigms we ought to know better. Warhol famously refused this expressive model by declaring himself to be a machine. Much process-oriented
and minimalist work appears hard and technical. Collaborative, participatory works can completely displace the artist's personality from his practices.
The figure of the emotional artist may still have pull in popular culture as well
as in the art press, and he may still draw crowds to the museum, but the *critical* cachet he enjoyed at the height of Abstract Expressionism (e.g., Jackson
Pollock) has dwindled.

In a polemical essay on the state of art criticism, James Elkins gives a useful portrait of the shifts in the place of emotion in writing about art.[1] Until
the middle of the twentieth century, much art writing could be described as
literary, as portraits of how the critic felt about the work of art. Such writing
could universalize the critic's reaction to artworks and usually ignored the
social, political, and historical implications of artworks, as well as the implications of the critic's own responses to them. In the middle of the twentieth
century, the orientation of art criticism began to change. As Elkins explains,
writers associated with the magazine *Artforum* (founded in 1962) and the
academic journal *October* (founded in 1976) established alternative models
that appeared to be more "rigorous," less personal in tone, and also more critically engaged with the question of how to discuss the material forces that
shape art, while keeping our attention on the work itself. In her work on
Artforum's formation and its influence, Amy Newman maps its increasing
reliance on models centered on what is "there" in the work, as critics reached
for a kind of scientific weight to anchor their observations. Critics wanted to
address the way artworks engage history and politics through form. Michael
Fried's essay "Art and Objecthood" (1967) is a particularly influential example
of the rhetorical opposition to that which feels "personal."[2] In an interview
with Newman, Rosalind Krauss, one of the founding editors of *October*, describes a move away from practices in which "poets would compose emotive

catalogue prefaces for artists" and a critical turn toward something that felt "*hard*, verifiable."[3] This led to the large-scale reconfiguration of art criticism in order to raise its level of seriousness, promoting contemporary art history, in particular, to the level of an academic discourse. Even in the past decade's endless discussions of the crisis in art criticism (in which art criticism is cast as compromised by the market and is distinguished from academic work, which one worries in turn has become almost unreadable in its density), seriousness is presumed to be one of the principal values most worth defending, although there has been little consideration in such discussions of what one means by that term, outside of an independence from market influences. Elkins writes, "Metaphors of intellectual labor, of difficulty, of challenge recur in *Artforum* discussions, beginning with Greenberg: when it is good the work is dry, hard, obdurate and irrigable. . . . It is not easy to imagine how these values could be transposed to the present, and even if they were, it is not easy to picture how useful they would be."[4] Because emotion itself has been associated in art criticism with a self-indulgent and naïve practice, it has been absorbed into the category of things one ought not take seriously. The serious art critic steers clear of anything resembling "a private history, a personal history."[5] A kind of austerity rules this body of writing, in which criticality has a narrow range of acceptable affect; whether the critic expresses a cool appreciation, clinical detachment, or critical disdain, she must be serious (unemotional), and she must address serious things (hard facts). Gavin Butt observes that "taking something seriously is in large part a morally sanctioned and habitually ingrained form of cultural response to something we take to be of value."[6] Seriousness is a disciplinary and disciplining stance that includes both a set of rules regarding the appropriateness of objects of criticism and the affective position that the critic takes in relation to the object of her writing. This is a particularly important question for critics working in queer studies. As Butt writes, queer culture is defined by a "troublesome relationship to serious appraisal" because it is profoundly defined by its capacity to "hold dear" that which is designated as the "non-serious, the trivial and the insubstantial."[7] As we shall see, this intertwining of affect, systems of value, and politics is also central to the work of artists working from other positions of marginality and exclusion. The call for serious criticism in mainstream contemporary art history (by which I mean the writing that grew out of *October* and *Artforum* after the 1960s) limited its ability to address the formal and political complexity of work that centers on the interface of the personal and the political. At issue here is a resistance to the sticky world of feelings and politics.

Emotion is widely assumed to make things easier to get and to pollute critical thought. Critical thought, conversely, is assumed to displace emotion. Even as he calls for a reexamination of the ethos of contemporary criticism, Elkins doesn't press this point. In an earlier examination of art and emotion, for example, he writes of his work as a scholar, "The piles of information smother our capacity to really *feel*. By imperceptible steps, art history gently drains away a painting's sheer wordless visceral force, turning it into an occasion for intellectual debate." He writes of the waning of the intensity of his own feelings for paintings under the disciplining pressure of his work as a historian. Inevitably, "in its cumulative effect history undermines passion. It smothers strong emotion and puts calm understanding in its place. It puts words to experiences that are powerful because they are *felt* rather than thought, and in doing so it kills them."[8] In more recent writing, however, Elkins makes it clear that the critical formations opposing passion and analysis, feelings and thought are no longer adequate: "Calls for a return to criticism that is serious, complex, and rigorous are indebted to the model provided by *Artforum* and its descendents. That means, in turn, that it is important to ask whether it makes sense to revive those particular senses of commitment, verifiability, and intellectualism. It seems to me the only defensible answer is that such values are no longer a good fit for art and the beginning of the twenty-first century."[9] These values were *never* a great fit for art. "Serious, complex, and rigorous" criticism can be passionate and personal. Art can be hard and difficult and also saturated with feeling; this is true of writing about art as well.[10] The rhetorical deployment of the personal and the emotional should not be assumed to be a retreat into an ahistorical, apolitical self; such explicit turns to emotion may in fact signal the politicization, the historicization of that self and of the feelings through which that self takes shape in relation to others. The blanket refusal to consider this possibility is itself a political failure, as is the pretense that a critical position can be taken independent of the author's networks of affiliation, friendships, and mentoring relationships, and as if it were not informed by his or her points of identification, estrangement, and institutional location.

The critical shifts mapped by Elkins had their impact on the artist: the romantic vision of the artist whose individual suffering transcends his time and place was long ago supplanted by a model of the artist and the art world as socially, politically, and institutionally situated. Artists engage this fact in diverse ways: by institution critique (e.g., Andrea Fraser's *Museum Highlights* [1989], Fred Wilson's *Mining the Museum* [1992–93]), by mapping the material context for the work of art (Hans Haacke's *Shapolsy et al. Manhattan Real Estate Holdings, A Real Time Social System, as of May 1, 1971* [1971]), by integrating art and activism (Suzanne Lacy and Leslie Labowitz's *Three Weeks in May* [1971]), and by engaging the question of history itself directly, making work that is a critically engaged historical practice (e.g., Jeremy Deller's *Battle of Orgreave* [2001], Ken Gonzales-Day's series *Erased Lynching* [2003–]). Concurrently, different models of artistic expression have also emerged, taking this politicization of the self as a starting point for recasting the very act of self-imaging (e.g., Adrian Piper's *Cornered* [1988], ASCO's *No Movies* [1972], Guillermo Gómez-Peña's *Border Brujo* [1988–89]).[11] This is where emotion makes things harder, more difficult, and more interesting. Such works speak to the complexity of feelings themselves, to their sociality, and to the fluidity of the self's boundaries. Finding the right language to access this is not easy because it requires a major shift in the vocabulary we use for talking about not only emotion but artistic expression itself. For some guidance in developing this vocabulary, let us turn to work in which emotion figures centrally, Franko B's *I Miss You!* (2003) and Nao Bustamante's *Neapolitan* (2006, 2009), in order to access the texture and complexity of emotion within performance, and James Luna's *History of the Luiseño People: Christmas, La Jolla Reservation (1990)* (2003, 2010) and Carrie Mae Weems's *From Here I Saw What Happened . . .* (1993–95), so that we may see how emotional complexity is played out within a work in order to problematize the association of the emotional weight of History with particular communities of people.

The Difficulty of Sentimentality: Franko B's *I Miss You!* (2003)

One can't talk about Franko B's work without addressing its emotional landscape. Like Ron Athey, Franko B works with his body. His actions leave a strong mark on his audience, and, as is also the case with Athey's work, what these performances say is by no means transparent. For over fifteen years (1990–2007) Franko B was largely known for "bleeding performances." These were live actions in which the artist bled either from wounds he'd created himself or from catheters that had been inserted into his arms by a medical professional before the performance.[12] For many, the very idea of such a practice is challenging. Photographs of his performances often show the artist naked and covered in white body paint that intensifies the visibility of his wounds. Many viewers, whether or not they are particularly squeamish, experience these documents as aggressive. Setting aside the reactions that some people have to blood (which can be independent of one's openness to this kind of performance), photographs of Franko B's bleeding performances can be harder to handle than the events themselves, largely because they conjure

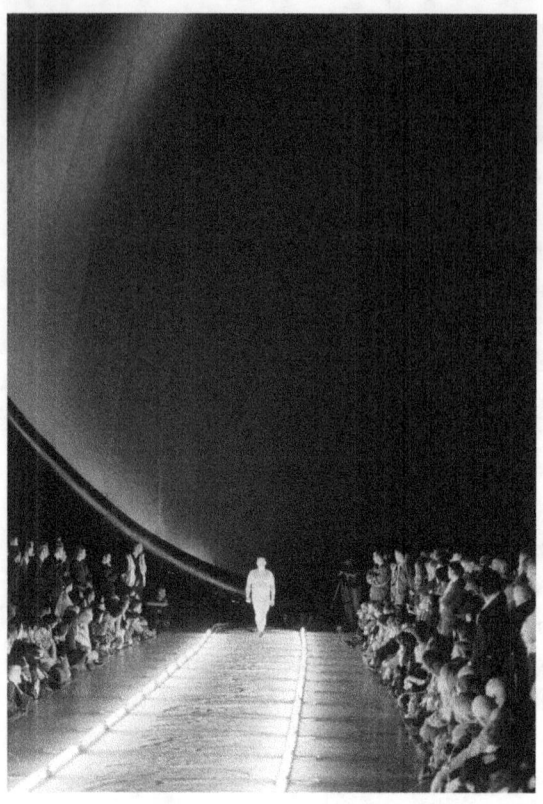

FIGURE 15. Franko B, *I Miss You!* Tate Modern / Live Culture. 2003. Photograph by Hugo Glendinning. Courtesy of Franko B and Hugo Glendinning.

an idea of the performance that is out of scale with the live action. At the live event, you can be present and also turn away. You can look at the floor and still be a member of his audience. Franko B has repeatedly declared that audience members are free to respond as they wish and as they need. Looking away is perfectly acceptable. I make a point of emphasizing this because I think many who are not used to such performances (a majority of readers) imagine attending a live event as being *forced* to look. But the experience of these events is not like that; they are hard, but they are not hard because of what you see.

I Miss You! was one of the last pieces to evolve from Franko B's practice of working with the process and spectacle of bleeding. In this performance, the artist bodies forth a single melodramatic gesture and frames it as a union with the audience. Naked, covered in white body paint, he walks a length of white canvas while bleeding from his arms (figs. 15–16). When he staged *I Miss You!* for the Tate Museum in 2003, he placed his runway lengthwise along its cavernous Turbine Hall, a cold, industrial space. At the time, the hall was filled

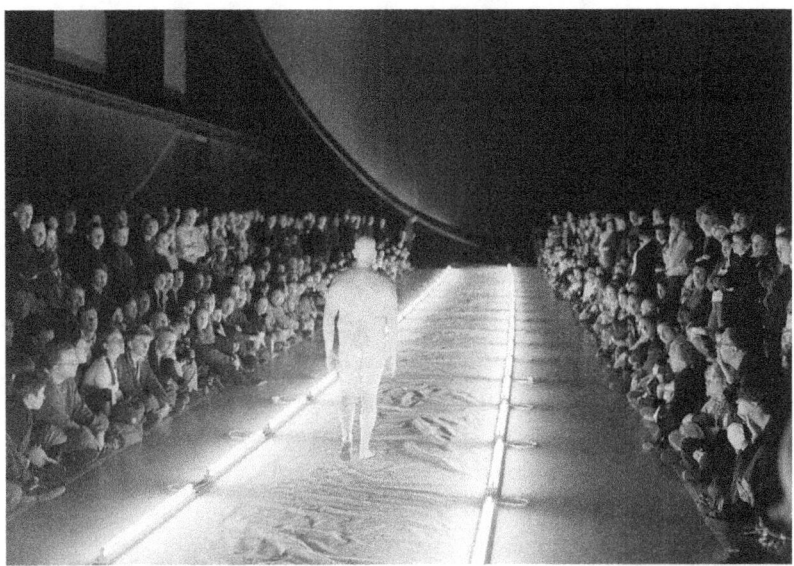

FIGURE 16. Franko B, *I Miss You!* Tate Modern / Live Culture. 2003. Photograph by Hugo Glendinning. Courtesy of Franko B and Hugo Glendinning.

with a suspended sculpture that looked like enormous fallopian tubes (Anish Kapoor, *Marsyas*, 2002). The performance was staged underneath this red structure, which arced across the hall. Franko B walked ceremoniously past his audience and toward a bank of photographers at the base of the aisle. The hall was dead silent, except for the mechanical whirring and clicks made by the cameras. He was lit up on both sides by florescent tubes edging the canvas aisle. Blood slowly dripped along the canvas and collected at his feet at each end of the catwalk, where he stood before turning around and beginning his march again. The performance was structured to resemble a fashion show or a wedding, and the blood-splattered canvas Franko left in his wake was used to make paintings, some of which he gave away to friends as keepsakes.

The experience of witnessing this performance was riddled with the questions you might expect: Should we be doing this? Is he okay? It seemed to take forever for Franko to complete his walk down the aisle, and he repeated this march several times. His body was ghostly, dwarfed by the enormous sculpture hanging over all of us and also by the scale of the space. The mood of the performance was intense; it felt like a silent opera. He seemed vulnerable, lonely. Although always composed, he was, near the end, clearly straining with the effort to keep up his march. Even knowing that he had medical assistance waiting on him, it was impossible not to feel moved and concerned.

I Miss You! is a stark enactment of a fantasy about love and its allure. It is about death, but only as the threat implied by love: Love me (Come back!) or I'll die. Franko B's walk alone down the aisle condensed into a performance the extravagant internal scripts we spin in our heads at the most harrowing points in the process of falling in love, teetering on the edge of abandonment. The scene was marital, but rather than celebrate the couple, we bore witness to the artist's isolation.

Franko walked out of our view, and the lights when up. Standing up, I felt a wave of intense emotion pass through me. I swallowed the urge to cry and looked around for a bar. *I Miss You!* is staged as the act of a desperate lover, an exploration of the aggression the lover feels toward his own body as an instrument of both desire and humiliation. Acknowledging this experience of love, recognizing that this experience registers in the body, is both painful and valuable. For a performance so obviously Catholic, it was also very punk. The artist learned his craft in London's anarchistic squatting scene and has long had a relationship with the queer music scene. If the performance felt punk, it was not in its aggressiveness (nudity, blood) but in the combination of the spectacle of the wounded body with the refusal of a redemptive gesture. As Tavia Nyong'o writes, punk represents "a withdrawal from the constraints of an affirmative culture": "Punk feelings help specify a radically passive and even masochistic orientation to the world."[13] Franko B's performances are staged as ritual but enact no salvation for either the artist or the audience. If we ask ourselves, Why would he do that to himself?, we might also ask, Why do we open ourselves up to anyone?

Many of us were surprised by the emotionality of the piece. For all the blood, for all the ways his performances have an edge one associates with punk, metal, or fetish scenes (his work overlaps with all of these), the thing that really unsettles the critic is the work's tenderness and sentimentality. *I Miss You!* is earnest. His work is often completely and unapologetically sentimental. In one performance, for example, he swings on a swing set, naked, to a melancholy piano score evocative of children's rhymes. In *I Miss You!* Franko B doesn't so much express himself as *leak*. We do not learn a thing about his biography in these performances. They are neither autobiographical nor confessional. He says nothing and in fact does very little. These events are nevertheless supercharged with emotion. Those feelings do not come from the artist so much as they circulate through the room and around his spooky body.

Sentimentality is generally unwelcome in institutional spaces associated with contemporary art; in its messiness, its direct assertion of the world of feeling, and in its hopeless association with the low and the popular (e.g., soap operas and pop music), the sentimental stands in opposition to the codes of conduct that regulate the social spaces of art consumption. In an essay on her experiences as the founding editor of the journal *High Performance*, Lynda Frye Burnham describes the abject status of emotion in discourse on contemporary art:

> Abstract art and fashion serve to remove feelings from art, to leave undisturbed the deep sleep we are falling into, where we feel nothing and nothing touches us.
>
> Let emotions belong to the theater, the art critics say. Artists can only be concerned with ideas and philosophies. And the real pursuits turn away from performance altogether because the very presence of the "hot" human body implies emotion, and emotion flows dangerously close to propaganda and self-indulgence.[14]

When Franko B bodies forth this maudlin gesture, walking alone down the aisle, bleeding for us and offering it as a declaration of feeling ("I miss you!"), he walks toward the steamy zone of sentiment, where the authenticity and value of emotion is always already in crisis. For a critic whose values are organized by the assumptions Burnham describes, his work is easy to dismiss as a kind of freak show entertainment, as mawkish and self-indulgent. And his audience's investment in the performance is even more suspect, as it appears to thrive on a vicarious thrill, a provisional identification with the idea of his suffering.

In his influential polemic opposing the avant-garde and kitsch, Clement Greenberg describes the latter as a category of "vicarious experience and faked sensation" and "the epitome of all that is spurious in the life of our times."[15] For Greenberg, the term *kitsch* signaled the recycling of feeling through popular culture at the expense of the new and the authentic. Many of the works disparaged using this vocabulary (*vicarious, fake,* and *kitsch*) fit easily under sentimentality's umbrella. Greenberg's complaint belongs to a broad rhetorical practice in criticism, in which the author gains the moral high ground by taking a stand against sentimentality. When such language is used in relation to contemporary art, it often wraps itself around a denunciation of political correctness, in which the artist's good intentions override his commitment to good art. In her essay "The Social Turn," the art critic Claire Bishop uses similar terms to denigrate contemporary collaborative, overtly political art practices as a form of sentimental liberalism. She writes, "The discursive criteria of socially engaged art are, at present, drawn from a tacit analogy between anticapitalism and the Christian 'good soul.'"[16] She attacks collaborative art practices that indulge this Christian ethic of self-sacrifice and good works. In another article she dismisses the work of Vik Muniz and Harrell Fletcher for "generating ripples of embarrassment through the audience for their reality TV sentimentality," a reaction she takes as synonymous with artistic failure.[17] Arguing in particular with Grant Kester's writing on collaboration and "conversation" (in which artists dissolve their authority in dialogue with specific communities), Bishop writes, "In the absence of a commitment to the aesthetic, Kester's position adds up to a familiar summary of the intellectual trends inaugurated by identity politics: respect for the other, recognition of difference, protection of fundamental liberties, and an inflexible mode of political correctness."[18] Her position represents a standard line in New York–centered, museum- and gallery-oriented art criticism on the relationship between art, identity, and politics. In *The Return of the Real* Hal Foster argues that "many artists treat conditions like desire or disease as sites for work. In this way they work *horizontally*, in a synchronic movement from social issue to issue, from political debate to debate, more than *vertically*, in a diachronic engagement with the disciplinary forms of a given medium."[19] He doesn't identify which artists "treat conditions like desire or disease" as sites for their work. It could be Athey. It could be Bob Flanagan and Sherry Rose (who expanded their S&M relationship, which was intimately related to Flanagan's cystic fibrosis, into a performance art practice). It could be David Wojnarowicz.

"Desire or disease" is, in Foster's formulation, a condition (an affliction?) from which no artist can achieve critical awareness. (Whereas once artists were engaged with art history, now, working from these "conditions," "the vertical lines appear to be lost.") Art of the period has become "dangerously political," grounded in issue and identity as the artist indulges an "over-identification with the other," which Foster forecasts as "a murderous disidentification from the other." "Today," he writes, "the left overidentifies with the other as victim, which locks it into a hierarchy of suffering whereby the wretched can do little wrong. . . . The right disidentifies from the other, which it blames as victim, and exploits this disidentification to build political solidarity through fantasmatic fear and loathing. Faced with this impasse, critical distance might not be such a bad idea at all."[20] Critical handwringing over the plight of the other is upstaged here by critical handwringing over identification with the other.

The antisentimental turn cuts across period and genre, and many of the most influential denunciations of the sentimental focus on this confluence of emotion and liberal politics. James Baldwin's essay "Everybody's Protest Novel" offers some of the most scabrous prose regarding sentimental fiction. Tackling the rigid political terms of the "race novel" (in which white and black characters battle over the humanity of the latter), Baldwin draws a deliberately polemical line from Richard Wright's *Native Son* backward to Harriet Beecher Stowe's *Uncle Tom's Cabin*. The movement from one to the other describes a liberal tradition that deploys (and exploits) black abjection in a national, self-serving rehearsal of racist paradigms. It is a controversial analogy: one novel (written by an African American man) offers a contemporary and hard critique of American dynamics of race and gender; the other (written by a white woman) is credited with having contributed to the Civil War and the abolition of slavery but also spawned an enduring tradition of minstrelsy and racist stereotyping. Baldwin's essay is an indictment of readers who feel their consciousness has been raised by *Native Son*'s violence as if such scenes bear out the full truth of racism's power. Baldwin works with terms and assumptions important to our conversation; namely, he presents sentimentality as a (bad) form of sadism, one ultimately complicit with the racist structures it purports to fight. He dismisses Stowe as a "pamphleteer." He calls *Uncle Tom's Cabin* "a very bad novel" and compares its "virtuous sentimentalism" with Louisa May Alcott's *Little Women.* The comparison needs no explanation, as, within the logic of the essay, the literary abjection of popular sentimental novels is treated as a given. Drawing from the presumption that one can name no genre more universally despised, he proceeds, "Sentimentality, the ostentatious parading of excessive and spurious emotion, is the mark of dishonesty, the inability to feel; the wet eyes of the sentimentalist betray his aversion to experience, his fear of life, his arid heart; and it is always, therefore, the signal of secret and violent inhumanity, the mask of cruelty. *Uncle Tom's Cabin*, like its multitudinous hard-boiled descendants, is a catalogue of violence."[21] The debate generated by Baldwin's essay was not provoked by his description of sentimentality but by his attempt to mark Wright's novel with its stain.[22] There is good reason for critical suspicion of sentimental practice: not only can such work package vicarious experiences of suffering as an enlightened form of entertainment, as Lauren Berlant explains in her writing on the subject, but the desire to make readers "feel right" (as Stowe herself once put it) can also look a lot like a desire for a world in which we all feel the same.[23]

The hard stand against the sentimentalist may be popular in criticism, but it frequently belies the complexity of the politics of feeling and identification, and it sometimes masks the critic's position, creating the illusion that she stands entirely outside the emotional economy she denounces. More problematically, it can support a critical practice that assumes that the problem is feeling, in and of itself, because in art feelings are always either not real or vicarious. (How many times have you seen an artist's, filmmaker's, or writer's lack of sentimentality cited as praise, as if the value of this were self-evident?) Complaints regarding the vicariousness of emotion in art have always struck me as Platonic, centering as they do on the problem that no emotion encountered in art is properly real, at least according to the standards by which such discourse measures realness.

The sharpest edges of antisentimental rhetoric are formed around words like *vicarious* and *inauthentic*. As Eve Kosofsky Sedgwick observed, "It would be hard to overestimate the importance of vicariousness in defining the sentimental." The anchoring point for a modern critique of the sentimental, she observes, is the identification of a "tacitness and nonaccountability of the identification between sufferer and sentimental spectator."[24] Threaded through such critical discourse are contradictory strands of thinking about art and emotion; it implicitly calls to mind the idea of an art form that does *not* depend on vicarious experience (for it is often vicariousness itself which the critic presents as the problem), while also banishing the juicy, nervous, and unpredictable dimensions of feeling triggered by proximity—especially where such proximity occasions empathy or identification. The feelings generated in the affective circuits between people are banished as always already suspect, for not being real, authentic, and truly one's own. The only solution offered by such rhetoric is the privileging of an anaesthetized version of the aesthetic encounter, from which the feeling body is banished. (On this point, I am tempted to see in Eakins's *The Gross Clinic* a sadistic emblem for the practice of criticism.)

———

Sedgwick observes that when we say something is sentimental, we describe a quality that pertains not to the text itself but to the reader's or viewer's relationship to it; in other words, there may be no such thing as an intrinsically sentimental text. She asks, "'Sentimental' with its quiverful of subcategories: don't they work less as static grids of analysis against which texts can be flatly mapped than as projectiles whose bearing depends utterly on the angle and impetus of their discharge?"[25] If sentimentality is presented as an overidentification with the other and if its abjection operates as a given in debates about the difference between good art and bad art, it is because that word embodies a singular truth about aesthetic judgment which must be disavowed in order for the disciplinary protocols of discourse on art to continue to operate. The line between good and bad art is fundamentally contingent (on class, for example) and deeply subjective.

The problem of sentimentality is not as easily dismissed in literary criticism as it has been in art criticism. Doing so would negate the value and influence of large communities of writers and readers (e.g., in the United States sentimental novels by Stowe and Rebecca Harding Davis, regional writing by Sarah Orne Jewett and Charles Chesnutt, the racial romances of Pauline Hopkins, and popular fiction by Horatio Alger, E. D. E. N. Southworth, and Helen Hunt Jackson).[26] Scholars invested in popular novels have a stronger voice within their discipline and have in fact reshaped its practice; we long ago gave up on using arguments regarding literary value as criticism's moralizing anchor. Interestingly, Foster's writing on these issues expresses anxiety that the practices of literary scholars might penetrate contemporary art history. His attack on the emergence of the ethnographic in art writing pivots on an unlikely reference to Janice Radway and her book *Reading the Romance*.[27] Radway asked readers of serial romances what they got from such novels and how they understood their reading practices. She was among the first scholars to take fans of feminine "trash" seriously. *Reading the Romance* was part of a wave of scholarship that moved beyond the assumption that consumers of popular genres are passive dupes to dominant ideology. To gesture back to John Vincent's work on difficulty and poetics: this kind of scholarship explores the question "What do readers want?" and also recognizes that not all readers want or need the same thing. This diversity in our investments and the text's enormous capacity to meet our interests are, in fact, what make the whole enterprise of literature interesting.

Radway is a cultural studies scholar who studies the formation of reading practices as well as institutional articulations of literary value. Her work is extraliterary, focused not on the text but on how it circulates. Diverse scholars — like Sedgwick, Jane Tompkins, Laura Romero, and Berlant — have spent quite a bit of time exploring how feeling can take on complex and productive dimensions in sentimental literature. The authors identified with this (porous) category were far from naïve about the textuality of their work, and sentimental writing is not always synonymous with the coercive dynamics that shaped its most celebrated (or notorious) examples. Some authors showed a remarkable optimism regarding the capacity for feelings in and of themselves to lead to action and social change. Others clearly saw the reader's feelings not as an end but as a means and as something that an author might manipulate to a wide range of purposes—sometimes even to stage an intervention against the habits of sentimental reading. Louisa May Alcott, famous for the intensely sweet *Little Women*, also wrote *Behind the Mask*, a potboiler and social satire in which an "old maid" pretends to be an ingénue governess and manipulates every member of the family through, of course, their sentimental investment in what they imagine to be her story (of some sort of suffering). Rebecca Harding Davis's "Life in the Iron Mills" quite clearly indicts its own middle-class readers who feel sympathy for the story's characters and do nothing regarding their real-world counterparts except read about them. The main character of that story, a factory worker with the soul of an artist, ends up in jail and slits his wrists in a scene that reads more like Poe than Stowe. Although the story has many of the hallmarks of the sentimental narrative, it is also acutely wary of the feelings it puts into circulation. Sentimental literature, in other words, is diverse, and a surprising amount of it is ambivalent about sentimentality itself.

As a number of literary scholars observe, there are countercurrents within sentimental culture in which sentiment and sincerity are redeployed in order to challenge exactly the sort of affective economy Baldwin described. Berlant uses the term *countersentimental* to describe texts that are "lacerated by ambivalence" and "withdraw from the contract that presumes consent with the conventionally desired outcomes of identification and compassion."[28] These works manifest a commitment to the transformative effects of emotion but also resist the universalizing imperative of sentimental traditions that use emotion to negate difference with the assumption that we all ought to feel the same. Countersentimental works explore the possibilities of feeling differently.

As live actions in which the artist appears to suffer before our eyes, *I Miss You!* and *Incorruptible Flesh: Dissociative Sparkle* both raise questions about vicariousness: within the space of art, it is hard to imagine how one might get closer to another's pain, and yet that proximity yields surprisingly little information about the other's experience. At such performances, I am very conscious of my own skittishness and unease, my own projection—but, above all, I feel acutely aware of the fact that there is a difference, a distance between not only myself and the artist but between myself and other spectators.

Although performances like Franko B's are worlds away from the nineteenth-century sentimental novel, we can think of the artist as having countersentimental practices in his commitment to "desire and disease" not only as content but as material (in some performances, he sprayed the venue with hospital disinfectant for its strange hygienic smell); in his reliance on a lateral (as opposed to vertical) poetics (refusing models that present a causal, linear narrative regarding feelings and politics); and in the open and unresolved structure of his performances, which throws his audiences back onto themselves.

The challenge of Franko B's work is connected to our suspicion that the pleasure we experience in being emotionally moved is structurally exploitative and sadistic; one might say that Franko B's and Athey's work explicitly stages the problem of the ethics of feeling for others. The overt masochism of Franko B's work in particular aligns a performance of bodily vulnerability with the world of emotion.[29] His performances are masochistic, but they also feel oddly sincere and nearly child-like. Tavia Nyong'o has used the term *punk feeling* to describe the sweet and rough masochism of queer and underground performance, its sometimes "truly shocking conflation of the sentimental and the obscene, the perverse and the innocent."[30]

Franko B's performances are staged at that punk intersection of "the sentimental and the obscene, the perverse and the innocent." The principal difficulty of his performance rests with his audience, with how *we* feel in relation to his display. The structural resemblance of *I Miss You!* to a wedding positions his audience as witness to his action and casts the performance as a ritual of transformation. Weddings give form to a relationship not only between two people but between that couple and a community (be it friends, family, or the state).[31] In walking down the aisle alone, Franko B performs a union with an absence, for an audience. In this sense, the performance locates itself in the agonistics of the melodramatic conclusion as one attempts to absorb loss, the gap between what one wants and what one has. If the loved one is missing from the artist, he is also missing from us. Franko B redirects questions about art and emotion away from the self-reflexive representation of the artist's emotional state to the production of feelings themselves within a social space. It's a risky move. In taking that walk alone, in marking the absence of the one he loves, he places the burden of filling the gap on his audience. He ask us if, and how, we plan to love him back.

The Strange Theatricality of Tears:
Nao Bustamante's *Neapolitan* (2009)

The emotional labor of Franko B's performances is visibly carried out by his weeping audience. To gain some perspective on how a critically engaged sentimentality might figure into an art practice, it is worth looking at artists who

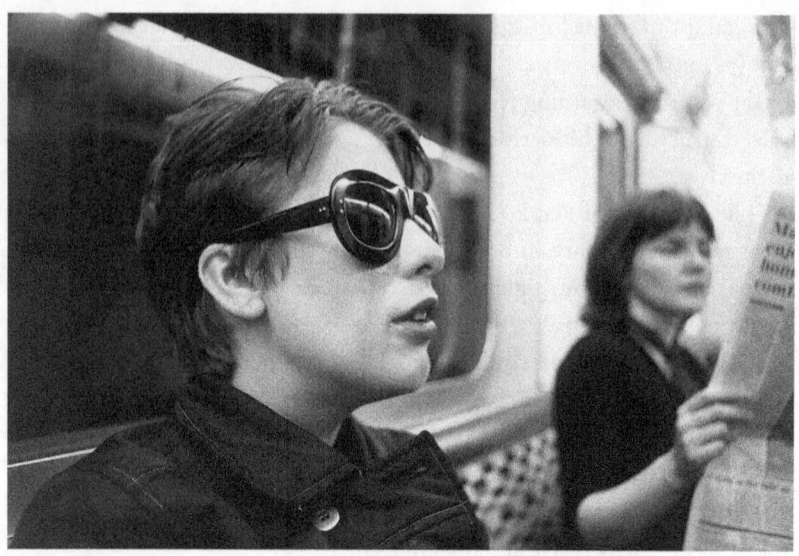

FIGURE 17. Hayley Newman, *Crying Glasses (An Aid to Melancholia)* from *Connotations Performance Images—1994–1998*. 1998. Photograph by Casey Orr. Courtesy of Hayley Newman and Matt's Gallery, London.

engage emotion more directly than he does. Tears are suspect, whether they are represented within a work of art or produced in the spectator. Tears seem to embody both the height of unquestioned emotionality and the depths of emotional manipulation.[32] Because of this, questions about the nature and sincerity of artistic expression figure prominently in works that feature a weeping subject. Hayley Newman's *Crying Glasses (An Aid to Melancholia)*, for example, shows the artist sitting in a subway car, wearing dark glasses (fig. 17). Tears appear to be streaming down her cheek. The photograph is accompanied by wall text that explains, "Over a year I wore the crying glasses while traveling on public transport in all the cities I visited. The glasses functioned using a pump system which, hidden inside my jacket, allowed me to pump water up and out of the glasses and produce a trickle of tears down my cheeks. The glasses were conceived as a tool to enable the representation of feelings in public spaces. Over the months of wearing glasses they became an external mechanism which enabled the manifestation of internal and un-identifiable emotions." The work belongs to a series of photographs and text called *Connotations—Performance Images*. Newman presents these images as documents of performances, but they are in fact staged images of fictional performances that never happened. *Crying Glasses* is therefore a false image of artificial tears. Although presented as "a tool to enable the representation of feelings in public spaces," within the larger context of falsified performance documents they become an uncomfortable allegory for the difficulty of "real" feeling (which the film director Krzysztof Kieslowski called "the fright of real tears").[33] Do we really want real tears from the artist? The photograph suggests that regardless of what we want from the artist, all the museum or gallery can offer us is a suspicious, unreliable record of performance—a third-hand record of emotions that may or may not be real. In fact all art, Newman suggests, is merely "a tool to enable the representation of feelings in public spaces" and not a tool to enable feelings themselves. Once emotion is absorbed into the sphere of representation, once a feeling becomes an image of feeling, its claim to authenticity (to being a real feeling) is thrown into question. Furthermore, the work mischievously implies that the disciplinary protocols of art history demand not sincerity from the artist ("real tears") but ironical distance. And so Newman offers a counterfeit version of *that*.

Marina Abramović's video performance *The Onion* (1995) calls attention to the difficulty of reading, bearing witness to, and responding to the artist's emotional display. In this piece, she holds an ordinary unpeeled onion to the side of her face and then slowly eats it, keeping her eyes pointed "up to the sky" (according to her own description of the performance) while we listen to a soundtrack of her complaining about her life. In a low, flat monotone, she recites a depressing litany of grievances, none of which is that grave or interesting: "I am tired of changing planes so often. Waiting in the waiting rooms, bus stations, train stations, airports. . . . I am tired of more career decisions, museum and gallery openings, endless receptions, standing around with a glass of plain water, pretending I am interested in conversation. . . . I am tired of always falling in love with the wrong man." This recitation (which is repeated several times over the duration of the performance) concludes with, "I want to understand and see clearly what is behind all of this. I want not to want anymore." The act of eating the onion begins as a perversely masochistic variant of using an onion to shed artificial tears—an external provocation to cry over a life not interesting enough to cry about. As the loop of complaints repeats itself, we watch her struggle over her own instinct as she takes one large bite from the onion after another. We hear her moan and whimper as she chokes it back, skin and all. (This aspect of the performance is almost erotic.) Over time she disintegrates before our eyes: her composed face collapses in abjection and grief.

This is a difficult performance to watch, even on a video monitor. You want to turn away, but you also want to keep watching to see if she finishes the onion. While at first the subject of the performance appears to be the artist's inability to feel, to care, to cry, as she gets deeper into the onion and is more and more overcome by the difficulty of eating it, her upset appears more and more authentic. In the end, it is not the authenticity of her tears that you question but their artificiality, in part because as you watch this video it is hard not to have a physical reaction in sympathy with the manifest difficulty of eating a raw onion while suppressing the impulse to gag. Importantly, the performance anticipates and interrupts the first question we usually ask of representations of crying: "Are those tears real?" Here what starts as a theatrical production of artificial tears appears to morph into real tears over the artificiality of the performance of her daily life.

Nao Bustamante's *Neapolitan* (2009) negates the question of whether or not her tears are sincere. The installation features a video of the artist sitting on a couch as she watches, rewinds, and watches again the end of *Fresa y chocolate* (Strawberries and chocolate), a moving film about the Cuban Revolution, whose drama revolves around the betrayal and exile of homosexual love (see plates 5–6). At the same point in the film's last scene, she starts to cry. When that scene ends, she rewinds and indulges in the same tears. She does it again. And again and again. The monitor is shrouded in domestic ornaments and grandmotherly doilies—not genteel white lace but a riot of garish orange and yellow. The monitor is cloaked in crocheted yarn; little tassels adorn every corner and dot the blanket that wraps around the monitor's base. The headphone's earpieces and wires have cute coverings, turning them into adorable caps. The bench is covered in its own tailored outfit. A black crow perches atop this mountain, wearing a crocheted hat. The installation is customized for each appearance. Electric cords, outlets, and power strips all wear yarn cozies that take the artist several days of continuous labor to fashion.

Abramović's tears appear unpleasant and painful, and, typical for the genre, her performance video is minimal: face, onion, blank wall, screened on a no-nonsense monitor. Bustamante's tears are, on the other hand, attractive. At the heart of *Neapolitan* is a scene of indulgence, the treat of a weepie. The installation is full of pleasure and care; we see this in the artist's obvious affection for the film and the loving hand applied to the installation itself, in which the television becomes a homey shrine. We also see it in the artist's desire to replay the scene over and over again and in the hospitality extended by the work to its own viewer. All those custom cozies invite the viewer to join her, to sit down and put on the headset. Usually video installations are hard to place in an exhibit; getting people to stop and put on headphones is hard enough, but getting them to stand or sit in a gallery for just five minutes is a real challenge. Not so with *Neapolitan*. The work is eminently approachable. In fact it's something of a scene-stealer: the bright colors, the plastic flowers and crow adorning its top demand the viewer's attention. In the artist's words, it's "showy."

Bustamante has said that when she sat down on the couch to record the crying performance for the camera, she expected that as she watched this scene over and over again, the tears would eventually stop flowing. But they didn't. The eleven-minute loop of the artist sobbing, making herself cry, is powerful and funny. She cries but doesn't seem (to me, anyway) unhappy. *Neapolitan* is oddly moving in its revelation of the momentum that tears have on their own, spilling over from the contrived scene of melodramatic spectatorship to suggest a self-sustained cycle, in which tears make more tears, in which tears migrate from screen to face and back again. This, the work reminds us, is what we want from melodrama.

The artist has lavished attention on the scene, looking after her television as if it were a sentimental object to be treasured. Crying, here, isn't something one stops but something one nurtures. The work has its own onion-like quality: layers of sticky-sweet sentiment collect around the story Bustamante watches. The work does not declare that the artist is sad because homosexuals were exiled from Cuba's revolutionary political community. It is not this history that makes her cry but a movie about it. It isn't even the whole film that works on her but just this one segment, this one swell in the film's affective score. Repeating this encounter and then looping these repetitions, Bustamante leaves no room for doubt: these tears are textual, squeezed from the film's melodramatic conclusion in which (classically) love must remain unrequited, in which the film's protagonist must let go of what he wants most. In melodrama, there is no solution, no resolution beyond the sacrifice of our happiness. There is no direct, linear relation between the story of *Fresa y chocolate* and that of *Neapolitan*. But one story, one scene, is wrapped around the other in an affective embrace.

The work contrasts nicely with Bas Jan Ader's *I'm Too Sad to Tell You* (1971), a three-minute silent black-and-white film of the artist crying (from which he also produced still photographs and postcards; fig. 18). Emotion here is both more intense and more contained. His eyes are wet, tears stream down his face, he tries to wipe his eyes dry, his face contorts into sobs, he holds his face in his hands, he grimaces. As the title reminds us, we do not know why Ader is crying; his sadness is cited as the very thing in the way of explanation, and so it registers as expression itself. As a male artist with a particular mythology (he disappeared while attempting to sail across the

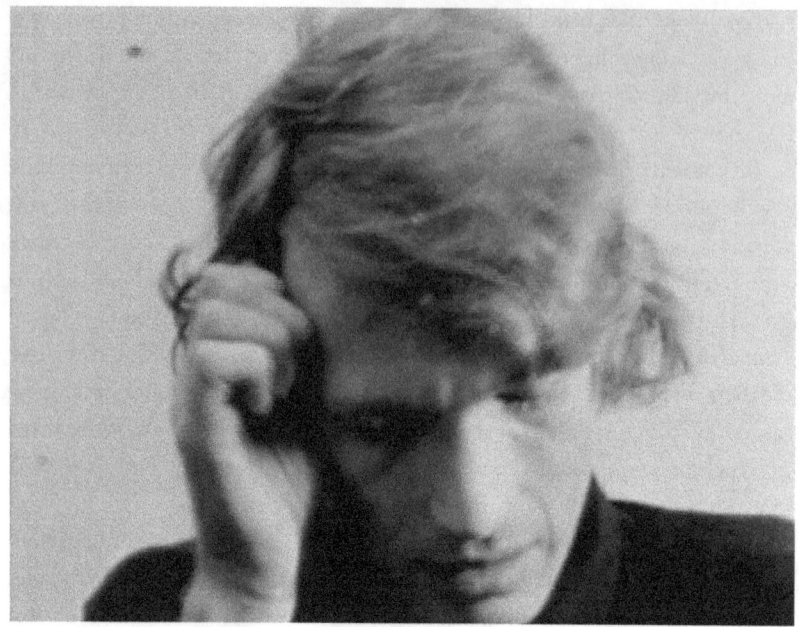

FIGURE 18. Film still from Bas Jan Ader, *I'm Too Sad to Tell You*. 1971. Black-and-white film in 16 mm. 3 min., 21 sec. Courtesy of the Bas Jan Ader Estate.

Atlantic in execution of a performance), Ader is closer to the eighteenth-century ideal of the gentlemanly "man of feeling" than he is to the female melodrama cited by Abramović and Bustamante—and this very gendered and classed difference signals the sociality of our feelings about feelings. We are ready to accept his tears as real, in part because there is a tradition of sad, melancholy white male artists that supports this response, a tradition Ader deliberately and ironically engages. His tears might register as real, and yet they are spared being marked as naïve.

I'm Too Sad to Tell You extends Ader's interest in exploring his own vulnerability as a performative subject, as in a series of quirky short films that document the artist falling over: riding a bicycle into a canal, falling from a tree, standing and swaying from side to side until he falls down. But it may also be read as a contemporary iteration of the self-representation of the male artist as emotionally injured, in which that very injury authenticates his artistic identity, as in, for example, Gustave Courbet's *Self Portrait as a Wounded Man* (1844–45) or *Self Portrait (Desperate Man)* (1943). When compared with Newman's photograph, Abramović's performance, and Bustamante's installation, Ader's film comes off as more directly seductive and also more private. Unlike our relationship with Abramović, we don't know the story behind his tears (other than that he's too sad to tell us). There is nothing in Ader's filmic performance to signal that we should read it as produced for the camera; in contrast, Abramović and Bustamante theatricalize the artificiality of their tears by showing us explicitly their cause. If the critic is tempted to read Ader's tears as performed for the camera, furthermore, he is likely to see in it not a story about how one can't trust the honesty of male emotion but rather a comment on the unreliability of cinema itself. As we look at a broader range of work in which crying figures centrally, we see that how we read emotion, and how emotion circulates, depends very much on the location and identity of the bodies shedding the tears. The emotionality of women is always already suspect, always already visible as performance, as imitative. Ader is a genius; the women are either acting or hysterics, or both.

Relational Aesthetics and Affective Labor

At this point, we should pause and consider the relational nature of emotion and its association with gendered forms of labor. It is widely accepted that since the early 1990s, the contemporary art world has increasingly invested itself in relational aesthetics. Nicholas Bourriaud's term was intended to describe the prominence of art practices that produce relationships (between the artist and the viewer, for example) as their object. Although Bourriaud's *Relational Aesthetics* was written as a response to a specific group of artists with whom he had worked (as is largely true of this book), the term *relational aesthetics* has wide application as a way to name the increasing centrality of relationships (e.g., of exchange, collaboration, and participation) to contemporary artistic practices. The historicization of relational aesthetics as a product of the 1990s belies the subjective, contingent, and relational structure of all aesthetic practices (even those that are object-based). But it does describe the increased visibility of work that evolved from the conceptualist and process-oriented art of the late 1960s and 1970s. The more a work looks like a relationship, the more important the place of affect and emotion may be to critical engagement with it.[34] This is explicitly the case with artists like Franko B and Adrian Howells (whose performances invoke structures of love, friendship, and intimacy), but it is also true of work that looks less personal.

Santiago Sierra is one of the most widely discussed and exhibited artists working along these lines. His work can appear totally complicit with the forms of exploitation that underwrite the privileged lives of his audiences. This often leaves the latter with no moral high ground from which they might pass judgment on the artist or his work. His signature installations re-produce, in gallery settings, the exploitation of day laborers (by, for example, paying undocumented workers to sit in boxes). The audience's relationship to those forms of exploitation is his subject. How can you judge Sierra for deploying underprivileged workers when much more violent forms of exploi-tation produce daily life as you know it? When you accept such relationships every time you buy a cup of coffee, drive to work, or put on your shoes? The outrageousness of his work grows from the banality of the crime at its core: the ideological submission of the consumer who acquiesces to these forms of inequity as inevitable.

Importantly, the affective orientation of Sierra's work is not toward the exploited performer but toward the guilt-ridden liberal art consumer. His installations of day laborers performing menial tasks (holding up beams or a wall or sitting inside cardboard boxes) for the city's going rate (usually pov-erty wages) thus interest Claire Bishop because they make spectators uncom-fortable with their complicity in the exploitation at the performance's heart, while also referencing art historical debates about minimalism; for example, in Sierra's hands, Michael Fried's discomfort with how much the minimalist cube feels like a body becomes a gallery installation of day laborers sitting inside refrigerator boxes. In terms of their emotional economy, Sierra's per-formance installations, in which the work is outsourced, performed by peo-ple hired by the artist, are the opposite of Howells's and Franko B's work.[35] Howells explicitly creates the feeling of being at home, whether or not his performances are staged in a gallery. When Franko B performed *I Miss You!* at the Tate Modern, it had the effect of defamiliarizing the museum's affec-tive space, of reminding you of the parts of yourself you normally check at the door. Sierra, on the other hand, draws from exactly that process of exclu-sion: the exploitative gestures that define his practices are already part of art's business, and that's his point. The feelings of those he exploits appears (at first glance, at least) irrelevant. This is not to say that those enlisted in these performances do not have feelings, but those feelings never factor into critical reception of his work; to examine them would approach the sociological and step outside of the concerns of the (traditionally defined) art critic.[36] Which is to say that the feelings of those deployed in Sierra's performances are not only irrelevant to the business of art, they have in fact been irrelevant to the practice of criticism.

The problem of the performer's feelings emerged dramatically in an instal-lation in 2002 for Deitch Projects in New York City. It is not easy to find day laborers in New York who will put up with being paid a meager wage to hold heavy beams for no apparent reason; most day laborers work in construction, help with moving, and do other familiar jobs and would be suspicious of something so out of the ordinary. The gallery hired the "performers" for their event from an employment agency. These workers organized during the opening and walked off the job, arguing that it was "demeaning to be used as props in an artwork."[37] In the workers' refusal to participate in Sierra's installation, we see something of the complexity of the actual work they were being asked to perform: they were hired to provide a complex service for Sierra's audience, a service closer to that demanded from the artist than to that asked of the manual laborer. Sociologists call this aspect of our work life "affective labor." The emotional economy of Sierra's installations exploits the overdetermined place of affective labor in the art world. This is what many of the people around artists do for a living: they work in a service industry, educating, writing, selling. The receptionist, the bartender at an opening, and the person parking cars all provide services that have an affective dimension, as do curators, critics, and teachers. This is what artists do as well; their work makes people feel good, smart, or important (for example). Work based in process or collaboration, work that presents itself as a service explicitly positions itself in relation to the affective labor already present in the production of the art experience.

Drawing from feminist sociological writing about the affective labor assigned to women (as mothers, daughters, and wives, but also as teachers, nurses, and secretaries), Michael Hardt and Antonio Negri argue that labor which revolves around the production of affect can be particularly alienating, for in this case we are alienated not merely from our time (as is the wage laborer) or from the product of our labor (as is the factory worker) but from our very emotional selves. They write, "When affective production becomes part of waged labor it can be experienced as extremely alienating: I am selling my ability to make human relationships, something extremely intimate, at the command of a client or boss."[38] The professionalization of affect is especially hard on those working at the margins of economic survival—life is hard enough without health care, job security, affordable housing, and transportation—but to have to produce the spectacle of a woman at peace with the world and her position in it while working at the very job that fails to pay a living wage or provide health insurance can be too much.[39] She is nevertheless expected to smile through it ("Welcome to Walmart!").

Affective labor is hard too because it is confusing. We are so used to thinking of our emotions as inside and private that this cultural shift unsettles not only how we understand work but also how we understand the very constitution of ourselves. Hardt and Negri argue that as the production of immaterial goods (services, information, knowledge, social relationships) becomes a larger and larger part of the global economy, affective labor and how good we are at it becomes increasingly important to how we understand our own value in the world; indeed it is transforming the boundaries of the self. We are bearing witness to the emergence of new models for the subject that are less bounded, and new hierarchies for labor in which the ability to connect becomes prized above, for example, the ability to make something. That said, our usefulness to others as emotional caretakers and surrogates—the availability of our time and space to the emotional needs of others—is wildly contingent and is an indicator of the kinds of privileges and entitlements we enjoy and from which we are barred by virtue of race, gender, sexuality, ethnicity, class, age, and (perhaps more than anything) location.

Hardt and Negri's observations regarding a transformation in how labor is understood helps to situate the emergence of relational aesthetics as a hot topic in art criticism at the turn of the new century. Just as skilled manual labor (the ability to make things) has waned as capitalism's ideal model for production, so it has in art. As affective labor (the ability to create and maintain relationships) emerges as the privileged model for the global citizen, we see models for art-making recast in these terms. What makes Sierra's installations challenging is not the demand that we keep company with manual labor but the awkwardness of keeping company with people who so powerfully make visible the economies of class exploitation that structure our experiences of labor and that draw the line between what kinds of work are valuable and what kinds of work are not. Sierra's installations work as long as no one thinks of his workers as artists, and this is, perhaps, his point.

The most visible discourse on relational aesthetics evolves out of a modernist investment in the art object as a site of ideological struggle (e.g., Clement Greenberg and Michael Fried). This mode of criticism scrutinizes the art object for signs of resistance to processes of objectification and commodification, for a critical engagement with itself as object. According to this modernist vein of thought, the object has by now been wrung dry of whatever oppositional value it might once have held for the critic looking for art practices that are aggressively defined by their self-awareness, their self-referentiality, and their resistance to market culture. Experiential artworks (e.g., conceptual art, performance art, some installations) seem to offer an escape route from art as commodity; certainly the artists making process-oriented work in the 1960s and 1970s saw their practice this way. For quite a long time, art criticism wrestled with the distinction between good objects (which exhibit a critical relationship to their status as objects) and bad ones (which are complicit with that objectification). Critics now have this argument about the relationships staged in these interactive, collaborative, participatory art practices (e.g., Bishop's arguments with Bourriaud; Grant Kester's and Liam Gillick's responses to Bishop's polemics in the pages of *Artforum* and *October*). The ultimate rhetorical aim of such a critical practice is the acquisition of a moral high ground from which one can arbitrate the distinction between modes of experience that are merely entertaining or merely representative and modes of experience that are critical and also have some sort of aesthetic value (thus Foster's call for "critical distance" at the conclusion of *The Return of the Real* as an antidote to the "ethnographic impulse"). Hardt and Negri help us to see that the important thing here is not the arbitration of which forms of relationality are best, which have more ethical or aesthetic integrity, but that this conversation is being staged around these terms at all. The fact that relationality itself has become the battleground for arguing the meaning and value of contemporary art confirms these global shifts regarding how people and the work they do are valued. Alarmingly, some of the criticism in this area mirrors the hierarchical logics of this service economy, in which the feelings of some communities (Sierra's audience) outweigh those of others (his workers) and in which the emotional register attributed to the work of some artists (Sierra, Thomas Hirschhorn) is valued as more complex, as having more integrity and intelligence than the emotional register of the work of other artists (invariably, women artists and artists of color). The same classifications map onto audiences too.

When Sierra's workers walked off of the job, they demonstrated their awareness of the difference between the labor that they were told they were being paid to perform (manual) and the actual labor that had been asked of them (affective). Their protest registers the offensiveness of the idea that they would not be aware of this difference and that they would be so economically vulnerable as to not care. These workers were aware, in other words, that service work is different and, in that setting, much more valuable than manual labor. It is hard to name their anger as a part of Sierra's work, as that anger seems to have been the very thing that brought the piece to an end and forced the art to walk out the door. But perhaps it should be seen as the natural extension of his practice: it forced into the light the intensity with which the emotional lives of the exploited are policed and negated, even (or especially) in art that purports to be critically engaged with this exploitation.

FEELING OVERDETERMINED

identity, emotion, and history

The Difficulty of Identity

Artists working from the margins find themselves burdened with a distinct form of affective labor: dealing with their audience's fascination and guilt as well as that audience's desire to absorb such works into prefabricated narratives about what it means to make work informed by, for example, discourse on race and identity. The deep suspicion of identity politics cited earlier (Bishop, Foster) may originate in an awareness of the problem of liberal formations around difference (e.g., its fetishization), but it has yielded a rather strange situation in art criticism in which the mere presence of especially race as an interpretive factor is enough to wipe out a work's difficulty and the complexity of its relationship to its context. Worse, that oblivion (which reduces work about racial discourse to a moment of racial identification on the critic's part) is more often than not presented as some sort of critical insight. Derek and Soraya Murray put it flatly: "Problems emerge when socially defined minorities become synonymous with the *political*."[1] Such artists are condemned by assumed proximity to having their work oversimplified, read symptomatically, and often enlisted in the very representational logics that their work contests. Grant Kester describes the critical logic behind the way that artists who overtly engage politics are most often positioned in art criticism, and the avenue by which their work is dismissed:

> Without the detachment and autonomy of conventional art to insulate them, [these artists] are doomed to "represent" in the most naïve and facile manner possible, a given political issue or constituency. This detachment is [argued to be] necessary because art is constantly in danger of being subsumed to the condition of consumer culture or "entertainment" (cultural forms predicated on immersion rather than on recondite critical distance). Instead of seducing viewers, the artist's task is to hold them at arm's length, inculcating a skeptical distance that parallels the insight provided by critical theory into the contingency of social and political meaning.[2]

In this model, in other words, the artist's level of attachment (indeed the artist's very comportment) is expected to mirror the critic's. Proximity, feeling, identification, and collaboration are lumped together as synonyms for each other, as complicit, "naïve and facile"—as, in other words, too easy. The reception history of works by artists of color bears this out, as questions of form and politics are frequently subsumed in criticism by racial metaphor. The artist ends up performing a kind of ideological service work in spite of herself, educating and helping audiences to work through their own racism. The artist may be praised or condemned for this. She might be ignored if the work does not conform to liberal protocols regarding what an antiracist practice might look like (as seems to be the case with William Pope L.). Worse, the work's politics will be put through a distortion chamber, and its critical dimensions will be reversed. In all of these cases, the artist's racial or ethnic identity will orient discussion of her work, resolving the work's difficulty by pointing to the artist's identity as its ultimate meaning. It is important to bear in mind that artists know all of this.

Darby English explains how this problem imposes a profound limit on the reception of contemporary African American art. He opens his book on this subject by discussing the critical reception of David Hammons's installation *Concerto in Black and Blue* (2002). His analysis of this case is worth reproducing here, because it points to the way that the difficulty of work about race is suppressed in much art criticism, and it points to the role that affect plays in that critical failure. In Hammons's installation, viewers walked through blacked-out rooms with only blue glow sticks to guide them (if they chose to grab one on their way in). English writes, "To perceive the work one had literally to become a part of it, all the while carefully negotiating a physically demanding circumstance."[3] It is not possible to see *Concerto* from the outside; to step away from it is to step outside of it. It is immersive, experiential, and restrained. It has a tight formalism that calls to mind the work of other artists using light as their medium, for example, James Turrell's framing of the sky in *Light Reign* (2003) or Miroslaw Balka's *How It Is* (2010), an enormous container that absorbs viewers in total darkness, but only as long as they have their back to the entrance. Hammons's title is nearly literal, but it is also rich with connotation: it indexes references to jazz and blues, the blues as mood, bruising, blackness (as race, as difference and color). English describes how reviews of the work stubbornly flattened its formal complexity, its politics, as well as the texture of its experience in favor of a clumsy racial reading. Ultimately, he argues, most critics were guided by an expectation of a story about blackness, rooted in their own projection of what kind of message an African American artist has to offer. He asks:

> What can explain *Concerto*'s reduction, in such accounts, to a thing of untroubled legibility, whether as a "gutsy public spectacle," a "confronting darkness," or, still more grossly given the piece's tranquility, an experience "reminiscent of police cars or bombs over Baghdad"? It is as if such an identification was a requisite exercise in fashioning a public reputation for *Concerto*. These reviews are not simply devoid of any detailed record of the complexities [of the work], *they appear to commit special critical energy to wishing Concerto's difficulty away*, thus relegating Hammons's obdurate design to its metaphors."[4]

It is incredible that such a quiet work would be narrated in terms of confrontation and assault, and it is very hard to imagine what would make viewers experience the work this way, other than the ideas about black masculinity or "art about race" they carried with them into the room. The work's *starting place*, English explains, is a critical engagement with the use of those metaphors as a mechanism for understanding the work.

George Steiner's typology of forms of difficulty (contingent, strategic, epistemological) help map the critical problem delineated by English. Hammons's title, *Concerto in Black and Blue*, invokes the desire to manage the work's difficulty by assuming a kind of transparency for it, in which the work's meaning can be accessed by what the viewer happens to know (or think he knows) about "black art" (this is a contingent form of difficulty, dependent on what the viewer is able to recognize in the work's references). Some critics might be generous enough to assign a kind of strategic difficulty to the work by pointing to Hammons's intention to frustrate the viewer's desire to interpret the work. For the critic who approaches this work as if blackness were knowable, however, the epistemological difficulty of *Concerto in Black and Blue* is completely inaccessible. This critical blindness takes the shape of a denial of the centrality of problems of difference and knowledge embedded in the immersive form of the work, and, ironically, it reproduces the logic of visual transparency that lies at racism's foundation. In this case Steiner's typology of forms of difficulty is complicated by how ideologies of difference inform or limit the critic's ability to recognize a work's difficulty as well as its politics. The critics English cites experience the work through their projection of the artist's identity. And so they see it as a metaphor for blackness (as if the meaning of that term were knowable and stable) rather than as a meditation on visuality and blindness (which has everything to do with the racialist discourse through which the work is invariably experienced).[5] The critic thus responds to the work literally, and with a literalism that is not even guided by the object, by what he sees. It is in fact guided by what the critic *feels*. That critic, English explains, scrambles to enlist on his behalf "a rhetorical triumph over the disorientations that are most elemental to the work," as if the declaration "It's about race" constituted some sort of meaningful insight, and as if that statement could contain the anxiety that the work provokes.[6]

Outside of the writing of those scholars who are actively engaged with work by artists of color, art critical awareness of how artists mobilize and respond to racial discourse in their work is dismal. Few in the field of contemporary art history (generically defined) seem to read even canonical work on race, representation, and politics, and many of the voices most prominent in contemporary art history reinforce the curatorial isolation imposed on artists of color, ignoring whole movements in their attempts to identify and theorize the currents of the past few decades. Even the most visible African American and Latino artists, for example, never seem to appear as representative of the decades in which they work; Adrian Piper, for example, might easily be placed at the center of practices of relational aesthetics (her cards and "funk lessons"), as might William Pope L. (The Black Factory truck, which collected articles people associate with blackness), but as long as such work appears to have something to do with discourse on race, for many critics that work represents a completely unexamined notion of Race, and its contributions to conversations about art practice are unexamined. Expressing the frustration of many scholars and artists, English writes:

> It is an unfortunate fact that in this country, black artists' work seldom serves as the basis of rigorous, object-based debate. Instead, it is almost

uniformly generalized, endlessly summoned to prove its representative-
ness (or defend its lack of same) and contracted to show-and-tell on behalf of an abstract and unchanging "culture of origin." For all this, the art
gains little purchase on the larger social, cultural, historical and aesthetic
formations to which it nevertheless directs itself with increasing urgency.
And in the long term, it runs the risk of moving beyond serious thought
and debate. Viewed this way, the given and necessary character of black
art—as a framework for understanding what black artists do—emerges
as a problem in itself.[7]

This situation may be particularly acute in limiting the reception of work
by contemporary African American artists, insofar as in the United States
blackness often comes to represent race itself. The problem is by no means
unique to black artists, however, and it is closely related to the literalism that
defines the reception of queer and feminist artists (described in the previous
chapter). From certain critical vantage points, as Derek and Soraya Murray
put it, artists who make work from a marked identity position "are intention-
ally locked in their bodies" by the critical apparatus.[8]

The case of Hammond's *Concerto* is stark because the work is stark; he can
withhold image and sound and ask his viewers to navigate a space with a blue
light, and the piece allegorizes the whole of African American history. Of
course, this is one of the points of the piece: the framing of art by the black
artist is, from a racialist vantage point, always already *raced*, always already
read as symptom (as, in fact, noise). But if that's where our thinking stops,
English argues, we have failed to engage the work itself and only replicated
the problem—the liberal humanist's romance with his own racism. It is one
of colonialism's most enduring legacies.[9] Within art history, colonialism lives
on this fantasy projection of the Other's literal body, which stands for all that
is outside the proper scope of the discipline.

James Luna's *The History of the Luiseño People (Christmas, La Jolla Reservation 1990)* (1990–1996, 2009)

Throughout his career, James Luna has consistently engaged the structural
difficulty of his location in contemporary art as a Native American artist. One
performance in particular frames the artist in terms of this political location
and places emotion and, more specifically, depression at its core. Live performances of *The History of the Luiseño People (Christmas, La Jolla Reservation
1990)* (1990–96, 2009) follow the same loose script. Luna installs himself in

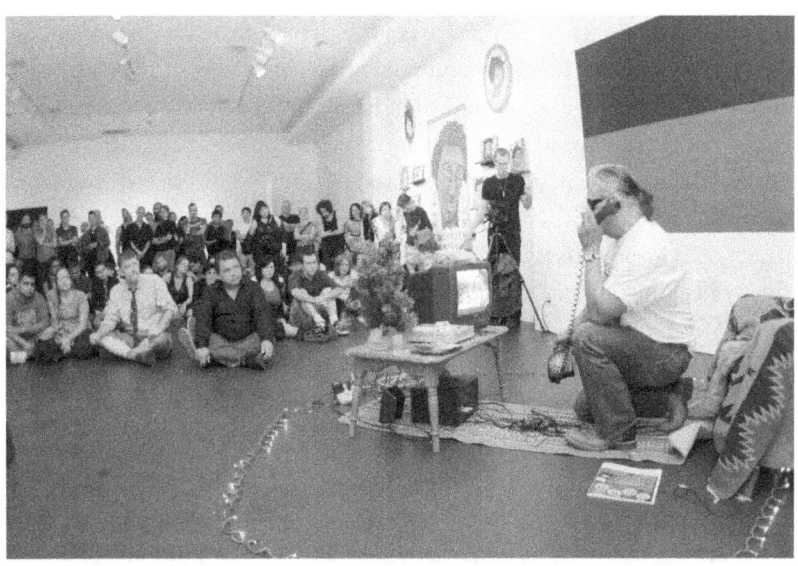

FIGURE 19. James Luna, *History of the Luiseño People, La Jolla Reservation Christmas 1990*. Los Angeles Contemporary Exhibitions. 2009. Photograph courtesy of James Luna and Los Angeles Contemporary Exhibitions.

an overstuffed chair in front of a flickering television monitor broadcasting the nostalgic holiday film *White Christmas* or trashy reality television such as *Cops* (fig. 19). The set is that of a bachelor's living room, and it remains in the gallery after his performance, as an installation. The furniture is cheap, worn, and ordinary. The recliner sits on a braided rug and is covered by a blanket. A small plastic Christmas tree is placed on a coffee table next to the television. A telephone is on the floor near the chair, together with newspapers and empty beer cans. (In the installation, the telephone rings periodically and goes unanswered.) Colored lights also lie on the floor in a circle around the installation. The work's title is written on the wall above the scene, in large text. In the performance, Luna sits in the chair and makes calls to family members, friends, and an ex-girlfriend. As he talks through these pretend conversations, he smokes cigarettes and drinks one beer after another. A drag is followed by a long gulp and the cracking open of the second, third, and fourth can. He seems drunk, and given how much he drinks in the performance, one has reason to believe that he is.

In 1996 Luna collaborated with the filmmaker Isaac Artenstein to translate these live performances into a performance video. It is choreographed to heighten the viewer's sense of proximity to the artist. We follow him from a convenience store, where he purchases a case of beer, to his cinderblock home on the reservation. He sets up camp in front of his television, cracks open another beer (he'd started drinking on the way home), lights a cigarette, and begins dialing. In the video the calls are awkward; at first they are nearly telegraphic. He is reticent and fumbles through clumsy and somewhat coerced performances of familial connection. "Hey, Mom," he begins, and then seems to run out of things to say. As he proceeds, it becomes increasingly clear that these calls are not made in an effort to reach out but as a way of absenting himself from the spaces of intimacy on the other end of the line. None of this looks very much like the nostalgic holiday broadcast on the television. And it certainly has none of the grandeur promised by the work's title.

As Luna drinks, his talk wanders more and more, particularly in his conversation with the ex-girlfriend. He knots up around references to their relationship and the problems he telegraphs as the whole "white-Indian thing." It is tempting to see this as some sort of revelation, as a confession of sorts, or a gesture toward the "white-Indian thing" that structures much of his work with art world audiences. But Luna does not resolve this story. Instead he says, "I think that way, but I don't feel that way," and drifts off in another direction. This provocative statement is nested in a twenty-seven-minute recording of depressed talk—talk in which the inebriated speaker seems detached from the words that pass his lips. But the work does speak to this suspension between thought and feeling, and not only through that remark. Kathleen McHugh describes the poetics of *History of the Luiseño People* as one of "radical estrangement." By this, she means not his failure to "connect" with the people he pretends to call but rather the estrangement between the artist and his audience, between the story he bodies forth and the "history" promised by the work's title. "What is not there in Luna and Artenstein's video," McHugh explains, "is *the* history of the Luiseño and Native Americans more generally—their subjugation, resistance, representation, and self-representation." History is marked as a defining absence.[10]

When Luna performs alcoholic masculine depression as *The History of the Luiseño People (La Jolla Reservation 1990)* it is to mark history as a problem—not only as the lingering trauma of settler colonialism but, more significantly (for Luna's practice), as the question of how one engages that past, how one narrates it, how one knows it, and how one feels it. All of those questions, however, are prefaced by the knowledge that Luna himself, as a Native artist, appears in art history as a living historical artifact, an atavistic reminder of an obliterated past. History structures his work as a lost past in an erased present, a multidimensional absence that he must continually negotiate. For Jane Blocker, the drunkenness that runs through his work thus "has more than a merely sociological significance. . . . It is not just an artifact of alcoholism [as a contemporary reservation problem], it is also metaphorical of history's inability to determine whether its memories really happened or are manufactured out of fiction, television, film, and popular art. It is a vivid reminder of history's tendency to pass out and forget the past."[11] Luna, an artist who once sedated himself so that he might be exhibited as an artifact under museum glass (*The Artifact Piece, 1987–1990*), is all too aware of the ways in which his forms of expression are always already enlisted in a romantic fantasy of a traumatic past. That work clearly comments on the art historical place assigned to him, no matter what kind of work he makes. (He might as well lie under glass, in other words, and do nothing. His work will be read the same.)

In 2009 Luna revisited *History of the Luiseño People* in a live performance for an opening of an exhibit that I curated for Los Angeles Contemporary Exhibitions.[12] His was an unsettling presence from the start. He arrived at the space hours before the performance with a group of friends. They hung out in the parking lot, drinking beer for the better part of the afternoon. Shortly before the gallery doors were opened, he purified the space by burning a bundle of dried sage. When it came time for him to take his place in the recliner, there were nearly a hundred people crowded into the gallery. He made his phone calls and improvised conversations with people in his life. Unlike the video of 1993 (the mood of which is subdued), this performance was animated with hostility and anger. There was a palpable awkwardness in the gallery, especially as people started to leave. It went on for ages, well past the point of comfort. As time passed, he seemed to lose his place, and his talk soured. He wobbled between an anger that felt faked (and was therefore a bad performance) and that felt real (and directed at his audience). More and more people left the room.

By the time he finished, there were about forty people left in the audience. Erwin (Junior) Osuna, one of Luna's friends and collaborators, stood up, moved to the front of the room, and began to sing. James Pax stood up, picked up a saxophone that had been resting against the gallery wall, and began to play a bluesy riff. Osuna and Pax traded off, extending Luna's work with hybrid forms, and the two men eased the audience out of the experience (fig. 20). Luna and his collaborators collected the noise of anger and depression and organized it into music. Those who had stayed were thanked with this song for sitting through the performance. As an audience, we had first been measured: How much could he trust us? Could we be trusted not with

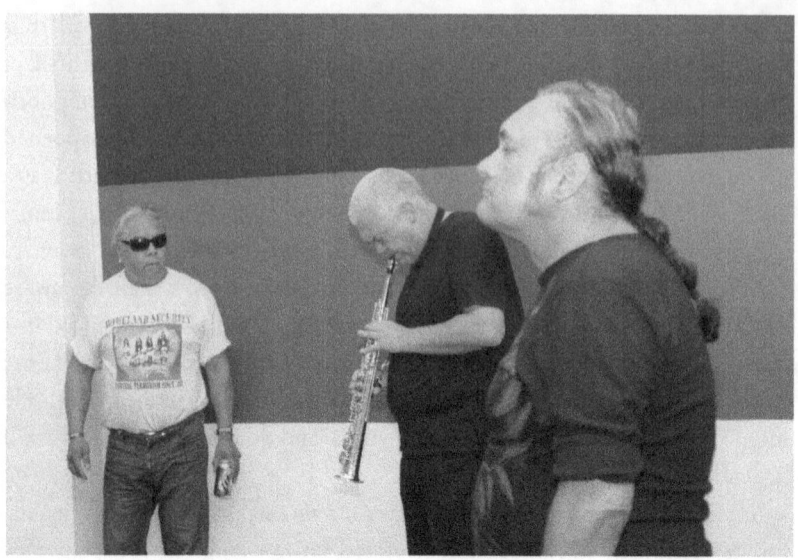

FIGURE 20. James Luna, *History of the Luiseño People, La Jolla Reservation Christmas 1990*. Los Angeles Contemporary Exhibitions. 2009. Photograph courtesy of James Luna and Los Angeles Contemporary Exhibitions.

what he had to tell us but to sit with his refusal to tell? This tension is necessary to understanding how *History of the Luiseño People* works, produced as it was on this occasion for a divided audience: an art world wanting a helping of authentic misery, an exhibit-opening crowd wanting to be entertained, and a different audience which knows far too well how misery is traded as Native artifact to take the performance literally. The last finds some aspects of Luna's work funny; he frequently tropes on Hollywood images of Indians, Indian consumption of pop culture, and the mass consumption of Native artifacts (like himself). He also works with things that are all too familiar to viewers with working- or welfare-class roots, the material details of the "sad" installation that fails to live up to the legend the artist assigns to it: the cheap rug, the pathetic plastic tree, the upholstered recliner; the grouchy old man watching hours of bad television, stewing in his anger but also working that anger up into a familiar routine. Luna pushes back against the pressure of making art as an Indian in part by making art with trash stewed in resentment. This opens up a world of ambivalence. If you couldn't get that, if you took it literally, looking for a real expression of anger and some sort of spiritual relief, or if you were looking for knowing irony and cool affect, the performance was impossible to sit through.

In the end, the performance *was* moving. Luna made a majority of the audience so visibly uncomfortable (bored? annoyed? repulsed?) that they moved on. Bearing witness to that exodus was painful. This only made more people look for the door. A lot of people just didn't want to watch the performance collapse. Trusting that there was something interesting waiting for us on the other side of that was hard for those unfamiliar with Luna's work, because it really did seem like it was all just falling apart.

A performance like this applies steady pressure to the bonds that tie an audience together. *History* experiments with the crowd. Luna does not aim hold the audience's attention for the duration of the performance. He does not explain or show us how he feels. The performance instead recasts our relationship to him; we move from being members of an audience to something more challenging, in which we find ourselves keeping company with a difficult (and drunk) man. In this regard it is hard to miss the way that Luna engages the structure and affective intensity of depression as crisis in affect and relation in which all forms of relationality become unbearable. For those around the depressive (who can radiate negativity), there is no easy way of being there for the other. How can one be present to a depressive who experiences that presence as an act of aggression, as the living embodiment of his failure to connect?

That depressive performance is set against the nostalgia that saturates mainstream, popular romance with Native American history, in which Native identity appears as always already "historical." Renato Rosaldo's term *imperialist nostalgia* names the sentimental economy that allows the imperial subject to weep over the bodies it has buried, to mourn the cultural practices it has annihilated. In her work on Native participation in and responses to pop cultural representations of Indianness, Michelle Raheja identifies within contemporary Native cultural productions a dialectical tension between that imperialist nostalgia and indigenous epistemologies and modes of relating to the past. Luna combats the depiction of Native Americans "as existing solely in the past as historical figures and in the present only as spectral entities." But such artists also, Raheja writes, "[take] spirituality and its attendant 'ghosts' seriously, without falling prey to [that] nostalgic, past tense vision of indigenous culture."[13] One might say that Luna stages a similar intervention here around affect and the mythology of the defeated "sad Indian." Depression and history are linked in *History of the Luiseño People*. But Luna does not present that relation as knowable, as a straightforward narrative of cause and effect ("history makes us sad"). Nor does he position his work as a compensatory form of healing, in which talking through the historical trauma of settler colonialism will make him and his audiences feel right. Instead the performance is structured by an affective loop not entirely unlike that which shapes Bustamante's *Neapolitan*.

The two works complement each other. Luna can't connect from his home and he can't show us how he feels or what that reservation is really like. Bustamante seems to connect too much to hers, and what feelings she shows are contradictory and dissociated from self-expression. Both installations are vulnerable to the same kinds of racial (mis)reading English describes. Knowing that this literal reading is always there informs the work's affective complexity. José Muñoz notes, for example, that a critic writing for *Artnews* made quite a lot of the kitchen towel that Bustamante used to dry her eyes, as it happened to be red, white, and green, the colors of the Mexican flag (Bustamante is Mexican American). This made the work "genuinely sad" for the critic, "expressing sorrow and mourning, perhaps, for the current world situation."[14] Muñoz rightly calls into question the logic by which this equation is drawn, as if the work's politics are visible only in the purely accidental alignment of this detail with Bustamante's ethnic location. Which isn't to say that Bustamante's work is not political; for Muñoz it is a performative investigation of "political depression," a more complicated social position than the liberal fantasy of ethnic sadness described by the art critic. Muñoz draws from scholarship on racial melancholia in his reading of affect in Bustamante's work to point to the way artists deploy negative affect to resist the social imperative for the minoritarian subject to produce a whole self and "be happy."[15] In that refusal to adjust, Muñoz identifies a critique of the system that would make happiness and a sense of wholeness prerequisites for full political participation. In the words of Antonio Viego (whom Muñoz cites in his writing on Bustamante), when we presume "a strong, whole, complete, and transparent ethnic-racialized subject and ego as the desired therapeutic, philosophical, and political outcome in a racist, white supremacist world . . . we fail to see how the repeated themes of wholeness, completeness, and transparency with respect to ethnic-racialized subjectivity are what provide racist discourse with precisely the notion of subjectivity that it needs in order to function effectively."[16] Such transparency motivates the misreading of a kitchen towel in Bustamante's work as evidence of her ethnicity and her politics, just as it facilitates the chain of associations that shape the reception of *Concerto in Black and Blue*. Indeed it structures the disappointment of the critic who expects from Athey's work "art about AIDS."

Entitlement's gift to the majoritarian subject is the psychic denial of the lack at the core of the self; it is the ability to operate with the illusion of wholeness and transparency.[17] It is, Viego writes, "one of [racism's] most generative internal principles: the undivided, obscenely full and complete ethnic-racialized subject, transparent to itself and others." The privileged, majoritarian and nondepressive subject disavows this (in the classic, psychoanalytic sense) and launches himself into the world. As desirable as such entitlement might appear, Viego warns that the desire for this kind of transparency, for this sense of an alignment between who and what one is, lies at the heart of racist (and sexist) paradigms. His caution is directed at perspectives within ethnic studies that present this model of the whole self as a critical and therapeutic goal. Viego writes that the ethical critical position is not advocacy for the minoritarian subject's "wholeness" but an insistence on the gap, the negative, the nonalignment and opacity of the subject. He writes, "Racism depends on a reading of ethnic-racialized subjects that insists on their transparency; racism also banks on the faith and conceit that these subjects can be exhaustively and fully elucidated through a certain masterful operation of language."[18] These points need to be absorbed into art critical discourse, for all too often the politics ascribed to artists of color are represented as exactly this quest for "wholeness" or "transparency" when, more often than not, the *opposite* is the case. Luna and Bustamante differently forward within their performances an ethnic or racialized subject that does not have (or seek) the privilege of disavowing the lack that lies at the center of the self. Depression, as a practice of maintaining an awareness of this, can have a deeply social, deeply political dimension. The depressive appears to be stuck not by virtue of a lack of understanding but rather by virtue of his or her inability to forget. Even as Bustamante and Luna cite traumatic histories (elliptically), those histories are not there to resolve the difficulty of their work—they are not there as causal elements. They are not there to fill in the gaps of what we don't or can't know. Furthermore neither installation could be called tragic in a classical sense, or even sad. As much as the artists appear to perform sad, that sadness is laced with and framed by a black humor. The emotional landscapes of *Neapolitan* and *History of the Luiseño People* are ambivalent.

Luna's presentation of the *History of the Luiseño People* as a performance of depression, ambivalence, and alienation intervenes against the rendition of History as a story of evolution and progress, and also against the construction of History as a knowable past. Luna's history is a portrait of the present, and it resonates with critical interrogations of the discipline.[19] History, Fredric Jameson writes, is not something we can know directly; it is available to the scholar only as a combination of traces or wounds. It "can be apprehended only through its effects, and never directly as some reified force"; it is constantly receding from us as an "untranscendable horizon." Rather than imagine the historian's job as filling in the gaps, he suggests that we should make those gaps visible. And so he calls for "a recontextualization of History which does not propose the latter as some new representation or 'vision,' some new content, but as the formal effects of what Althusser, following Spinoza, calls an 'absent cause.' Conceived in this sense, History is what hurts, it is what refuses desire and sets inexorable limits to the individual as well as collective praxis, which its ruses turn into grisly and ironic reversals of their overt intentions."[20] "History is what hurts" is one of the most well-known turns of phrase in Marxist criticism, and for good reason. The hurt he describes is manifold: it continues on as a structuring absence within the practice of history. The historian who attempts to redress the wound by "filling in the gaps" with more and more information succeeds only in transferring that pain down the line. Luna is as much a philosopher of history as he is an artist. His work takes on not a literal history of the Luiseño people, and not even "the problem of history," but rather the relationship between the individual and the social, between the present and the past. His work is structured by these competing narratives regarding Native presence and its configuration as absence, and it throws this contradiction against the disciplining gear works of Art History. The result is not the sad Indian of history but history itself as a sad and inadequate picture.

Difficulty and Ideologies of Emotion

As I have argued, one of the problems limiting the reception of works of art by artists of color is that almost no level of irony, self-reflexivity, ambivalence, or complexity seems to ward off the urge to read the artist's work as naïve, earnest forms of self-expression with no awareness of the complexity of representation, art history, or political institutions. "The identity artist," Derek Murray writes, "is coded as ahistorical, and thus irrelevant to both the formal progression and the intellectual evolution of the art object."[21] In such critical discourse, the difficulty of the artist's work is actively disavowed by the literal-minded critic, who projects that literalism onto the artist and her work, as is also sometimes the case with the reception of the most challenging feminist and queer work. I have already suggested one set of problems with this mode of analysis: it recasts racist logics in terms of art critical judgment, negates the complexity of racial discourse itself, and makes it seem as if the recognizable presence of race or ethnicity within an artwork is itself a sign of critical naïveté. All of this is scooped under the umbrella term *identity politics*, usually in order to be dismissed. There is a second problem at work, however, which also serves to mask the difficulty that emotion presents to critical engagement with contemporary art. When literal misreading responds to the emotional intensity of an artwork as a form of intellectual shutdown, the work's affective economy is read simply as an expression of how the artist feels. If one engine of that misreading grows from critical naïveté regarding identity, it is twinned by a flawed model for understanding how emotion works.

There is a false assumption in much art writing that we can be smart about emotions only if we are being cynical about them. (Jaded is the default attitude one strikes in the social space of the art gallery about nearly everything.) If we struggle to find ways to adequately consider how emotion works in art, if it is easier to dismiss the artist or the audience's emotionality as naïve or as a critical failure, it is partly because we have been working with inadequate models for what feelings are and how they work.

It is worth taking a moment to analyze how commonly assumed models for emotion limit our conversations about how they work in art. People generally operate with what the philosopher Rei Terada describes as an "expressive" model for emotion, one in which feelings are assumed to originate inside the body and to find expression on or outside the body. This "ideology of emotion," she writes, "diagrams emotion as something lifted from a depth to a surface." It leads us to measure representations of emotion according to how well we are convinced that those feelings represent the subject's interior life, and according to how those feelings correspond to the interior lives of the audience. (Thus an audience member might experience Luna's performance as a failure if she didn't find his performance of anger convincing or if she thought it was misdirected or inappropriate.) This model shapes even the most sophisticated criticism. As Terada argues, Jameson's writing on the "waning of affect" in postmodern art and culture describes a formal turn to a disorienting play of surfaces that displaces the interior, emotional world of the subject. Famously, he pointed to Warhol's *Diamond Dust* shoes to make his point: they are pure objects, glittery commodities, there is no trace in this work (he argues) of the people who might wear these shoes. Pop Art flattens out not only the image on the canvas but the subject, abandoning all pretext to describing the subject's interior life. (So Warhol described himself as "a mirror.") Postmodern art thus appears in Jameson's narrative to announce the "waning of affect." Terada explains, "It is so conventional to think at once of 'expression and feelings or emotions,' as Jameson puts it, that attacks on expression look like attacks on emotion."[22] Thus, in his reading of the aesthetic of Warhol's paintings, for instance, Jameson describes Warhol's dismantling of models of expression (e.g., his use of mechanical reproduction, the flat and graphic style of his paintings, the impersonal and emptied-out appearance of his portraits) as the "waning of affect" itself.

Terada takes a different view. The critique of the idea of "authentic expression" and a refusal of an expressive model of emotion need not be treated as the same thing as a total negation of affect and emotion. If Warhol's work appears as a simultaneous attack on authenticity and expression, it is because paintings like *100 Campbell's Soup Cans* (1962) work against the models of subjective experience through which expression (of what is inside the artist) and emotion are articulated as one and the same process. Some of Warhol's work, however, can be quite provocative. The intensity of both positive and negative responses to the first exhibitions of his signature Pop works demonstrates that viewers often had strong emotional reactions to his work. His portraits of Marilyn Monroe, made in response to her death, for example, have a powerful affective charge, as do other images from his *Death and Disaster* series (e.g., *Suicide* [1962]); that charge belongs not to the artist (they are not his feelings), and not specifically to the person looking at his work (viewers don't necessarily see their reaction to Warhol's work as personal). They belong instead to the public sphere constituted around these subjects: celebrities, brands like Campbell's soup and Coca-Cola, iconic newspaper photos, daily newspaper stories of "death and disaster." These works are about the way our own feelings can seem like they belong to someone else, as if they are scripted, particularly when they feel quite sincere.[23]

The assumption of a depth-model geometry for emotion, expression, and identity bears on the reception and institutional placement of nearly all of the artists I have pulled into this conversation. Critical narratives regarding contemporary art generally assume a depth model for all three terms: emotion as contained within and externalized as expression; identity as a correlation between who and what one is. But just a glance at Warhol's work demonstrates that while it might refuse a depth model for expression, it is nevertheless loaded with affect and also very deeply concerned with identity. For the Pop artist, identity is interesting as a surface effect and a social phenomenon. This is one reason his sexuality is not incidental to an analysis of his practice as an artist. It is in fact integral to a full understanding of it, insofar as that identity appears in his work as a profoundly social phenomenon.

The sense of interiority that seems to come with emotion should be thought of as one of emotion's effects. Work that openly explores emotion as a surface effect upends our ideas of what comes first, feeling or expression. This can in fact be the very thing that makes an artwork moving. For example, as Terada explains, Jacques Derrida found that a novel could be moving exactly because the ownership of emotion is troubled and displaced from the reader onto someone else. The reader doesn't always experience her reactions to novels as proper to her; those feelings seem to live within and around the novel, belonging to the author, to characters, to scenes, situations, and other readers. This perspective considers the mediatedness and the sociality of emotion. Terada writes that Derrida thus "suggest[s] that we feel not to the extent that experience seems immediate, but to the extent that it doesn't; not to the extent that other people's experiences remind us of our own, but to the extent that our own seem like someone else's."[24] In this model, emotion is not communicated so much as it is circulated, transferred, modulated, and amplified. An expression does not represent an already existing feeling; it is the very thing that makes emotion happen, or, more nearly, it is the thing that sets emotion into motion. Tears migrate.

Emotions are profoundly *intersubjective*. They do not happen inside the individual but in relation to others. As Sarah Ahmed explains, most of our models for thinking about emotion treat it as something we have, as something that rises up from inside (the expressive model cited by Terada), or as something that "sinks in" from the outside—as the outside world makes us "feel bad." "Emotion," she argues, however, "is not simply something 'I' or 'we' have. Rather it is through emotions, or how we respond to objects and others, that surfaces and boundaries are made." For Ahmed, it is important to understand that "emotions are not 'in' either the individual or the social, but produce the very surfaces and boundaries that allow the individual and the social to be delineated as if they were objects."[25] Emotion actually does more than mark the boundary between the self and the other. Emotion brings those boundaries into being, and artists frequently explore the poetics of this fact in their work.

Adrian Howells explores this aspect of emotion in *14 Stations in the Life and History of Adrian Howells*. Staged as a one-on-one autobiographical "confession," Howells escorts his audience through set pieces describing his childhood, his relationship to his mother, his first loves and the disaster of those attempts at intimacy, his performance history, the collapse of a long-term relationship and his culpability in that relationship's end. (Howells is not "too sad" to tell us.) About midway through these "chapters," he escorted me into an alcove in the space's basement. He put headphones on and listened to music from a personal CD player while the image of a young man whom he had loved but who could not return those feelings was projected on the wall behind him. Facing me, listening to this music (which I could not hear), he started to cry. Facing me too was the image of the man who was the source of this pain: the unrequited love. Instead of being moved to tears, I felt myself shut down. A cold curiosity took over; he was making himself cry, for me, and I didn't care. I felt obliged to give him a hug when he took off the headphones, more as compensation for the fact that I felt nothing when confronted with those tears, produced on cue, for me. Tavia Nyong'o describes such scenes (which abound in queer performance) as *extimate* for how they "[palpitate] with the felt absence of connection."[26] Howells exploits this, stretching the distance between himself and his viewer into a sadistic relation. As the performance progresses, the expectation is that the artist and his "confessor" will grow closer. What happens, however, is that the two become more and more estranged, as the relationship between us grows more and more confusing and abusive. At a later station in the performance sequence, Howells asked me to pour him a drink. I filled a glass, using a pitcher of what I thought was water. It was vinegar. He drank it, spitting out what he could not swallow. Then, at his request, I poured ice water on him. I could have refused—but I didn't. The evolution of our dynamic reproduced the story of seduction, love, betrayal, and hostility that he had been recounting. It mirrored one of the stories Howells recounts, in which he handled the end of a relationship badly, hurting a man who had loved and been loyal to him. If he had just told the story, the performance would have been confessional. But the structure and poetics of Howells's performance implicates the spectator in the artist's injury. The participant's detachment makes her into the artist's tool. Guilt and anxiety circulate through this performance much the same way that tears migrate around the artist in the artworks described earlier. They do not (at least in my experience) lead to empathy, however, or even pity. My affect shifted according to the artist's, and, I presume, his was informed by mine. The experience was intimate and alienating, like the end of a relationship.

––––––––––

Emotions are not in and of themselves things. They are not the property of people or objects. Ahmed warns that when we think of emotion as property, as objects, we fetishize feelings as if they were independent of the processes that produce them. "Feelings become fetishes," she argues, "only through the erasure of the history of their production and circulation."[27] That erasure is a form of political violence, if not its engine. There is a link between Ahmed's warning about the de-historicization of emotion and Baldwin's diatribe against the sadism of sentimental culture. It's the ethical knot in the fact that we have feelings for, about each other. Echoing Baldwin, Theodor Adorno argues that the invocation of "pure feeling" is "society's alibi for the domination of interests, [bearing] witness to a humanity that does not exist."[28] When we lean on romantic fantasies of feeling as beyond the reach of social and political structures, as independent of historical and political flows, we become the very agents by which exploitative forces naturalize themselves.

Contemporary artists have long demonstrated a critical interest in emotion as a "product" they are expected to produce. Bas Jan Ader's *I'm Too Sad to Tell You*, for example, withholds the story behind his tears, and in so doing he isolates his affect as art object. His sadness appears as the work itself, and this may have been his point. For Howells, sadness is a given and a starting place. As he moves us through his *14 Stations*, he subjects himself to the sadomasochistic framework of the confessional. The work explores the emotional dynamic of this kind of one-on-one encounter as he navigates our reactions to him and our graduated implication in the story he tells. The story he tells is in fact ancillary to the dynamic set into motion by that tale (not that the two can be entirely divorced). Emotion marks the points at which we announce our difference from him, and his from us; those differences, furthermore, are not stable or absolute. That is the point of the work—not the stability or authenticity of the artist's feelings. Luna's work situates alienation, depression within a historical context not as an affective disorder "caused" by history but as an affective disorder through which we come to experience our oblique relationship to it.

Terada's and Ahmed's contributions to the critical analysis of emotion are particularly useful for thinking about art. Not all emotionally intense work is difficult, but some is difficult exactly insofar as it questions what emotion is, where it comes from, to whom and to what it belongs, and even whether it can be thought of as "belonging" at all. Artists take this on not only by making emotion itself their subject but by bringing the context for those feelings into the field of representation, as a means to resist exactly the kind of fetishization of emotion Ahmed describes. This is the effect of Abramović's performance video, which theatricalizes the production of tears to make us wonder when her tears become real. Bustamante and Hayley Newman both locate the production of emotion within story itself, within representation itself. The attempt to disarticulate emotion and expression poses a specific kind of difficulty in art. It leaves us in a strange place when we attempt to talk about the experience such works generate, as we struggle with the question of what a nonexpressive model of emotion looks like. This, I believe, is one reason so much of this kind of work gets simplified in criticism: the expressive model for emotion is so powerful that work which explores strong feelings looks to many critics like an assertion of simplistic, essentialist models for identity, even when such work self-consciously refuses those very ideologies. It is easier to shrug off the challenge of such work as merely the artist's feelings (as merely cultural studies or simply autoethnography) than it is to map the braiding of feeling and politics in work that challenges our most basic assumptions regarding what it means to make art about identity and the histories through which it is constituted.

Carrie Mae Weems's *From Here I Saw What Happened and I Cried* (1995–1996)

Carrie Mae Weems's *From Here I Saw What Happened and I Cried* (1995–96) is a photographic essay, and so its structure and tone are quite different from the other works I have discussed so far. Like Luna's *History of the Luiseño People*, this work is produced from a site of historical overdetermination that the artist mines for its emotional density. As Weems digs through the archive, the pressures on affect and emotion escalate. The work asks how you feel about feelings that seem to come from you but that are not quite your own, or at least are (within certain contexts) never yours alone because a national culture is always already feeling your feelings for you. Economies of witnessing structure this work, in that it traces the circle of one's feeling regarding another's experience. It is also an intertextual work. *From Here I Saw* is staged as an explicit dialogue with the images and representational practices of other photographers; it is a conversation with and between various sets of witnesses.

The work originated as a commission from the J. Paul Getty Museum, which wanted an artist to respond to its exhibit *Hidden Witness: African Americans in Early Photography*. This was the Getty Museum's first artist's commission. Originally exhibited as "Carrie Mae Weems Reacts to *Hidden Witness*," *From Here I Saw What Happened and I Cried* (1995–96) is a counterbalance to an exhibition of mid-nineteenth-century photographs of African Americans. *Hidden Witness* is a complicated project in its own right. Centered on Jackie Napolean Wilson's private collection, *Hidden Witness* spans the invention of photography and the end of slavery. Some of the photographs are portraits of white families in which black men and women appear as background figures, and in some of those images the black people in the frame are plainly slaves. (The show's title is taken from the name Wilson gave to one such portrait.) A great many of the images in *Hidden Wit-*

ness are of free men and women, however. There are mothers pictured with children, men in uniform, and portraits of musicians, dignified elders, and political leaders. They are surprising to those viewers who are raised on a history of this period that presents all African Americans living in the antebellum years as subjugated or enslaved or as escapees. The American canon admits few works of antebellum African American cultural production. Unless it is a course in African American history and culture, representations of nineteenth-century African American life encountered in the classroom are mostly authored by white people (e.g., Harriet Beecher Stowe, Mark Twain). Popular cinematic depictions of life in the antebellum era swing between plantation fantasy and plantation nightmare. The viewer instructed in this tradition approaches antebellum photographs of African Americans expecting a record of victimization and trauma.

Wilson's collection (and the Getty Museum's framing of it) identifies these men and women as witnesses to a historical trauma; that trauma, however, provides the frame more than the content for the individual photographs. Wilson's collection tracks a quieter story of self-possession and forbearance. Most of the images have a domestic and sentimental texture that to date remains largely invisible in popular representations of black life during the period. A critical fraction of these images are photographs made for one's circle of intimates (as is generally the case for studio portraits). These portraits are a dramatic contrast to work from the same period of African American subjects produced by and for white viewers. The exhibit title suggests the marginal position of the community pictured in these images. The portraits themselves suggest a history of African American self-representation, grounded in available codes signaling dignity, accomplishment, and domestic stability. *Hidden Witness* has a particular importance for the African American viewer. The portrait's subjects are evidence that "we are here" and "we were there." They leave the viewer with lingering questions about how much more there is to know about what we see and what we don't. *Hidden Witness* empowers black subjects of representation as not objects but owners of the gaze and of the camera itself.[29]

If the existence of the studio portraits in *Hidden Witness* is surprising to some viewers, it is because these personal portraits differ from the nineteenth-century images of black men and women that have circulated in American cultural history. The obscurity of these images relative to available histories of photography is itself evidence of the disciplinary production of the image of blackness as one of subordination, in which histories of black authorship and self-imaging are suppressed and forgotten.[30] Within contemporary visual studies, the topic of historical representations of African Americans in photography often begins with brutally clinical studies of black men and women, stripped for the camera as evidence of racial difference. Fifteen such daguerreotypes were discovered in the attic of Harvard's Peabody Museum in 1975. In 1850 the South Carolina daguerreotypist J. T. Zealy was hired by the notorious racist Louis Agassiz to produce a series of images that would visually demonstrate his theory that people of African descent belonged to a different species. Since their discovery, Zealy's images have become powerful emblems for the fraught relationship of the African American subject to the disciplinary (and disciplining) practice of photography.[31] In the hands of this scientist, the camera is an instrument of a colonial vision fixing the racialized subject in its gaze, immobilizing and epidermalizing that person into an object of study. But as a number of scholars point out, the photographs also document the noncooperation of its subjects in relation to the camera and the limits of photographic evidence. Molly Rodgers describes one subject, Delia, who faces the camera, her dress having been pulled down to her waist: "Physically, she was fully exposed, every detail of her upper body on display and minutely recorded by the camera, but at the same time there was a complete lack of emotional presence in the picture, as if the woman had put on a mask to conceal her identity."[32] These images alone can't body forth Agassiz's racist views; they work only within an apparatus that decides for the viewer what they mean. In other words, that apparatus may have had power over the bodies of these men and women, but it does not hold absolute power over their image. These particular images have become paradigmatic, emblems for the collaboration of photography, science, and racist ideologies.

Hidden Witness excavates an altogether different view of the relationship between African Americans and the camera, absorbing photography into African American history as a process in which black men and women are not only subjects of the camera but agents in creating and consuming the picture. The explicit charge of the commission from Weems was to give *Hidden Witness* a context. Although that kind of historical project has long been Weems's craft, it is hard to imagine an artist approaching such a commission with relish, especially when we consider the time and location of the exhibit.[33] (The artist described her first reaction to the invitation as "Why me?")[34] The J. Paul Getty Museum is tucked away in Malibu, in deliberate remove from black and brown Los Angeles. *Hidden Witness* opened three years after the Los Angeles uprising in 1992 that was sparked by a white jury's decision to exonerate the Los Angeles police officers who brutally assaulted the African American motorist Rodney King as he lay on the ground.[35] Photography figured centrally in that trial: a man videotaped the beating (at the time, such recordings were rare), which was widely broadcast and became the focal point of a national conversation regarding racism and police violence. The officers' defense lawyers used slow-motion excerpts and still images from that same tape to argue that King (prone on the ground, arms clearly raised to protect himself) posed a threat. The lawyers aggressively reframed images of a group of white men assaulting a black man as images documenting police officers attempting to protect themselves from the threat of violence embedded in the black man's body, regardless of its position. That narrative manipulation depended on the same disciplinary practices of framing with and against which Weems works in her installation.[36]

It is hard to overstate the importance of these contexts for reading the work's emotional landscape. There is a harmony between the layers of reaction with which Weems's installation is coated and the intensity of the city's (and the nation's) awareness of its own reactions to the conclusion of the trial of the officers who assaulted King. This was the first artist commission from the Getty Museum. At that point, it was a big deal for the museum to show work by a living artist, so it is significant that this inaugural invitation was offered to an African American woman who works with discourses of race, gender, and history.[37] The paired exhibitions, named as a dialectical exchange of witness and reaction, pointed directly to the city's recent history and to an ongoing national confrontation with its racialized varieties of class warfare. The project unfolded within a public conversation regarding the ethics of bearing witness, of testimony and perspective—one in which the political geometries of spectatorship and power could not have been more visible or contested.

The photographs in Wilson's collection bear witness to a suppressed history *and* to a history of oppression; Weems reacts with yet another form of bearing witness: an art historical survey of what Elizabeth Alexander describes as "narrative dominion," meaning the deployment of images of black bodies, of black experience in the service of someone else's narrative.[38] As important as is the historical context for the commission, the installation hardly need have been exhibited in Los Angeles at that moment in order to be weighed down by history. *From Here I Saw* sketches a familiar (and depressing) lesson. The work is explicitly didactic. (Weems worked closely with the education department through the commission.) The installation's thirty-three frames each redeploy an existing photograph that takes black men and women as its subject.[39] Some frames use Zealy's daguerreotypes; some are images from *Hidden Witnesses*'s archive of studio portraits; many are more recent and familiar works, frequently included in surveys of the history of American photography: photographs of Harlem nightlife, works of contemporary art, documentation of the civil rights movement. The first and last images are seen through a cool blue lens, the color of the work's glass. The rest pulsate with an angry, blood red. Those images are framed by round charcoal matting, described by one art historian as "telescopic."[40] Text has been sandblasted onto the surface of the glass of each work in the series. "I SAW WHAT HAPPENED" is written across the first image of an African woman in profile (one of two covered in a cool blue). This is followed by four of the Zealy daguerreotypes of enslaved men and women from South Carolina, identified as Delia, Renty, Jack, and Drana. "YOU BECAME A SCIENTIFIC PROFILE" is written over Delia, posed shirtless and in profile. Renty is inscribed as having become "A NEGROID TYPE," Jack "AN ANTHROPOLOGICAL DEBATE," and over Drana the text reads "& A PHOTOGRAPHIC SUBJECT."[41] Much of the text is blunt and flat in tone (see plates 7–14).

The original photographic perspective for the images deployed in Weems's series is that of the unmarked viewer, in which a naturalized, distanced, and objective point of view organizes the presentation of racial difference within the visual and narrative field, situating the viewer without requiring, however, that she feel this positioning. Such positioning precludes or suppresses the possibility of identifying with the image's subject.[42]

An interest in the ideological work of documentary photography has been a constant across Weems's career. As Lisa Gail Collins has argued, in this installation the artist intervenes against the "visual empiricism" of the camera's historical relationship to the black subject.[43] The unmasking of this "neutral" position as the hallmark of white supremacist ideology is one of the signature critical interventions of antiracist projects, be they visual, literary, or scholarly. The subject of *From Here I Saw* is partly how, in the artist's words, "white America saw itself in relationship to the black subject."[44] It is a lesson in the affective density of the historical project, in which bearing witness might be a critical act, but it might also be a form of complicity, depending on the spectator's location. At what point does witnessing switch from being a point of resistance to being a point of collusion? How does one know the difference—is it a matter of how we look at something, how we feel about what we are looking at? What is the relationship between one and the other?

———

From the opening series of Zealy's images, a longer story of subjugation and resistance unfurls across the rest of Weems's frames. The installation enlists the spectator in an exchange between word and image, between artist, spectator, and photographic subject. In some instances, the text surfaces the ideological work of the colonial gaze. The phrase "DESCENDING YOUR THRONE TO BECOME FOOTSOLDIER & COOK" is written over a grandfatherly man with a gray beard and wearing a floppy hat. Other statements describe twists in that colonial relation: "YOU BECAME MAMIE, MAMA, MOTHER & THEN, YES, CONFIDANT — HA" is written across the image of a heavyset older woman wearing a white head-wrap. A young boy is reduced to "DRIVER." Four women in sequence stare back at us through the words slapped over them: "HOUSE," "FIELD," "YARD," "KITCHEN." Already the agency of the photographed subjects is complicated: if one becomes a house slave, it is because one is *made* that. The saturation of these images in red, the punch of each word combined with the stony expressions of the women suggests a kind of push back. One might become mammie *and* a confidant, and in doing so cobble together an important if limited kind of power: thus the snap of "HA."

As already indicated by the use of the Zealy daguerreotypes, many of the source images have an important place in both African American history and the history of photography. One of the most confrontational panels redeploys "The Scourged Back," a widely circulated image taken in 1863 of a man's back crisscrossed by raised scar tissue.[45] That scourged back belongs to Gordon, who escaped slavery and enlisted with the Union army during the Civil War. He is positioned for the camera so that the viewer can survey the extent and depth of the traces of the whip on his skin. In an early use of photography as propaganda, the image was mass-produced as a carte-de-visite and used in abolitionist lectures to provoke moral outrage in the spectator.[46] Weems's speaker does not see this image so much as she hears it:

BLACK AND TANNED
YOUR WHIPPED WIND
OF CHANGE HOWLED LOW
BLOWING ITSELF — HA — SMACK
INTO THE MIDDLE OF
ELLINGTON'S ORCHESTRA
BILLIE HEARD IT TOO &
CRIED STRANGE FRUIT TEARS

She moves quickly from the visual ("BLACK AND TANNED") to the howl and moan of Ellington's orchestra and then to Billie Holiday's performance of "Strange Fruit," which is itself a story of an affectively intense performance reacting to racist violence. (Holiday closed her performances with this song about lynching, sometimes refusing to sing it for audiences who didn't deserve it.)[47]

As we move deeper into the series, Weems conjures scenes in which subjection is transformed into expression, in which pain is translated into music and myth. The photographed subject becomes "A WHISPER / A SYMBOL," "JUJU MAMA / VOODOO QUEEN / HOODOO DOCTOR." In the last seven frames, the dialogue turns back onto itself with increasing force:

YOU BECAME
THE JOKER'S JOKE &
ANYTHING
BUT WHAT YOU WERE
HA
SOME LAUGHED
LONG & HARD & LOUD
OTHERS SAID
"ONLY THING A NIGGAH
COULD DO WAS SHINE MY SHOES"
YOU BECAME
BOOTS
SPADES &
COONS
RESTLESS AFTER
THE LONGEST WINTER
YOU MARCHED & MARCHED & MARCHED
IN YOUR SING SONG
PRAYER YOU ASKED
DIDN'T MY LORD DELIVER DANIEL

The photographs underneath this sequence range from nineteenth-century studio portraits and ethnographic documentation to iconic images from twentieth-century art history, such as Robert Mapplethorpe's *Man in a Polyester Suit* (1980; a picture of a black man whose penis hangs from his unzipped trousers and whose head has been cropped from the image) and Robert Frank's *Charleston, South Carolina* (1955; a picture of a black woman holding a white baby). This last movement within the installation's text seems to take us from Jim Crow and minstrelsy ("YOU BECAME THE JOKER'S JOKE") to the civil rights movement ("YOU MARCHED & MARCHED & MARCHED"), from debasement to uplift—or, at least, a righteous struggle on its behalf.

Weems bookends the red emblems with twinned blue-toned portraits of an African woman, over whom is inscribed the work's title: "FROM HERE I SAW WHAT HAPPENED . . ." / " . . . AND I CRIED." Her profile turns inward, facing the history that it sandwiches. Visually she is located in the series in an African space. (Formally, the panels of red and black subjects sit on the wall as a kind of Middle Passage.) Her isolation from the series she frames and the association of the first-person point of view with her image lends a density to the work's perspective: is the "I" (and the feelings that accompany it) hers, or the artist's? Or does it belong to the viewer, who inserts herself into the text by identifying with its speaker and is, technically, the one doing the seeing? Who is "you," and how does she or he become this image? If the viewer sees "spades and coons," isn't she also collaborating in, contributing to that becoming?

Clearly, *From Here I Saw* presents itself as a kind of history: it is linear, book-like in its physical structure, and the text links one image to the next. That linear structure ought not be taken to represent a narrative of progress; although a sense of forward motion animates the installation, it is an effect of its physical structure, the text's causal syntax ("I SAW WHAT HAPPENED," "YOU BECAME," "I CRIED"), and the linear movement of photographic time as the image produces its past for the viewer's present. The narrative and the organization of the images in relation to each other are cyclical. The photographs are not organized chronologically. The series begins and ends with the same image (in a mirrored reversal). We end up, in other words, in the same time and place, that of the witness. Furthermore each frame in the installation is treated as a work unto itself. They are all titled by the text that appears on their surfaces. In criticism, the entire work is rarely grappled with; it is hard to describe in part because each frame stands on its own as an emblem. This is in fact integral to its difficulty: there is a tension in the work between the snapshot that fixes the image to a caption ("YARD") and the dynamic and circular motion implied by its larger narrative structure ("I SAW," "YOU BECAME," "I CRIED").

The full series is mournful and asks questions about the relationship of the museum to the historical traumas archived within it. Is the ultimate aim of African American art history, for example, the inclusion of things like Wilson's collection into the museum? (What sort of museum?) What do we do with Zealy, then? And the long string of images of black subjects, framed for white viewers and racialist consumption? Weems's installation analyzes not just the place of African Americans in the history of photography but the role of photography in what Toni Morrison calls "American Africanism," the denotative and connotative blackness that African peoples have come to signify, as well as the entire range of views, assumptions, readings and misreadings that accompany Eurocentric learning about these people. As a trope, little restraint has been attached to its uses. As a disabling virus within literary discourse, Africanism has become, in the Eurocentric tradition that American education favors, both a way of talking about and a way of policing matters of class, sexual license, and repression, formations and exercises of power, and meditations on ethics and accountability. Through the simple expedient of demonizing or reifying the range of color on a palate, American Africanism makes it possible to say and not say, to inscribe and erase, to escape and engage, to act out and act on, to historicize and render timeless.[48]

From Here I Saw produces that series of "readings and misreadings" in the gap between the image and the text etched onto each work's surface. The reification (fixing) to which Morrison refers is made visible in Weems's work as the violence of the emblematic logics of racialist vision, in which a person doesn't get to *be* but must *represent. From Here I Saw* is positioned as testimony, bearing witness to the processes whereby a person becomes an image, an image becomes an emblem, and that emblem becomes "a mechanism for testing the problems and blessings of freedom."[49] It also takes its viewer on a tour of the set pieces through which the American viewer comes to know his or her emotional depths in relation to black feeling.

Writing about the reception of Kara Walker's work, Christina Sharpe describes this ideological landscape as one in which the black figure becomes the "sole site on which the signifying power of slavery in the past and present is put to work."[50] The sadness announced by the title of Weems's series might represent not a breakthrough, or even a working-through of emotion, but the disciplinary articulations of African American history for the national subject as grief-ridden, as if African American history were itself the lone reservoir of national trauma. *From Here I Saw* might thus be read as indexing anger, frustration, and exhaustion, a depression by dint of routine: theft, exploitation, appropriation, resistance, grief, mourning, and recovery—followed by the requirement that the artist produce that cycle within her work.

Individual works from the series operate as condensations of this process: the fixing of an individual becomes an emblem for the whole of African American history and, by extension, for the "problem" of African American art history, insofar as it is produced in art critical discourse as a disciplinary failure to transcend identity. When *Art in America* put the artist's work on its

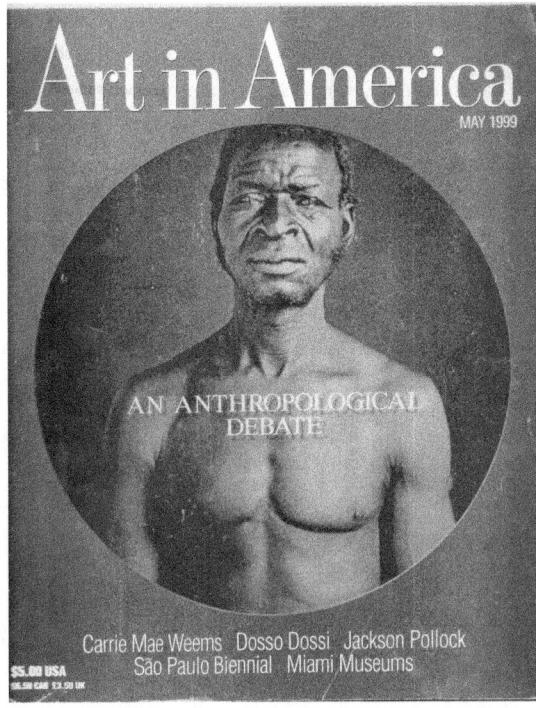

FIGURE 21. Cover of *Art in America* (May 1999). The image is Carrie Mae Weems's *An Anthropological Debate* from *From Here I Saw What Happened and I Cried*. 1995–96. Thirty-three toned prints. Courtesy of Carrie Mae Weems and Jack Shainman Gallery, New York.

May 1999 cover (fig. 21), it selected "An Anthropological Debate," creating a triple emblem in which Jack stands in for Weems's work, in which Jack's face and body appear as the incarnation of a debate about race, while also bodying forth debates within art history about its proper object (art? ethnography?). Jack's work never stops.

In his "Theses on the Philosophy of History" Walter Benjamin asserts, "There is no document of civilization which is not at the same time a document of barbarism. And just as such a document is not free of barbarism, barbarism taints also the manner in which it was transmitted from one owner to another." For the philosopher, there is nothing quite so suspect as the historian committed to reliving the past; such a practice risks confirming the status quo as inevitable, as always meant to be what it is. In such cases "a secret agreement" is struck "between past generations and the present one. Our coming was expected on earth." Within the naturalizing logics of history as progress, the present redeems the past, enlisting "even the dead" in its service. The desire to relive the historical past betrays an "empathy with the victor" and a cooperation with "the triumphal procession in which the present rulers step over those who are lying prostrate. . . . The spoils are carried along in the procession. They are called cultural treasures, and a historical materialist views them with cautious detachment. For without exception the cultural treasures he surveys have an origin which he cannot contemplate without horror."[51] *From Here I Saw* negotiates with this basic problem in the protocols of museum culture. Weems gives us a portrait of the shadow that stretches across art history, not only in terms of the thievery practiced by museums in its acquisition of "treasure" (the J. Paul Getty Museum being one of the most notorious examples of this) but in the very shape of the aesthetic, insofar as the horizon that gives it shape and definition is marked by the bodies it has freighted with the symbolic weight Morrison describes, a weight that relegates those bodies to the subspace of the discipline (ethnography) where they do the heavy emotional lifting (embodying the trauma of history itself). The aim of *From Here I Saw* is not a reconstruction of the past but, as Thelma Golden writes, a proper "reckoning with the present."[52]

Adding to its difficulty, Weems's installation both recalls and comments on the ways that African American history has its own disciplinary protocols and counterpressures. There is a mandate to demonstrate a certain respectability, a control and evenness in one's tone, a call to represent well which develops as a counterpressure to the racist discourse that produces African American history as an abject disaster, a story of victimization, licentiousness, and failure. In the face of those kinds of supremacist narratives there is a script one is expected to follow as a defensive measure and at times as a matter of necessity. Roderick Ferguson describes it as "a way of writing and imagining community" in which "invisible blemishes" are "withheld from conversation and kept out of sight."[53] The contrast between *Hidden Witness* and Weems's installation speaks to this dialectic within African American history and art history. *From Here I Saw* is directly engaged with the gruesome dimensions of disciplinary structures in ways that *Hidden Witness* can't be; even the title of that exhibit suggests its position of constraint. *From Here I Saw What Happened and I Cried*, on the other hand, is openly didactic, propagandistic, and at points anxious, rebellious, and ambivalent. It participates in a critical tradition of working against the ideological and disciplining structures of history and also of naming one's location ("Here"). (Other contemporary artists who produce work engaged with African American history, discourse on race, and the disciplinary structures of art history include Kerry James Marshall, David Hammonds, and Glenn Ligon.) The "political imperative" of this tradition, Fred Moten writes, "is never disconnected from an aesthetic one." Such projects engage in "a necessary reconstruction of the very aesthetics of photography, of documentary, and therefore, of truth, revelation, and enlightenment as well as of judgment, taste, and therefore, the aesthetic itself."[54] They are didactic and propagandistic, and they are *about* didacticism and propaganda.[55]

Each of the photographs appear in this series as reclaimed spoils deployed against history's grain.[56] Where the J. Paul Getty Museum exhibits nineteenth-century images of African Americans to give its audience a reparative encounter with a repressed photographic archive, Weems takes as her focus the story of how photography is deployed within what W. E. B. Du Bois called "the propaganda of history."[57] Weems's installation is overtly committed to making the politics of Art *and* History visible, as disciplines engaged in ideological work, and she locates that work in affect and economies of perspective.

The installation's original title ("Carrie Mae Weems Reacts . . .") and its revision both frame the work as having something to do with emotion. It has a complicated mood. *From Here I Saw* makes no effort to produce a sense of intimacy with the photographed subjects, other than to suggest what happened to them. Weems centers the installation's narrative not on what the imaged subjects feel but on what the viewer bears witness to: the emphasis is on the spectator's feelings. The framing narrative may describe an expression of emotion but, as a statement, "From here I saw what happened and I cried" is not expressive in and of itself. It is in fact as spare a statement regarding emotion as one can imagine producing. The titular declaration is flat, matter of fact, and superimposed over a woman who is far more a picture of restraint and self-possession than a picture of grief. The work's overall affect is hard, even stifling. As saturated with emotion as the work appears at first glance, on closer examination it is incredibly controlled. In spite of the tears promised by its title, the work is anticathartic.

Weems's installation inventories the affective project within which these photographs have been deployed as emblems for subjection, dignity, humiliation, and freedom. Through its use of writing, the work also folds into its archive a series of intensely emotional texts: the sentimentality of *Uncle Tom's Cabin* and the biting satire of Mark Twain; Billie Holiday's blues performances of "God Bless the Child" and "Strange Fruit"; the grisly comedy of minstrel performance and the liberating strains of gospel. The speaker of the series breaks up the work's mournfulness with a periodic "HA" (for example, "YOUR RESISTANCE WAS FOUND IN THE FOOD YOU PLACED ON THE MASTER'S TABLE—HA," is written across a portrait of a white man, his two children, and a black woman servant). These HA's bite and slice through the work as controlled breaks. The feelings in circulation are framed and indexed as having already happened (thus the text is in past tense). The speaker's tears are shed not over what happened to her but about what happened to others. The speaker's "you" might call out the photographed subject or the viewer (as addressed by the work's use of second person) or both (interpolating the viewer as subject of the sentence and the image). The work produces history as an affective feedback loop, in which now and then, here and there, "I" and "you" are locked in an embrace.

The emotions drawn out in the work articulate a distance. This is not the distance of the neutral or the objective—of critical disinterest. It is instead an affective portrait of the dead space that such distance produces (objectivity, detachment). The work's difficulty comes from our confrontation not with what we see but with what seeing fails to give us. The work's emotional economy is organized around that blockage; we are left with the feeling that something has happened, some kind of disaster, but we sense it only partially as a presence lurking behind the frozen expressions that greet the camera. Like Luna's *History of the Luiseño People*, Weems's installation explores the poetics of depression, anger, and alienation that unfold around the moment America turns to specific communities when it needs permission to *feel*, in which the spectacle of one's reaction is always already working on behalf of someone, something else. ("Why me?")

All of this work points to what it might mean to practice art history according to counterhegemonic models described by writers like Du Bois and Benjamin. Such scholarship would not ask that we deaden our feelings, and it would not dismiss the feelings that we do have as precritical, superfluous, as so much vicarious feeling. Nor would this work present politics as structured by either the vertical or the horizontal axes Foster describes (as if one can choose between the past and the present). That sense of verticality—be it the depth model of expression critiqued by Terada or the deterministic logic of historicism critiqued by Jameson—is an ideological effect that disguises the terrible complexity of the surface. Those figures that we project back in time (the slave, for example) exist ideologically in the present as haunting signs of a traumatic past. They are the mediums through which that trauma is carried forward.

The affective intensity of the space around works of art marks not a limit but a starting point for critical engagement. "Feeling and emotion," writes Deborah Gould, "are fundamental to political life, not in the sense that they overtake reason and interfere with deliberative processes, as they are sometimes disparagingly construed to do, but in the sense that there is an affective dimension to the processes and practices that make up 'the political,' broadly defined."[58] The feelings imagined as outside art history have been mystified as that which is inside, as personal, and as therefore belonging neither to the art object (because they belong to the artist) nor to discourse about it (because they are private and are therefore not historical). Franko B, Nao Bustamante, James Luna, and Carrie Mae Weems help us to understand how this apolitical take on art, emotion, and history is a product of both the ideology of emotion Terada critiques and the ideology of the historian who imagines her job is to provide more and more facts. Each of their works demonstrates how political work is done in and through emotion as a site of connection and intimacy, of alienation and radicalization.

CONCLUSION

"history keeps me awake"

David Wojnarowicz's *Untitled (Hujar Dead)* (1988–1989)

The base for David Wojnarowicz's *Untitled (Hujar Dead)* (1988–89) is a nine-panel collage of black and white photographs of Peter Hujar's face, hands, and feet (plate 15; fig. 22). The artist took those photographs moments after Hujar had died from AIDS in 1987. Before he took those pictures, Wojnarowicz panned the length of Hujar's body with a Super 8 camera. Between 1987 and 1992, the year Wojnarowicz died, he would return again and again to the scene of his friend's death—in poems, writings, in notes toward a never-finished "film for Peter Hujar."[1] *Untitled (Hujar Dead)* belongs to that cycle of works. The text covering the portrait's surface ("If I had a dollar") was deployed by the artist in other works: it appears in *Close to the Knives: A Memoir of Disintegration* (in the chapter "Postcards from America: X Rays from Hell"); he performed the text live (and recorded those performances); an audio recording of the artist reciting it appears in *ITSOFOMO* (a multimedia performance collaboration with Ben Neill); and he reads the text from *Untitled (Hujar Dead)* in a television appearance, *The Eleventh Hour*, in 1989. In that broadcast, his back is turned to the camera as he reads directly from *Untitled (Hujar Dead)*, which is hanging on the wall (see fig. 23).

Much of the art Wojnarowicz produced during these years evidences the

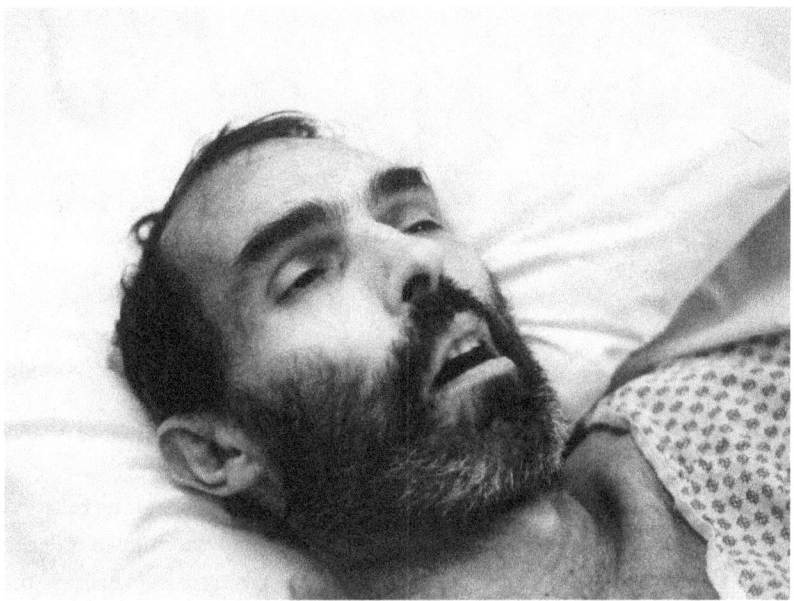

FIGURE 22. David Wojnarowicz, *Untitled (Peter Hujar)*. 1987 (taken), 1989 (printed). Courtesy of the Estate of David Wojnarowicz and PPOW Gallery, New York.

unfinished work of grieving Hujar. He wrote extensively about Hujar's illness and death. In his journals he turns over the idea of making work dealing with Hujar's death—work that might register something of what it felt like to survive the man he described as the most important person in his life.[2] Peter Hujar was the artist's closest friend. They had been lovers, they became family to each other, and Hujar (himself an influential photographer) was a mentor to Wojnarowicz. Wojnarowicz cared for Hujar throughout his illness and documents some of the most harrowing moments of their last months together in his published writings.

The misery of watching Hujar's decline and rage at the indifference of the public to the suffering of a generation is boiled down into this intensely personal and acutely political tableau.[3] The overall image is chaotic. Hujar's body is framed by the chopped-up graphics of supermarket posters and dollar bills, over which float blood cells and sperm cut from money and maps. The nine photographs are buried under another layer of information: a *cri de guerre* is stamped across the work's surface. Standing in front of *Untitled (Hujar Dead)*, it takes time to read that text. This writing functions like the soundtrack for Linda Montano's *Mitchell's Death*: one repels the casual viewer

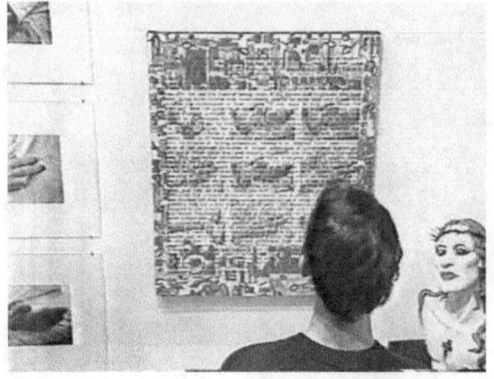

FIGURE 23. David Wojnarowicz reading from the surface of *Untitled (Hujar Dead)* in a broadcast of *The Eleventh Hour*. 1989. Courtesy of the Fales Special Collections Library at New York University.

with an ascetic drone, the other with a wall of words. The text intervenes directly in the structure of spectatorship: the artist deploys writing in order to force the spectator to become a *reader*, and that reading is hard because the text is written as a breathless rant. To cite only its conclusion:

> I've been looking all my life at the signs surrounding us in the media or on peoples lips; the religious types outside st patricks cathedral shouting to men and women in the gay parade: "You won't be here next year—you'll get Aids and die ha ha" . . . there's a thin line a very thin line and as each T-cell disappears from my body it's replaced by ten pounds of pressure ten pounds of rage and I focus that rage into non-violent resistance but that focus is starting to slip my hands are beginning to move independent of self-restraint and the egg is starting to crack America seems to understand and accept murder as a self-defense against those who would murder other people and its been murder on a daily basis for eight count them eight long years and we're expected to pay taxes to support this public and social murder but I say there's certain politicians that had better increase their security forces and there's religious leaders and healthcare officials that had better get bigger dogs and higher fences and more complex security alarms for their homes and queer bashers better start doing their work from inside howitzer tanks because the thin line between the inside and the outside is beginning to erode and at the moment I'm a thirty-seven foot tall one thousand one hundred and seventy-two pound man inside this six foot frame and all I can feel is the pressure all I can feel is the pressure and the need for release.[4]

It is easy to feel suffocated by the work's visual density and affective volume. C. Carr describes Wojnarowicz's writing as a Ginsbergian howl, "built on the long breath that leaves one body to engulf the endless world and, returning, sees the universe in a single action."[5] Terry Allison and Renée Curry describe the text as a "stockpiling" of outrage.[6] The writing pours out of the artist. It appears so unmediated that at first there seems little for us to grab onto. Lucy Lippard explains, "Even now, years after I started to love his paintings, I find it difficult to describe their robust poetics. They map a territory I recognize but don't really know. They blow me away."[7] Approaching this work as a critic, one is confronted immediately by a hesitation: to treat this work formally would seem to do it a kind of violence, to reduce its urgency to a question of style rather than a question of history or crisis.[8]

There is a tendency in art criticism to feel that one must choose: style *or* politics, form *or* content. This is especially true for works whose style is grounded in popular and expressive genres. (In Wojnarowicz's case, that would include graffiti, punk, and DIY aesthetics.) If we buy into that binary, then yes, the tension between the work of art and its context, between its form and its subject has been stretched in *Untitled (Hujar Dead)* to a breaking point. Accepting that formula backs the critic into a corner, however, because in such a framework art produced within and about social injustice has no meaningful value for either the art critic (because it is "bad art") or the activist (because it is "only art"). It's a devil's choice. We can see that most powerfully in the work of artists like Wojnarowicz, for if art and politics are so incompatible, then we must wonder what would motivate an artist to make so much work in the middle of something as terrifying as the AIDS crisis in the late 1980s and 1990s, when, for an overwhelming majority of people, a diagnosis was a death sentence all but gleefully issued by a homophobic and racist public.[9]

"If I had a dollar" and a handful of phrases and images from Wojnarowicz's archive have become emblems for the AIDS crisis itself.[10] Statements like "When I was told I'd contracted this virus it didn't take me long to realize that I'd contracted a diseased society as well" appear frequently in writing about AIDS and homophobic culture.[11] An image of his mouth sewn shut, a photograph of his face almost completely buried in sand, an image of buffalos being driven over a cliff, all circulate widely as a visual shorthand for the deadly effects of the prohibition against talking about sexuality and AIDS, for the experience of living with a death sentence and a declaration of the AIDS pandemic as a form of "social murder."[12] Wojnarowicz was one of an astonishing number of artists who died from AIDS within a decade of each other. Their absence registers in art history and performance studies as a terrifying erasure: Peter Hujar, Robert Mapplethorpe, Keith Haring, Jack Smith, Marlon Riggs, Derek Jarman, Sylvester, Leigh Bowery, Scott Burton, Cookie Mueller, Félix González-Torres, Paul Thek, Essex Hemphill, Freddie Mercury, Klaus Nomi—these are just a few of the influential artists who died from AIDS-related illnesses. It is not just that the lifework of these artists was cut short but that, in some cases, their work was transformed by the AIDS crisis (explicitly or implicitly). Their absence registers not as a quiet disappearance but as an explosion.

One of the readers of the first draft of this book remarked that nearly all the artists I discuss come from Wojnarowicz's generation. (Shvarts and Bustamante are exceptions.) This was the result of an unconscious drift in my attention to the artists who came of age at least a decade before I did and whom I watched from a distance, trying to imagine a future for myself. A number of critics of my generation have been thinking and writing about the future, questions of time and timing, and utopia; this is in part because in our early adulthood, it seemed as if there was no place in the world for the people we wanted to become.[13] As we move through our forties and fifties, we are growing older than the artists whose work inspired us. Perhaps writing about their work is a way for us to mark that passage—and perhaps my desire to link Wojnarowicz and other queer artists to oppositional figures who are still here (to nod to the choreographer Bill T. Jones's work on this very topic) is a way to critically imagine futures for work that is usually framed in relation to stories of disappearance.

It is not possible or responsible to ignore the AIDS crisis as a context for understanding the difficulty of Wojnarowicz's work. In an interview about their friendship, Kiki Smith recalled that when she "was making work that was based in the body," Wojnarowicz "was doing work that was based in his experiences."[14] It is a smart observation, for it suggests why Wojnarowicz's work has become such an integral part of what Ann Cvetkovich has described as the "archive of feeling" for the AIDS crisis; his work is perhaps one of the most frequently referenced when writers need to distill what things were like. They describe the life-world of a community doubly traumatized, by the disease and by the vicious public policy and homophobic discourse that took shape around AIDS in the late 1980s and 1990s.[15] Works like *Untitled (Hujar Dead)* capture the emotional world of AIDS activism. They have an urgency and intensity that one might describe as a survival poetics, in that the work feels *necessary*, grounded in a need for the things that make life not just pleasurable but possible. It *is* driven by desire and disease.

Wojnarowicz performed "If I had a dollar" as a fire-and-brimstone sermon. In recordings of him reading this text he can hardly keep his breath as he pushes the words out; its recitation exhausts him. (Again, I think of *Mitchell's Death*: Montano's control over her own voice represents a different strategy for channeling intense feeling.) For the viewer, reading *Untitled*'s text is only slightly less tiring and uncomfortable than watching recordings of Wojnarowicz perform it. It bodies forth the affective world of a man who wants to live, a man who can feel the basic elements that life requires being withdrawn not from him but from the world. Blood, sperm, and money stand in for oxygen, sex, and access (to health care, political representation, and power). But laced through the work is something less easy to decode: a global panic (here meaning full-body and also worldwide), a sense of one's body as both nothing and gigantic, a pressure both described in the text ("and all I feel is the need for release") and produced by the text as it takes over the work and pulls the breath out of its reader.[16] It may be a two-dimensional static art object and therefore quite traditional in terms of the kinds of things a museum, art gallery, or critic can accommodate. But *Untitled (Hujar Dead)* is atmospheric, environmental, and like all narrative writing, it demands time from the viewer. Because of this, it works against the grain of the spectator's habits in relation to the visual; in a museum or gallery, we want to move over the image, to take it in at a glance, to step back and appreciate it. Wojnarowicz asks us to step closer and read. He forces the viewer to decide if she will commit to this aspect of the work. Like *Mitchell's Death*, *Untitled (Hujar Dead)* centers on the absence of the dead and is structured by an ambivalence to the dynamics of display, to the implicit requirement that a visual work seduce the viewer with the promise of showing her something. Wojnarowicz and Montano respond to this problem by turning the viewer into something else: a listener, a reader, and a witness.

In visual art, text can operate as a disruption or intrusion, a refusal to privilege the forms of knowledge and pleasure associated with the gaze.[17] That interference is aligned with forcing us to turn our gaze away from Hujar's body, for you can't read the words and look at the images under the words at the same time. This text forces us to get physically close to the work, but it also pushes us away from the image at its heart. The wall of words asserts a fundamental distance between the event of Hujar's death and our encounter with Wojnarowicz's representation of it. As immediate and unmediated as this rant may feel when we read it, it appears in the work as a literal mediation of the image. The text ushers us away from the intimacy of the moment captured by Wojnarowicz's camera. Its words stand between us and the image, and they do not describe Hujar's death.[18]

This work does not memorialize Hujar in a traditional sense. *Untitled (Hujar Dead)* layers rage over grief. The work speaks to what Douglas Crimp describes as an "antagonism to mourning" within the AIDS activist community, a discomfort with the quieter "rituals of grief" that seemed to risk easing people through a sense of loss rather than activating people to fight against the processes which created that loss in the first place.[19] This sense of conflict was aggravated by the demand that one be quiet about both the disease and homosexuality: the social rituals of mourning added another psychic injury to friends and lovers in the frequent requirement that those left behind not acknowledge the sexuality of the person they had buried. In other words, at the funeral for your lover, partner, or friend, you may be expected to be "polite" and "respectful" of the family's silence by denying the nature of your love and your experience of loss. The simple equation "Silence=Death," which became a defining slogan of AIDS activism, captures the collaboration of one with the other. "The violence we encounter is relentless," Crimp writes of this awful erasure, "the violence of silence and omission [is] almost as impossible to endure as the violence of the unleashed hatred and outright murder. Because this violence also desecrates the memories of our dead, we rise in anger to vindicate them. For many of us mourning *becomes* militancy."[20] For those barred from public displays of grief (or even from attending the funeral), public mourning becomes a powerful and necessary form of activism.

Wojnarowicz has long been central to conversations about this aspect of AIDS activism. In "Postcards from America: X Rays from Hell," he records his resistance to joining a community of "professional pallbearers . . . perfecting the rituals of death." Instead he fantasized making each death as public, as noisy as possible: "I imagine what it would be like if, each time a lover, friend or stranger died of this disease, a lover, friend, or neighbor would take the dead body and drive with it in a car a hundred miles an hour to washington d.c. and blast through the gates of the white house and come to a screeching halt before the entrance and dump their lifeless form on the front steps."[21] This vision was realized by interventions like *Ashes Action* (October 1992 and 1996), in which activists threw the ashes of people who had died from AIDS onto the White House lawn.[22] His own death sparked a demonstration, as people took to the streets of New York carrying signs bearing his words and images. They marched behind a banner declaring, "David Wojnarowicz

(1954–1992) died of AIDS due to government neglect." His partner Tom Rauffenbart threw Wojnarowicz's ashes over the White House fence in 1996.

Work about AIDS and illness shares a common vocabulary in its necessary preoccupation with the process of dying, the moment of death, and the need to politicize the rituals of grief.[23] That work is shadowed by problems of representation: how to make the crisis visible when it impacts "invisible" communities; how to make the crisis feel real and urgent to those not directly impacted by it; how to properly grieve for the people you love when they are dying en masse; how to keep in view people who are gone, in a world that disavows the nature of your relationship with that person. It was also important that people with AIDS not be represented as victims isolated from their context, and that dying from AIDS not be dressed up in the sentimental dynamics that Baldwin described as "the signal of secret and violent inhumanity." In the push for visibility, artists and activists were conscious of the risk of turning the "AIDS victim" into a consumable object of pity and struggled overtly with the challenge of integrating subjects like sex, desire, love, and friendship into a narrative about the politics of illness, medicine, insurance, and discourse on public health. Nicholas Nixon's "humanizing" portraits of people with AIDS, for example, won praise from some art critics and drew fire from others. Crimp writes that such photographs reproduce a narrative always already out there, which represents people with AIDS as "ravaged, disfigured, and debilitated by the syndrome; they are generally alone, but resigned to their 'inevitable' deaths."[24] These portraits, he argues, confirm that death as inevitable. They figure an impending death as if it has already happened. Art about AIDS constantly navigates these different pressures: to represent the specificity of what being HIV-positive and having AIDS means, but also to refuse to reduce a person to the story of a virus and a disease, not only because such reductions are dehumanizing but because they risk mirroring the phobic equation of homosexual desire with disease.[25]

Photography is always already structured by some of these concerns; this has been observed by nearly every philosopher of the medium, but nowhere more memorably than in Roland Barthes's *Camera Lucida*. "With the photograph," he writes, "we enter into *flat Death*." He associates the camera with shifts in the social place of death in the nineteenth century: "Contemporary with the withdrawal of rites, photography may correspond to the intrusion, in our modern society, of an asymbolic Death, outside of religion, outside of ritual, a kind of abrupt dive into literal Death. *Life/Death*: the paradigm is reduced to a simple click, the one separating the initial pose from the final print."[26] It was one of the things that drew Wojnarowicz to the medium long before the AIDS crisis took over his life. A few years before *Camera Lucida* was published, Susan Sontag observed, "Photography converts the world itself into a department store or museum-without-walls in which every subject is depreciated into an article of consumption, promoted as an item for aesthetic appreciation. Photography also turns the whole world into a cemetery."[27] She wrote this in an essay accompanying *Portraits in Life and Death*, a collection of Peter Hujar's photographs. Cynthia Carr tells us that when Wojnarowicz first went to Hujar's apartment, Hujar handed him a copy of that book: "David was stunned to see a volume he'd been drawn to years before."[28] The series features eerie portraits of Sontag, Divine, Edwin Denby, and Paul Thek, all definitive figures in the queer New York underground. These are juxtaposed with photographs that Hujar took of corpses displayed with loving care in Italian catacombs. Those Palermo images, in turn, were produced on a trip to Italy to visit Thek, who at that time was Hujar's friend, lover, and collaborator.[29]

Untitled (Hujar Dead) is about Hujar's death—that much is brutally clear. Less obvious is the place of this work as the last in a series of photographic exchanges between the two artists, in which death is explored as a scene of intimacy and identification, a conversation that itself unfolded in a broader context of queer appropriations of scenes of mortal suffering. *Untitled (Peter Hujar)* (1982), for example, pictures the photographer on the ground, on his back, as if he were asleep or dead (fig. 24). The pose repeats that of a few of the subjects in *Portraits in Life and Death* (including Sontag's). Wojnarowicz used that image of Hujar in a host of works, including his first paintings—most notably, *Peter Hujar Dreaming / Yokio Mishima: St. Sebastian* (1982), a work that explicitly places both artists in a genealogy of queer desire, death, and martyrdom. (The Japanese writer committed a ritual suicide in 1970; St. Sebastian is a long-standing image of queer identification; see plate 16).

Wojnarowicz had been drawn to Hujar's explorations of the entanglement of life and death even before the two had met, through his work in *Portraits in Life and Death*. In one sequence in the unfinished "film for Peter Hujar," Wojnarowicz sits at a window in Hujar's loft and flips through the book's pages, carefully, from the very first to the last (figs. 25–28). It could be the same copy that Hujar handed to Wojnarowicz the first night they went to Hujar's apartment.[30] The book is a point of connection to the prehistory of their relationship, to a moment when Hujar didn't know Wojnarowicz, and to the erotic collaborations of Hujar and Thek. Elisabeth Sussman describes that relationship as "a complex erotic/intellectual performative relationship for the camera."[31] Thek, Sussman explains, modeled for Hujar; they experimented

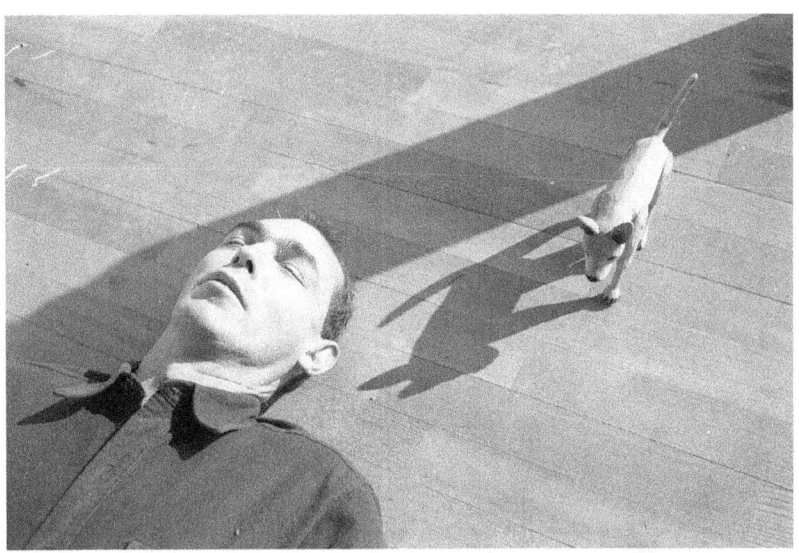

FIGURE 24. David Wojnarowicz, "Untitled." 1982. Courtesy of the Estate of David Wojnarowicz and PPOW Gallery, New York, and the Fales Special Collections Library at New York University.

with the conventions of commercial, artistic, and cinematic photography in sessions that could be serious, playful, and overtly erotic. Thek eventually integrated photography into his own practice, but in the 1970s and 1980s he was known more for his work exploring corporeality in meat-like sculptures (e.g., *Meat Piece with Warhol Brillo Box* [1965]), in works that looked like body parts (hands, fingers, and a "death mask"), as well as an installation centered on a complete effigy for himself (*The Tomb* [1967]). Hujar produced a series of photographs of Thek standing next to and working with that effigy. These reproduce the movement between life and death implied by *Portraits in Life and Death* and by Hujar's portrait of Thek standing next to stacks of ornately decorated corpses. (Wojnarowicz knew Thek and dedicated several works to him.) Although the AIDS crisis shapes *Untitled (Hujar Dead)*, the work's difficult relationship to the image of Hujar's corpse should also be placed within two interlaced contexts: the larger context of their relationship, which, like Hujar and Thek's, included visual meditations on love and loss, and the place of photography within grief culture, a tradition that itself informs the place of memorial and postmortem images in art about AIDS.

A number of scholars have observed that in Europe and the United States the postmortem photograph was an integral part of nineteenth-century grief

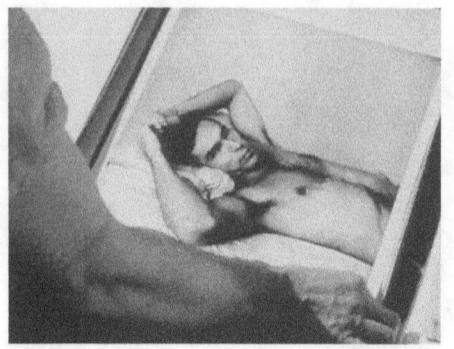

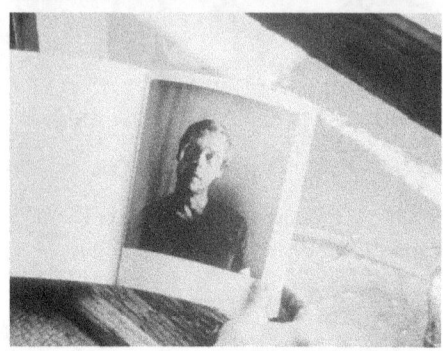

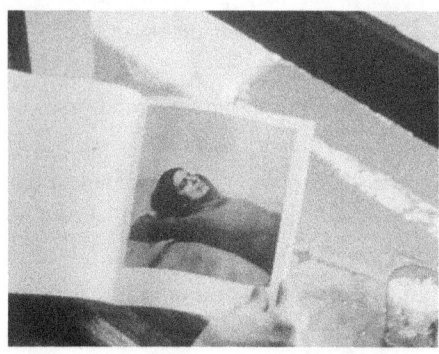

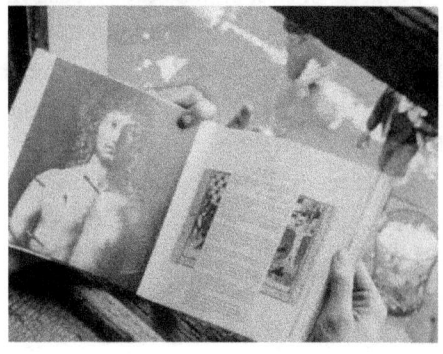

FIGURES 25–28. David Wojnarowicz, four stills from an unfinished
film for Peter Hujar. Courtesy of
the Estate of David Wojnarowicz
and PPOW Gallery, New York,
and the Fales Special Collections
Library at New York University.

culture. At a time when you were far more likely to die in your own bed than in a hospital, and when your ailing body was looked after by family and friends, death was intricately woven into domestic life.[32] Families who could afford it photographed the bodies of children, spouses, and parents, and kept those images close: above the hearth, near the bed, in lockets together with pieces of hair. Franny Nudelman, for example, writes that the practice of photographing a person after death "testified to the ongoing devotion of the living who washed, groomed, and posed the corpse in preparation for the photograph." Nudelman makes this point within her reframing of Civil War photographs of the war dead. Traditionally, scholars have credited those images for their realism, arguing that they raised awareness about the grim nature of warfare. Contemporary viewers tend to assume that the brutality of the images rested in the fact that they made death visible. Nineteenth-century viewers, however, were not undone by the image of a corpse. What shocked them, Nudelman explains, was the lonely anonymity of the bodies pictured on the battlefield and the public circulation of photographs of the dead, outside the community of their family and friends. These kinds of photographs preclude "individual grief" and instead "threatened to build national community bound not by common sorrow but by a newfound detachment in the face of death." Those photographs were difficult, in other words, because they revealed a death torn from the sentimental spaces that gave death—and, by extension, life—meaning. Nudelman writes, "These images, and the commentary surrounding them, used the corpse to demonstrate how war destroys ways of managing, honoring, and understanding the dead, practices that, to a certain extent, shape the very contours of reality. . . . Out of the reach of intimates, the corpse could not provide a medium for expressing the sadness and desire of grieving individuals. Instead, it fell into the hands of professional journalists who, documenting its woeful isolation, intimated a future in which portraits of dead strangers, wrenching and complete, would tell us all we need to know about the circumstances of distant suffering."[33]

In her sweeping history of death and grief culture during the Civil War, Drew Gilpin Faust describes how "soldiers and their families struggled in a variety of ways to mitigate [war's] cruel realities, to construct a Good Death even amid chaos, to substitute for missing elements or compensate for unsatisfied expectations." A good death implied that the dying person was surrounded by people who loved him, that he was reconciled to his death, at peace with himself and with his fate. The manner and context of a person's death in essence "epitomized his or her spiritual condition. The dying were not losing their eternal selves, but rather defining them for eternity."[34] Dying was a social process, woven intimately into both domestic space and public culture. At home the postmortem photograph supported the staging of the good death for the dying and the bereaved. At war, photography did exactly the opposite: it made it impossible to think of these deaths as good, and it made painfully visible war's annihilation of the networks of relations that give death meaning as a shared social experience. Today those of us living in societies that manage death for us (removing death from the home) tend to be more comfortable with visual images of the anonymous corpse as a representation of the "distant suffering" of others than we are with postmortem photographs staged within a circle of intimates.

Some postmortem photographs function as talismanic substitutes for the bodies of the dead. They remind the person for whom the image was made that she was there, that she bore witness to the moment of her loved one's passing, that she groomed this person's body and gave that body a familiar and supportive context. Other photographs, Nudelman argues, substitute for death itself: they remove one's death from one's life as a subject of overt representation and ritual. In its difference from this sentimental photographic practice, Nudelman argues, war photography became a powerful medium not for making the dead real and for bringing the war home (as we tend to assume) but for materializing in both its composition and its form the distance between the home and the battlefield.[35] Barthes describes this shift as "the abrupt dive into literal Death." Sontag saw this dynamic at work in Hujar's *Portraits in Life and Death*. The photograph participates in the removal of death from life. Death becomes abstract and absorbed into the image as the camera's secret—a sort of knowledge that haunts even photographs of the living. Sontag writes, "We no longer study the art of dying, a regular discipline and hygiene in older cultures; but all eyes, at rest, contain that knowledge. The body knows. And the camera shows, inexorably."[36] Hujar's photographs of the catacombs explore a tradition that has disappeared from mainstream American cultural practices regarding death and dying.[37]

Untitled (Hujar Dead) navigates the dual capacity of photography to function as a continuation of the care one extends to the dying and as a mechanism that abstracts death, turning it into a consumable object. The text covering the work's surface may be intensely expressive, but on the subject of Hujar, it is silent. Confronted with Hujar's body, what is there, after all, to say? "When someone dies," Georges Bataille writes, "we, the survivors, expecting the life of that man now motionless beside us to go on, find that our expectation has suddenly come to nothing at all. A dead body cannot be called nothing at all, but that object, that corpse, is stamped straight off with the sign 'nothing at all.' For us survivors, the corpse and its threat of imminent decay is no answer to any expectation like the one we nourished while that now prostrate man was still alive; it is the answer to a fear. This object, then, is less than nothing and worse than nothing." This awful confrontation with the lover's body does not shut down desire; it takes us to its most primal scene: "Love raises the feeling of one being for another to such a pitch that the threatened loss of the beloved or the loss of his love is felt no less keenly than the threat of death. Hence love is based on a desire to live in anguish in the presence of an object of such high worth that the heart cannot bear to contemplate losing it. The fever of the senses is not a desire to die. Nor is love the desire to lose but the desire to live in fear of possible loss, with the beloved holding the lover on the very threshold of a swoon."[38] Hujar's, Thek's, and Wojnarowicz's repeated self-presentations as corpse-like bodies for their lover's camera is much more than a forecast of what was to come (and comes for all of us). It is an embrace of love's shadow—this fantasy of loss. These living images move the body back and forth across a line marking loss and recovery.

There is an awful finality to the photographs of Hujar dead because they record the last act of intimacy between Wojnarowicz and Hujar's body. In an elegy for his partner, Philip Brett, George Haggerty asks, "Is it possible to eroticize the loss of so dear a friend? Can I eroticize this loss of Philip? In some ways it is impossible not to. The dying form of one so loved does not resist this eroticization, in my experience; rather, death itself becomes a scene of an unspeakable intimacy."[39] This is to say that even as it becomes "nothing at all," the lover's body still holds a personal, an intimately shared history. This history remains with that body. *Untitled (Hujar Dead)* approaches Hujar's body ambivalently: it refuses to represent Hujar's dying as a good death, and it also resists "remembering" Hujar. It bars the possibility of looking on Hujar's body with pity and obscures (but does not erase) the image's personal context. There is no "good" photograph to be made here. Wojnarowicz covers Hujar's body with rage—but that rage also functions as a blanket, which we might think of as one way the artist continues to look after the person he described as "the most important man in my life."

Contrast Wojnarowicz's ambivalent use of the image of Hujar's body with the artist AA Bronson's postmortem portrait of Felix Partz, his partner, lover, and collaborator. *Felix, June 5, 1994* (1994/1999) is closer to the older sentimental practices described by Nudelman. "He is arranged to receive visitors," Bronson explains in the text accompanying the portrait. He is at home, surrounded by colorful blankets and pillows. His tape recorder, the remote control for his television, and his favorite brand of cigarettes are all there. The work is seven feet by twelve; the blown-up digital photograph is so pixilated that the image has a snowy texture, as if it were dispersing. Bronson offers us a picture of Felix's body at home, where he is surrounded by the things he loved and, implicitly, the people who loved him (see plate 17).[40]

Bronson, Partz, and Jorge Zontal worked together as the artistic collaboration General Idea from 1969 until Partz and Zontal both died in 1994. Their partnership was a romantic and creative enterprise that expanded the horizons for imagining what domestic intimacy and partnership, as well as collective authorship, might look like. General Idea was a twenty-five-year experiment in deep collaboration. Partz's death marked the end, then, of a person, a love relationship, and a collective identity. In text that accompanies this image, Bronson writes, "Dear Felix, by the act of exhibiting this image I declare that we are no longer one mind, one body, I return you to General Idea's world of mass media, there to function without me."[41] Although both works grapple with a very similar moment, the emotional textures of *Untitled (Hujar Dead)* and *Felix, June 5, 1994* are very different. *Untitled (Hujar Dead)* takes up a defensive relationship with the viewer. Text covers the photographs of Hujar like a shroud. They take care of Hujar's image, as if we can't be trusted to do the same. *Felix*, in contrast, is disarmingly open and beautiful. All those warm colors and cozy patterns make the viewer feel at home. The image's pixilation gives the work a painterly effect. In its right-hand corner is the camera's time stamp. Bronson invites us to let our guard down, which is perhaps the only way we can spend time with the image of Partz's body, which is devastated by a wasting disease. It is hard to accept this as the body of a man who has just died. Already he looks so decomposed. It seems more and less real than a photograph: more, in the level of detail given to the things around Felix, and less, in that it is hard to accept Felix's body and face as real.

In November 2010 Wojnarowicz and Bronson became linked in controversy when the director of the Smithsonian Institute withdrew Wojnarowicz's *Fire in My Belly (Film in Progress)* (1986–87) from an exhibit at the National Portrait Gallery.[42] *Hide and Seek: Desire and Difference in American Portraiture* was one of very few major museum exhibits to center explicitly on work by gay and lesbian artists.[43] Wojnarowicz and Bronson figured prominently in the section of the show devoted to the subject of AIDS, and Bronson's startling, monumental portrait of Felix was one of the exhibit's anchors. That fall a fundamentalist Catholic organization complained about an image of an ant-covered crucifix that appears in *Fire in My Belly (Film in Progress)*. This group described Wojnarowicz's images as "hate speech."[44] In a letter to G. Wayne Clough, the Smithsonian's secretary, the offended Catholic group threatened to reignite the NEA wars of the 1990s (in which Wojnarowicz figured, as had Athey). Ignoring the advice of the exhibit's curators, Clough pulled the work from the gallery even though it had been seen at that point by thousands of viewers and had provoked no other complaint.

The Smithsonian's actions were universally condemned by the art world. Although letter-writing campaigns, teach-ins, and public statements from museum directors increased awareness of Wojnarowicz's work, the Smithsonian failed to put that work back in the show. They also failed to forward a meaningful conversation about Wojnarowicz's work. A few seconds of film showing ants crawling over a crucifix might offend a handful of people, but it is actually one of the easier things in his archive; it is nowhere near as challenging as *ITSOFOMO* (which includes gut-wrenching readings from Wojnarowicz's writing) or the segment of *Fire in My Belly* used in Rosa von Praunheim's *Silence=Death* and scored by an excerpt from Diamanda Galás's *Plague Mass*, in which Galás shouts and screams a passage from Leviticus.[45]

There has been little acknowledgment of the institutional conditions that made it seem easy for the Smithsonian to pull the work from the exhibit. Wojnarowicz is not here to defend himself; the work exhibited was an edited collection of footage associated with an unfinished film called *Fire in My Belly*; the footage was shown on a monitor that was awkwardly integrated into the gallery, accompanied by a soundtrack chosen by the organizations handling Wojnarowicz's archive and estate; this material is not mentioned in the exhibit's catalogue. Reviewing the exhibit after the work was censored, Holland Cotter argued that given how heavily it had been edited, "the video was missing even when it was here."[46] The soundtrack that had been imposed on the super-8 footage was an audio recording of an ACT-UP demonstration found in Wojnarowicz's archive. These compromises (shortening the film, adding a soundtrack) were made at the request of museum administrators who felt that visitors would not watch all of the footage associated with the unfinished *Fire in My Belly*.[47] The irony of the "Hide/Seek controversy" is that it had nothing to do with the challenges the piece actually presented to the curators: a silent film featuring a nonnarrative series of gruesome images is, quite simply, hard to work with.

An earlier draft of *Fire in My Belly* was evidently a lot tougher. James Romberger, a friend of and collaborator with the artist, describes his experience of the first cut of *A Fire in My Belly* as both intense and disquieting:

He showed it to me privately at his apartment. . . . He had me sit in front of his big TV, next to his baby elephant's skeleton and insisted that I watch his Mexican film [the footage was shot while on a trip to Mexico]. What followed was an assault on my senses, a view of a world completely out of control. The strobed, often violent scenes of wrestlers, cock and bull fights, lurid icons, impoverished dwellings, clanking engines, an enslaved monkey, cripples begging for coins, for bread, a burning, spinning globe—it was a picture of indifference to the value of life, Mexico as a grinding machine of poverty and cruel spectacle. I didn't enjoy the experience. The images and soundtrack combined to create a powerful feeling of unease and angst. I was obviously shaken when it ended, but David just laughed. . . . He told me later that he had disassembled that first version.[48]

Romberger goes on to contextualize the film in relation to Wojnarowicz's work from this period and describes the soundtrack for this first draft as "loud" and a mixture of "incidental noise" and "industrial music, which was equally as chaotic as the images." The imposition of a recording of a demonstration over the edited selection of film footage lessens the material's difficulty. That soundtrack explicitly orients the work's frame of reference to the AIDS crisis (the longer version suggests a more elemental and more global disaster).[49] The posthumously selected soundtrack suggests a desire that Wojnarowicz's work be *more* political than it already is. Although the choice of this audio recording was made with the best of intentions, this is the same line of thinking about art and politics that was pursued by the *Artforum* writer who saw in Ron Athey's performance a failure to be properly political. The "political" soundtrack doesn't make *Fire in My Belly* more political but less, by mobilizing a familiar sense of the political rather than demystifying our notions about the boundaries of the political in order that we may see where ideology does its most intimate work.

The most powerful intervention regarding the censorship of *A Fire in My Belly* came from AA Bronson. *Felix, June 5, 1994* was on loan from the National Gallery of Canada. In December 2010 Bronson issued a public statement, asking that the work be withdrawn from the National Portrait Gallery exhibit. In correspondence with the museum, Bronson identified emotion as central to the story of the importance and the difficulty of Wojnarowicz's work: "As an artist who saw first hand the tremendous agony and pain that so many of my generation lived through, and died with, I cannot take the decision of the Smithsonian lightly. To edit queer history in this way is hurtful and disrespectful."[50] His statement reminds us that the decision to remove Wojnarowicz's work in order to protect the sensibilities of an openly homophobic religious organization closely mirrors the structures of hate and silence that conspired to make AIDS what it was then and is today. It also suggests that when Bronson sent *Felix* out into the world, it was with the hope that those who took in the work would look after it, that they would care for *Felix* and what it—what he—represents. *Felix* is jarring: an image of intense suffering nests in a scene of ordinary comfort. If a context of love and care is there for us to see, the limit of that palliative care is unavoidable. Bronson's declaration, "By the act of exhibiting this image I declare that we are no longer one mind, one body, I return you to General Idea's world of mass media," bestows on the photograph a quality like that of early memorial portraits. While marking a separation (of life and death, of Bronson from General Idea), it also bodies Felix forth—projecting a parallel world in which he circulates freely, to do a new and different kind of work. Writing of the shape of "fundamental questions of mourning and memory in our own time," Molly McGarry asks, "How can the dead speak through the living as something other than the haunting, seething presence of absence?" Bronson and Wojnarowicz negotiate this question through their portraits of Partz and Hujar. Other artists I've discussed in this book (Athey, Luna, Weems) are similarly working through this question of how one makes work about loss, grief, and historical trauma *without*, however, reifying their subjects as *gone*. In their direct use of postmortem photography, *Felix* and *Untitled (Hujar Dead)* consider the relationships between what McGarry describes as different "techniques of remembrance": from haunting to "the technology of photography" and "history, the secular discipline of memory."[51] When Bronson withdrew his permission for the exhibition of *Felix* in *Hide/Seek* he made visible the disciplinary layers that frame and condition our encounter with *Felix*; a conflict emerged, then, between different "techniques of remembrance" such as that represented by his use of postmortem memorial photography, that represented by the exhibit as an official representation of gay and lesbian life in art history, and that represented by a national museum as an official organ of history making.

The National Gallery of Canada supported Bronson's request, even knowing that this countered its contractual obligations to the Smithsonian and that the Smithsonian would likely never agree to remove the painting from its gallery. Bronson's intervention sent a ripple of fear through the museum world. I attended one workshop on the "Hide/Seek controversy" and watched local curators and gallery directors shake their heads in worry at the implication of Bronson's action. (It seemed as if all of the artists in the room, however, found the whole idea exciting.) The managerial personalities discussed drafting a memo or white paper to which museums might refer in situations like these and mulled over the problem of artists and the feelings they have about how their work is displayed. It is hard for administrators to resist the impulse to manage and neutralize challenges to the authority of cultural institutions like museums, galleries, and schools. But perhaps they should.

I saw *Hide/Seek* after *Fire in My Belly* was removed and after Bronson's request had been refused. *Felix* floated on the gallery's back wall, stuck like a ghost doing his work, without Bronson—for in a very material way, *Felix* was not his to control.

In that context, the work acquired a new kind of difficulty: it was now held hostage by contracts and conventions, by a disciplinary and institutional need to secure the integrity of the exhibit, as if that integrity had now become *Felix*'s burden. This allowed me to see other things: the conversation between Bronson and the museum drew from the shadows the deeper story of all that has to be left out, left behind in the production of a museum exhibit like this—a thousand decisions about what will work and what won't. *Hide/Seek* was a compromise; we see this in the very title of the exhibit, from which the words *gay*, *lesbian*, and *homosexual* were excluded not only to smooth its movement through the museum's bureaucracy but to avoid exactly the politicization of the exhibit that was instigated by religious extremists (as if one could, or should). Even as the exhibit used portraiture to explore the question of homosexual relationships and gay and lesbian identity (a wonderful idea), homosexuality could be named only obliquely, as something to be hidden (in the phrase "desire and difference"). Another hidden witness.

Every exhibit is a compromise, of course, as is every museum, every institutional and disciplinary structure. There are some people who work from inside those structures. There are agents of stabilization, and there are agents of change there too. Some of us work on the edges of those structures, and others work from outside. All of these boundaries are moving all the time. Bronson moved one when he expressed the need to withdraw *Felix*. Revoking his permission to display the work, he gave it another context than that within which it had been curated. The surviving member of General Idea turned the portrait into a protest, one quite literally channeling "agony and pain" as well as love, leaning backward to remember those who are gone, while also making explicit *We are still here* and that there are responsibilities to the past which come with that fact.[52]

Returning to *Untitled (Hujar Dead)* with the problems of *Fire in My Belly* and Bronson's unheeded request in mind, I now see another dissonance in the relationship between the overtly political text of the surface and the intimate history that lies beneath it. Wojnarowicz thought a lot about the relationship between the body, the world, and what we call history and politics. There is a poem in his archive called "History keeps me awake some nights." It opens with the speaker looking at photographs of himself and his lover and spirals outward in a galactic sweep:

> On the floor of the unused room
> there's a scattering of photographs
> of both of us walking in the sands
> of a weekends wintered beach
> through the light of late skies
> wanting time and history to forget us
> though we have such fears of not existing
> we fuck constantly so as not to forget ourselves
> this burning hunger for life not death
> close up the world is so terrible and sad
> that we invent small fictions of loving
> on the edges of those cold oceans
> while the cities lose themselves in evening
> and stray dogs patrol forgotten streets
> we have come out of our mothers bellies
> to find ourselves at the end of ropes
> strange how this sleep overtakes us
> how we move sideways as our love dies
> how you were once some guy
> who knew neither my present or my past
> whose eyes and hands worked in silence
> as you turned me over and over
> in the dim light of dusk
> removing articles of clothing
> watch these wet bodies on the sheets
> watch how they slowly become history[53]

The poem is tender and grim. Love fades and we go on; people leave, or they die and love becomes history. Once Peter Hujar didn't know that David Wojnarowicz existed; these are not master narratives "but small fictions" spun "on the edges of those cold oceans" ("you were once some guy"). The political force of *Untitled (Hujar Dead)* is not confined to its diatribe regarding health care, homophobia, and AIDS, nor to the images of Hujar's corpse.

It lives somewhere in the space the work creates between these things and in our confrontation with the fact that we are still here, living in that zone in between one death and another, where things are becoming political, in which we are being undone.

It is in this turn toward the living that these works take on a kind of urgency—for if we turn to art at such a limit, isn't it because, really, this is where we "feel how we slowly become history"? There is something absolutely obvious about the necessity of this work. It reveals the brutality, the cruelty of the notion that art is a luxury, practiced and consumed only by the rich, in times of contemplative peace. It peels away too the frightfulness of the ongoing political movement toward defunding whatever structures are left that support the production of difficult, confrontational works of art. As if doing so will make difficulty itself disappear.

The works with which I have opened and closed this book explore what it means to be responsible to the unyielding surface of these facts. Wojnarowicz is still here in *Untitled (Hujar Dead)*, standing at his lover's bedside, as is Bronson in *Felix*. We know Mitchell's death only through the sound of Montano's living voice.

Wojnarowicz converted the wave of death moving in on his world into a heightened awareness of presence, in a poetics of scale that is at once eschatological and intimate. *Untitled (Hujar Dead)* is intensely historical, not only because it is openly engaged with the AIDS crisis but because it is structured by an awareness of the historical dimensions of experience itself. That is, I think, what Kiki Smith meant when she said that experience was Wojnarowicz's material. This in fact names the practices of all of the artists I've described in this book, insofar as they each differently explore how it feels to occupy a position, to be in a specific kind of body, to belong to a certain community, to survive, to experience, or to be asked to embody experience for others. Experience here is not an unquestioned zone of personal truth to which one retreats but a site of becoming, of subject formation—it is an ongoing process that produces the conditions of possibility for recognition, understanding, and difference.[54]

This work addresses the political and historical dimension of our personal selves; it also expands the sphere of the intimate. It isn't moving because it is about hard things but rather because it makes us feel history moving through us, and *that* is hard.

NOTES

Preface

1 A transcript of this performance is published in Montano, *Letters from Linda M. Montano*, 220–26.

2 "An Astral Interview: An Email Exchange between Linda M. Montano and Jennie Klein," Montano, *Letters from Linda Montano*, 6.

3 Throughout this book I use the terms *emotion*, *feeling*, and *affect* rather loosely. In general, I privilege the words *emotion* and *feeling* over *affect* when describing how people experience works, and use *affect* to highlight the diffuse nature of emotion and feeling, in which a mood can saturate a space, for example, or in which an institutional setting such as a museum might impose its own set of rules regarding proper comportment, expressivity, and emotionality. Following the example of Rei Terada's work in *Feeling in Theory*, I resist the identification of categorical differences between these terms. In my view, such efforts belie the complexity of the experiences I am describing—or, at least, a typography clearly delineating one from the other would not forward the kind of conversation I am staging in this book if only because it would give the reader the idea that the difference between emotion, feeling, and affect is one of the subjects of this book. (It is not.)

4 Adorno, *Minima Moralia*, 172.

5 Vincent, *Queer Lyrics*, 1.

6 Contingent difficulty requires a willingness on the reader's part to do home-work—to look up words one doesn't know, research references one doesn't rec-ognize, and then reread the poem, taking this new information into account. This form of difficulty is more complex than it seems at first glance. It seems like the resolution of this form of difficulty is straightforward: one needs to read more, to familiarize oneself with technical and obscure terms used by the poet to animate the writing. One just (just!) needs to learn more: understanding a seventeenth-century Italian poem requires knowing more about the discursive universe in which the poet lived. It means knowing more about the resonance of that universe with ours. The particular complexity of this form of difficulty lies in the illusion that there is a limit to that homework. Steiner writes, "The 'look-ing things up' does not stop because the context pertinent to a major poet or po-etic text is that of the whole ambient culture, of the whole history of and in the language, of the mental sets and idiosyncrasies in contemporary sensibility. . . . Moreover, there is an inevitable feedback: with every particular clarification, comes a motion of return to the poem" ("On Difficulty," 267). There is a fur-ther complication. In practice, this is a never-ending process—the horizon of knowledge that informs the text is ever expanding. But, he writes, in theory, "there is somewhere a lexicon, a concordance, a manual of stars, a florilegium, a pandect of medicine, which will resolve the difficulty. In the 'infinite library' (Borges's 'Library that is the Universe') the necessary reference can be found" (267). So, yes, we know the critical work of explaining these things will never be finished. And yet there is something about these kinds of references that gives us the sense that there are specific questions than can be answered with concrete information. He calls this form of difficulty "epiphenomenal" or "contingent," in that the difficulty appears to lie outside the boundaries of the text, in what we happen to know or not know. In chapter 2, where I discuss Thomas Eakins's painting *The Gross Clinic*, we get a glimpse of how this kind of difficulty can ensnare the viewer in an encyclopedic project of figuring out the painting by seducing us with the promise that there is something—a truth—beyond the canvas that we might access if we just look closely enough. Ironically, this way of looking at an image—in which we decode the figures and marks on the canvas, in which we evaluate the painting for its fidelity to an original scene for which it is a record—can lead to a disavowal of what is there, a disavowal of the surface of the painting and the formal practice that creates the illusion that the painting is a recording. How artworks are shaped by this kind of difficulty varies widely.

Steiner's next category for difficulty in poetics is the modal, the sort of dif-ficulty that can't be eased by a dictionary or an interpretive key because the plea-sures of those texts are deeply bound up with the tastes of another time and place. "Here," he writes, "there are no answers to be 'looked up'" (269). This is a harder form of difficulty to resolve, partly because its very nature can discourage interest; one can look up every strange word, read the scholarly footnotes, and still not really understand the point. "The experience of obstruction is at once banal and elusive," Steiner continues. "We 'get the text' but we don't 'dig it' (and the suggestion of active penetration is exactly apposite). The poem in front of us articulates a stance towards human conditions which we find inaccessible or alien" (267). Interestingly, he says (writing in 1978) that today we "are ashamed to concede any modal inhibition, to confess ourselves closed to any expressive act however remote from our time and place." Speaking of scholarship on poetry, he calls out the lie of this: in spite of an imperialism of taste that would have us imagine that we can empathize with works produced by any historical or geographic context, "large, sometimes radiant bodies of literature have receded from our present day grasp. Who now reads, who experiences at any adequate depth of response, the tragedies of Voltaire, which once dominated the European canon?" (267). Like the first order of difficulty he describes, this category becomes more complex as one looks at it more closely, for it refers to the conditions of possibility that make a work disappear without our feeling its absence as such (and also the reverse: the conditions of possibility for a work's visibility, for the general acceptance of our favorite texts as somehow universally interesting).

The modal differs from the contingent in the following way: whereas the latter provokes interest, leaves you with the feeling that there is always more to know, more to discover, the former deadens one's interest, leaves you with the feeling that there is nothing there. The disappearance from critical discourse of these "radiant bodies" of literature is hardly noticed. Not only do we not read and engage such works, but we don't notice that we don't read them. This kind of difficulty is invisible; it marks an ideological limit. It is more than a question of taste—or rather, it is the rubric by which we learn that taste is historically conditioned. Within this project, modal difficulty expands horizontally across the present to account for the material conditions that support our attention—the social pressures that move our attention toward some works and away from others. In Steiner's words, it describes a "failure of summoning and response" that "lies wholly outside the categories of 'liking or disliking'" a work, although it is in fact one of the things that conditions "liking or disliking." We encounter a good example of a modal problem in Steiner's essay, incredibly, in the section on modal difficulty. He writes, "Learning, the suspension of reflex, can make us understand at the cerebral level, the dynamics of judgment which made of Rosa Bonheur a painter more highly valued than Cezanne or which induced Balzac to set the novels of Mrs. Radcliffe above those of Stendhal (whom he was one of the first to praise). But we cannot coerce our own sensibility into the relevant frame of perception" (269). It is at this point that he conjures the image of large, radiant, disappearing bodies.

Today Rosa Bonheur is in fact appreciated again, understood in relation not to Cezanne but to the history of European women painters and the generic corners they inhabited, largely in exile. Ann Radcliffe was a popular and influential Gothic novelist whose work fell out of favor for a long time largely because it was not supported by the critical apparatus that supported the reading of works by her male contemporaries writing in more "serious" genres. But she is now very much the object of critical interest and is widely read, at least in universities, where students perhaps enjoy reading Radcliffe over Stendhal. If Steiner felt he could take as a given the difficulty of understanding the past popularity of work by these women, as well as their critical irrelevance to the present, it was because he was writing in 1978, before feminists had a voice in the critique of canon formation and the contingencies of literary taste, before feminists had fully raised awareness of the sexism embedded in the dismissal of genres associated with women artists for their sentimentality and excess in feeling. We may understand how, writing with unexamined patriarchal assumption, Steiner might have felt the point to be obvious, but it's not a point that makes sense today, at least not to this reader. The tone in which he makes the comparisons is in fact somewhat offensive. In the contrast between the irritation one feels reading that statement and the breezy tone in which it is written (as if his puzzlement were universally held) we see something of the "archaeology of feeling" required by any critical project that tackles modal difficulty and the set of problems that "lie with the beholder" and the limit of his emotional alphabet. Amazing how things can turn around in just thirty years—and, to give Steiner credit, that was his point. But where for Steiner this issue was a matter of timing (of historical location), for us this is a matter of community—evidencing the gaps and ideological conflicts between different interpretive communities that may exist not only in the same historical moment but in the same discursive space. Modal conflicts—disjunctions between the "archaeologies of feeling" that define different communities, different spectators and audiences—are acted out constantly in art criticism.

The third type of difficulty offered by Steiner is tactical. Poets can be strategic about difficulty: they can make their work harder to read, leave things deliberately ambiguous, paradoxical, and strange. It is here that their writing pushes up against our habits and expectations, often to make us notice that those habits and expectations are there. The aim is to make language feel new and strange: "tactical difficulties endeavor to deepen our apprehension by dislocation and to goad into new life the supine energies of word and grammar" (273). This is perhaps the difficulty we discuss in the classroom most often because it is where "the literary" is felt most keenly by the reader, where we, as readers, conjure the figure of author.

The last and, for Steiner, the most compelling form of difficulty is ontological: this form of difficulty calls poetry—indeed representation itself—into question. It is connected to the strategic, but where strategic difficulty holds forth the possibility of interpretive resolution, ontological difficulty insists on a fundamental crisis within the linguistic field. "Ontological difficulties confront us with blank questions about the nature of human speech, about the status of significance, and the necessity and purpose of the construct which we have . . . come to perceive as a poem" (273). For Steiner, writing that explores this form of difficulty rejects convention, seeking out in its stead an authenticity of expression imagined as both prior to and beyond the representational forms we know. Here poetry seeks not quite communication with the reader but something more like a communion with Art. (Perhaps some abstract painting could be imagined along these lines.) "In ontological difficulty, the poetics of Mallarmé or Heidegger . . . express their sense of the inauthentic situation of man in an environment of eroded speech" (274). This degree of difficulty, like the modal, is often historically charged. On this point, he gestures toward the example of Paul Celan "and the specific discomforts of a survivor of the holocaust writing . . . poetry of the utmost personal compulsion, in the butcher's tongue" (274). Steiner argues that Celan's poetry is deeply informed by its impossible linguistic place (written by a German-speaking survivor of internment). In his work, "it is not, as in the case of tactical difficulties, that we are meant to understand slowly or to stand poised between alternatives of signification. At certain levels, we are not meant to understand at all, and our interpretation, indeed our reading itself, is an intrusion" (275). Celan's poetic practice is thus shaped by "anguish at writing poetry, at having to write poetry 'after Auschwitz' and in the language of the devisers of Auschwitz" (275), an anguish expressed by carving out spaces of privacy which no interpretive drive can penetrate. This is more than catachresis, the gesture toward experiences (of pleasure, of pain) that can't be written. It is more properly a confrontation with the strange and haunted nature of language. Here, Steiner suggests, we do not "read" a poem like this; we "bear witness to its precarious possibility of existence in an 'open space' of collisions, of momentary fusions between work and referent" (275). One might see this level of difficulty shaping *Mitchell's Death*, insofar as no number of viewings will bring us any closer to the events it describes; its emotional intensity is amplified by this fact.

7 One might align it with Roland Barthes's *The Pleasure of the Text* (1973), for example, or his essay "The Death of the Author" (1967). Other very influential works that put the reader at the center of critical practice include Janice Radway's analysis of the interpretive practices of specific groups of readers in *Reading the Romance* and her work on the production of literary value and taste in *A Feeling for Books: The Book-of-the-Month Club, Literary Taste, and Middle-Class Desire*; Elizabeth McHenry's *Forgotten Readers: Recovering the Lost History of African American Literary Societies*; Barbara Herrnstein Smith's critique of canon formation and notions of the literary in *Contingencies of Value*; Stanley Fish's argument for the primacy of the reader in generating meaning in *Is There a Text in This Class?* Hal Foster cites this turn toward cultural studies in literary studies in his polemic against the emergence of ethnographic models in art practices and in art criticism in *The Return of the Real*. I discuss Foster's polemic and a broader discomfort in art history with this kind of scholarship in chapter 3.

A similar expansion of the critical scope has been unfolding in film studies: Laura Mulvey's "Visual Pleasure and Narrative Cinema" (1975) politicized spectatorship by turning our attention to the gendered structures of vision in classical Hollywood cinema. Her manifesto begins with the question "What does the spectator want?" and proceeds to tease out the politics of that economy of pleasure. Feminist film theory now offers the most complete bibliography of scholarship exploring the dynamics of spectatorship, display, and power. Mary Deveraux describes the importance of that bibliography to art history in the following terms: "Feminism asks us to replace the conception of the artwork as an autonomous object—a thing of beauty and a joy forever—with a messier conception of art. On the new view, the artwork moves from an autonomous realm of value to the everyday realm of social and political praxis" ("Oppressive Texts, Resisting Readers and the Gendered Spectator," 344). This was the first essay on feminist scholarship published by the *Journal of Aesthetics and Culture*.

As the date of Deveraux's essay (1990) indicates, the critical activation of the viewer is more recent in art history, but since the 1990s that field has been dominated by conversations about participation and relational aesthetics (e.g., Nicholas Bourriaud's *Relational Aesthetics* [1998], Jacques Rancière's *The Emancipated Spectator* [2009], Grant Kester's *Conversation Pieces* [2009], Claire Bishop's *Artificial Hells* [2012]). That said, this vein of theoretical analysis of the politics of contemporary art suffers from a kind of amnesia: with a few exceptions (e.g., Kester), most forget that feminists have been staging this exploration of the relational dynamics of art production and consumption since the 1970s (in criticism and in art practices themselves).

The entire field of performance studies is structured by attention to the social space around performance, and so scholars like Amelia Jones and Jane Blocker (who are also art historians), Peggy Phelan, Fred Moten, Diana Taylor, and José Muñoz might all be cited in conversations exploring the presence of the spectator or viewer to the work of art. This book should be seen as a part of this project, which considers artworks within the broader scene of our encounters with them.

8 Vincent, *Queer Lyrics*, 3.

9 Barthes, *The Pleasure of the Text*. Vincent's questions elicit the resonance of the refusal of closure for queer readers. For such readers, figuring something out, finally, can take on a rhetorical violence that rhymes with the experience of having one's self explained by a diagnostic label. "Poetic difficulty lives at the site of poetry's central node," he writes, "at the conflict between what can and cannot be said" (*Queer Lyrics*, 1). For the queer reader, that line—that space in between—is charged with feeling and with politics. For the queer poet, creating this space in between, a space of contradiction and possibility, is vital for a sense of play and necessary for his or her survival.

10 Vincent, *Queer Lyrics*, 3.

11 Visual and performance studies scholars and some art historians are already heading in this direction. Art's intersubjective dimensions have become more and more central to scholarship. Where criticism once relied on binary models of viewership, it is now committed to models that approach the work of art as an event, shaped by fluid social dynamics. Critics, of course, are following the lead

of artists themselves. See Crary, *Techniques of the Observer*; Jones, *Self/Image*; Phelan, *Unmarked*; Rogoff, "Looking Away"; Rancière, *The Emancipated Spectator*; as well as Butt, *Between You and Me*; Blocker, *What the Body Cost*; and the Barthesian work of Carol Mavor (e.g., *Reading Boyishly*). This kind of expansion of the art critical field is also the subject of Bourriaud's *Relational Aesthetics* and Grant Kester's *Conversation Pieces*.

12 Richard Meyer reviews the fantasies about sexuality and art that are embedded in conservative attacks on gay and lesbian artists in "The Jesse Helms Theory of Art." For an earlier essay offering a provocative discussion of the relationship between desire, fear or paranoia, and fantasy in these censorship battles, see Butler, "The Force of Fantasy." In 2011 PPOW (the gallery managing Wojnarowicz's estate) mounted an exhibit on spiritualism in Wojnarowicz's work as a counterbalance to the charge that his work is anti-Catholic.

13 Froma a 1988 journal in the David Wojnarowicz Papers, Fales Collection, New York University Library.

14 It neighbors what Maggie Nelson describes as "the art of cruelty."

1. Introducing Difficulty

1 Jon Cairns, "Public Intimacies: My Audiences with Adrienne," paper presented at Performance Studies International 16, Toronto, June 2010.

2 Key works in this vein are Pierre Bourdieu, *Distinction: A Social Critique of the Judgment of Taste* (Cambridge: Harvard University Press, 1987); Barbara Herrnstein Smith, *Contingencies of Value* (Cambridge: Harvard University Press, 1991); Janice Radway, *The Book of the Month Club and the Making of Middlebrow Culture* (Chapel Hill: University of North Carolina Press, 1991).

3 González, *Subject to Display*, 99.

4 Lyn Gardner, "An Audience with Adrienne," *Guardian*, 10 August 2007.

5 Cairns, "Public Intimacies." Berlant introduces the term *intimate publics* in *The Queen of America Goes to Washington City*. For Nyong'o's writing on "extimacy," see "Brown Punk."

6 Chris Ofili's painting was the subject of a huge public outcry when it was exhibited at the Brooklyn Museum of Art's installation of the *Sensation* show. The painting depicts an African female figure, surrounded by butterfly-shaped collages made from cut-outs from pornographic photographs. The beautiful and eye-catching painting also includes elephant dung. For a polemic on this work, see Fusco, "Captain Shit and Other Allegories of Black Stardom." An excerpt from David Wojnarowicz's video *Fire in My Belly* (which is an unfinished work and exists in multiple forms) was withdrawn from a National Portrait Gallery exhibit in 2010 after an extremist Catholic organization protested its use of the image of the crucifix. I discuss this in the book's conclusion and discuss the controversy surrounding Athey's *Four Scenes in a Harsh Life* in chapter 2.

7 Nelson, *The Art of Cruelty*, 174.

8 For an early overview of the ramifications of the NEA crisis, see Kim Shipley, "The Politicization of Art: The National Endowment for the Arts, the First Amendment, and Senator Helms," *Emory Law Journal*, Winter 1991, online. See also Mysoon Rizk's account of Wojnarowicz's battle with the American Family Association, "Regulating Desire and Imagination: The Art and Times of David Wojnarowicz," *Studies in Law, Politics, and Society* 37 (2005), 3–32.

9 Steiner, *The Scandal of Pleasure*, 3, 4.

10 Cited in Lippard, "Out of the Safety Zone."

11 Lippard, "Out of the Safety Zone."

12 It also reflects the ethnic and racial segregation of the art world. For example, the affective dynamics of African American and Latino art are quite different from that of mainstream art. Curatorial projects centered on artists from communities of color are often treated by museums as a form of social work; art history remains one of the most Balkanized of the humanities. It remains entirely possible for American academic departments to not just marginalize but exclude these fields; mainstream scholars ignore both the art and the theory that engages the politics of race. This issue is taken up in chapter 4.

13 For a more specific discussion of the rhetorical outrage in public debates about art practices like Athey's, see Sigman, "Self-Mutilation, Interpretation and Controversial Art." This essay is focused on Stelarc but discusses the controversy surrounding Athey's Minneapolis performance. Sigman examines the expression of moral outrage in public discourse about especially the use of self-mutilation in performance practices. She focuses furthermore on what the discipline of philosophy offers to an understanding of the emotional landscape of this public discourse. The series of questions and observations she offers are provocative, though oriented around somewhat different sets of values than this book. (Sigman seems to accept that all representations of a sexualized body are demeaning, for example.) But her call for a more sophisticated argument in defense of work that "offends" is well placed. She writes, "Ultimately, what will convince people of the value of such works is not simply asserting that they are valuable or 'morally uplifting' but show[ing] how under some interpretations they might not be demeaning or what we might learn from them even if they are. And what will protect art in our culture is demanding of its critics an articulate account of the interpretations they tacitly hold" (114). For a comprehensive and detailed survey of the NEA and NEH battles, see Koch, "The Contest for American Culture."

14 See Shockley and McNeely, "A Seismic Shift in U.S. Federal Arts Policy." This essay examines the politicization of art funding, though here that politicization is more precisely an effect of the "culture wars" and the demand that public funding engage a broader range of the population and promote access to arts education and development resources. Richard Meyer's *Outlaw Representation* explores how homosexual artists in particular anticipate censorship, building the dynamics of prohibition into their work itself. See also Adler, "Post-modern Art and the Death of Obscenity Law." Adler gives a very useful overview of the state

of U.S. obscenity law up to 1990 and ends with an extensive discussion of the challenges facing performance artists like Karen Finley and Annie Sprinkle.

15 See Electronic Disturbance Theater / b.a.n.g.lab's *Sustenance: A Play for All Trans [ ] Borders* (Printed Matter Inc., 2010), http://www.thing.net/~rdom/Suste nance.pdf; Evan R. Goldstein, "Digitally Incorrect: Ricardo Dominguez's Provocations. Art or Crimes," *Chronicle of Higher Education*, 3 October 2010, online.

16. Electronic Disturbance Theater / b.a.n.g.lab, *Sustenance: A Play for All Trans [ ] Borders*.

17 For a cogent summary and analysis of the state of performance art in the United States, see Gómez-Peña, "Disclaimer."

18 And so, for example, the conservative critic Robert Hughes expressed Schaden-freude at the NEA's demise, as it had, in his view, come to privilege "access" to museums by gay and lesbian artists, artists of color, and feminists over "excellence": "Under the rubric of 'self-esteem' ['multicultural' programs] foster mediocre art for a populist mentality that contents itself in the jargon of supporting ethnicity and gender differences in the arts, instead of the harder one of looking for real excellence." Cited in Shockley and McNeely, "A Seismic Shift in U.S. Federal Arts Policy," 13.

19 See, for example, Phoebe Hoben, "How Far Is Too Far?," *Artnews*, 1 July 2008.

20 Rogoff, "Looking Away," 119.

21 Ibid., 121.

22 For sustained discussions of art and censorship, see, for example, Meyer, *Outlaw Representation*; Mitchell, "Offending Images," *What Do Pictures Want?*, 125–44; Steiner, *The Scandal of Pleasure*. The controversy of Kara Walker's work grows from its explicit dialogue with the racist imaginary, as well as from the challenges it poses to some members of the African American arts community who have found its popularity with the (white) mainstream problematic. Some of her critics balked at watching an African American artist play into the art market's demand for sensational, abject black bodies. This issue makes the work more difficult within the African American arts community than within the whiter spaces of the commercial galleries selling her work. As Gwendolyn DuBois Shaw explains in her writing on the artist, within the African American community, Walker's work can be harder to program even though her commitment to confronting racism would suggest otherwise. Thus in some contexts, Walker's work is both controversial *and* difficult. See Shaw, *Seeing the Unspeakable*, especially the chapter "Censorship and Rejection."

23 Most recent writing on the artist emerges from performance studies and from scholars explicitly concerned with S&M practices. Only a few articles offer in-depth discussion of his work. See McGrath, "Trusting in Rubber"; Jones, "Rupture"; Blocker, *What the Body Costs*, 111–12; Carr, "Washed in Blood," *On Edge*, 336–40; Sikes, "The Performing Genome"; Richards, "Ron Athey, AIDS and the Politics of Pain." See also Johnson, "*Perverse Martyrologies*," for a literature review.

24 Johnson, "*Perverse Martyrologies*," 505."

25 Kateri Butler, "Ron Athey: In Extremis and in My Life," *Los Angeles Times*, 28 January 2007. For another good overview of the artist's perspective on the NEA controversy, as well as a good discussion of *Four Scenes in a Harsh Life,* see Spurrier, "Blood of a Poet." Jan Tumlir offers one of the best discussions of Athey's performances in the mid-1990s in "Ron Athey, Bob Flanagan and the Practice of Secular Sacrifice."

26 It seems likely that the trigger for the national scandal was the presence of a phrase and a sentence on the face of the event's program: "The Walker Center presents" and "This program is funded, in part, by The National Endowment for the Arts." This, and Athey's reputation and the images inside the program, would have been enough for conservative media and politicians to grab onto. In the controversy that followed, Jane Alexander, then head of the National Endowment for the Arts, went on the record in support of the program at Patrick's Cabaret. She said Athey's work "isn't everybody's cup of tea," but that doesn't mean it shouldn't be funded. That people seemed grateful for this crumb says a lot about how bad things were at the time.

27 I programmed a performance by Athey in Riverside (*Self Obliteration Solo*, February 2009). It was well attended and was received positively by the audience. We heard not one complaint regarding the event and received quite a few positive emails from people who were moved and inspired. Nevertheless, when I approached a curator at the campus arts complex about working with them again, I was told there were "risk management issues" and "You can never do something like that again," meaning program Athey's performance. As it happens, I had worked closely with the campus's risk management office, the director of which told me he was not at all nervous about the performance. From a risk management perspective, he explained, an art opening at which alcohol is served and a basketball game are both much riskier than performance art. Art isn't really dangerous, I learned, and when it is, there's a waiver that artists can sign to cover the venue's liability. The real issue was the administration's fear that the venue would be associated with the idea of Athey's work and the audiences who appreciate it.

28 Foster, *The Return of the Real*, 199, 183.

29 For an excellent overview of the erasure of the political and formal complexity of artworks by a community of artists working with and around identity, see Chon Noriega's discussion of contemporary Chicano/a art in "The Orphans of Modernism." He opens with the following passage from artist Harry Gamboa's writings: "When someone does not belong to the dominant culture and yet comes up with concepts and/or theories that are equal to other ideas in the market, he is generally overlooked and not taken seriously by those who are in fact agents provocateurs of that culture, such as art critics, curators, and museum directors" (Chon Noriega, ed., *Urban Exile: The Collected Writings of Harry Gamboa* [Minneapolis: University of Minnesota Press, 1998], 48). As Noriega points out, some of that marginalization grows from the rejection of modernist tropes by many Chicano artists (thus Gamboa's description of him-

self and his collaborators as "orphans of modernism"). As much art criticism remains committed to modernist values, progressive work that draws from different cultural genealogies and that takes a critical view of modernism's colonial flavor simply doesn't show up on its radar. This is a subject of nearly constant complaint from art historians, visual studies scholars, and art critics who are engaged with feminist, queer, Chicano, African American, and Asian American art (for example).

30 Some of the artists I discuss here developed their work in clubs, in close proximity to this kind of music. Athey's initial performances unfolded in collaboration with Rozz Williams, the founder and lead singer for the influential band Christian Death. While still teenagers, the two initiated a collective project titled *Premature Ejaculation*. These performances (staged in Pomona in 1981) are infamous in the lore of LA's punk and queer scenes; Athey has said that they were inspired by the performance artist Johanna Went (who opened for hardcore punk bands like Black Flag and the Germs) and COUM Transmissions (Cosi Fanni Tutti and Genesis P-Orridge's performance and music collaboration, which later reformed as Throbbing Gristle and then Psychic TV), which staged an epic scandalous performance (involving enemas, blood injections, farting—you name it) at the Los Angeles institute of Contemporary Art in 1976.

31 Attali, *Noise*, 28.

32 In *Pop Modernism* Juan Suarez explores the copresence of noise and popular culture in modernist works and argues that traditional art historical narratives regarding modernism and the avant-garde have made it particularly difficult to acknowledge or critically engage with certain kinds of practices. In the opening pages of this work, he describes the limits of art historical rhetoric regarding modernism and postmodernism and the place of popular culture in both (in which the two are opposed in the former and entangled in the latter):

This sharp distinction between modernism and postmodernism rested on a partial conception of modernism—a conception that reduced the experimental ferment of the beginning of the twentieth century to a small canon and privileged the most self-reflexive moments of modern art. Gone from the picture were the alternative perspectives of women, queers, and artists from the peripheries; the fascination with machinery, fashion and cities; and the modernist immersion in the pop life of the times. This reductive account drove a wedge between avant-gardes and ignored the existence of many overlaps between the two, but it also simplified the work of canonical figures. . . . Their connections to modernity's material, sexual, political, and popular cultures, where they found much of their inspiration, were regarded as anomalies or marginalia that had little bearing on aesthetics. As a result, modernism appeared strangely disembodied and sublimated, unhinged from some of its most vital contexts. (2)

I cite this observation at length because nearly all of the work discussed in this book has been faulted at some point for its apparent disregard for aesthetics;

such criticism is of course grounded in disciplinary discourse organized around the exclusion of popular culture and the methodologies developed around its analysis (e.g., cultural studies, sociology, ethnography). Noise figures in Suarez's work as a representational subject, as a thing figured within artworks. I am using *noisy* as a term to describe the disruptive, antidisciplinary nature of certain artworks themselves.

33 McClarey, "The Politics of Silence and Sound," 157.

34 In fact when I told curators and art historians that I was writing a book about difficulty and contemporary art, they universally assumed that I was writing about minimalism. Minimalist sculpture can be notoriously hard to get, but it has nevertheless inspired a wide range of terrific writing and enjoys much support from art institutions. Art historians, in fact, love minimalism's difficulty. The challenges it poses seem to be good for us: it makes us think about "objectness" and space. It can make us feel questions of scale in our bodies and consider form qua form. It must be understood in relation to the history of genre and in the context of the critical debates that have unfolded around it.

35 Julie Tolentino, personal correspondence with the author, September 2011.

36 In Athey's words, "I feel differently about how the show went in Minneapolis from how I read it in print—I still feel like it was a good show, it was well received, and included a better than excellent post-performance discussion. I've been told that [the performance, not the controversy] was something that 'was waiting to happen'" (Steger, interview, 8).

37 Ron Athey, "Artist's Commentary," performance program, Patrick's Cabaret, Minneapolis, 5 March 1994.

38 Ibid.

39 Writing by people who have attended performances by Athey and his company abounds with descriptions of people fainting, but those accounts also marvel at the fact that many of those people stay with the performance when they come to. The performance studies scholar John Edward McGrath described his own fainting spell as "like that of a religious possession" ("Trusting in Rubber," 37).

2. Three Case Studies

1 In the past, Karen Finley has taken on abortion and reproductive rights across a range of her performances and installations, as in the twinned installation *Memento Mori* (1992–94). The "Women's Room" portion of that exhibit featured controversial works like *The Virgin Mary Is Pro-Choice* and positioned the fight for reproductive freedom as parallel with the fight against AIDS. In general, recent scholarship about abortion and art focuses on feminist artists who trouble the distinctions drawn between art and activism by raising awareness, distributing educational information, and even facilitating women's access to abortion. Woman on the Waves, for example, is a Dutch activist organization that sends a small ship to locations around the world to offer abortion services to women in

countries that severely restrict their access to birth control and pregnancy termination. Their work bears a strong resemblance to AIDS activist projects that used the creative expertise of members to both raise awareness about homophobia and HIV/AIDS and to educate and offer services to the local communities; as these artists did so, they used visual and performance-based actions to imagine other possibilities to the world within which they worked. As Carrie Lambert Beatty explains in her essay on the group, Woman on the Waves "tacks between art and politics in much the same way it moves between actual human rights mission and media-political campaign, legality and piracy, fact and myth" ("Twelve Miles," 316). It is a cutting-edge example of the most visible way that feminist artists engage abortion through activism and consciousness-raising. Without taking away from either the material opposition to their project or the interestingness of such work as a practice that breaks down boundaries between art and political action and that embodies the ethos of collaborative and relational art practices within art criticism, it is also perhaps one of the most socially sanctioned ways an artist might take up this particular topic. We know how to talk about this kind of work, as a form of activism, as a form of participation within specific communities. See also Crimp, AIDS Demo Graphics, for a comprehensive map of the political actions staged by Gran Fury and other AIDS art activist groups. The book invites readers to adopt the strategies they used and to reproduce the images included in the book.

2 Ludlow, "The Things We Cannot Say," 32, 33.

3 So, for example, in a pro-abortion film like Four Months, Three Weeks, and Two Days (Cristian Mungiu, 2007) the pregnant woman seeking an illegal abortion (Gabriela) is represented as a helpless baby, even as the film makes clear that in Romania during this period the most basic forms of contraception had been criminalized. Gabriela's pregnancy is presented as the result of her passive relation to the world. The protagonist of the film is not the pregnant woman, but Otilia, the highly competent, savvy friend who takes care of Gabriela (and is raped by the abortionist for her troubles). The pregnant woman is thus represented as a child-like screw-up. The moral center is anchored in the friend's mothering of the abortive woman. These protocols regarding representations of unwanted pregnancy articulate themselves largely around the policing of affect—a mandate that the offending woman produce the proper amount of regret, incompetence, and apology. Motherhood is recovered symbolically in a story about how a woman takes care of her friends.

4 Details of Shvarts's project are from her statement about the project cited in Martine Powers, "For Senior, Abortion a Medium for Art, Political Discourse," Yale Daily News, 18 April 2008. Shvarts has also written about this performance in "Figuration and Failure, Pedagogy and Performance."

5 Email discussion with the artist, June 2008.

6 The deployment of ambiguity as a means of denaturalizing reproductive ideology and its hold on the body is not unheard of in visual work about abortion. In

her analysis of Aline Mare's experimental video *S'Aline's Solution* (1991), for example, Valerie Hartouni traces how the artist asks if "what are, in effect, pro-life representations, meanings, and practices [can] be (re)deployed and oppositionally inflected to tell precisely the kind of story their deployment has otherwise worked to silence" ("Fetal Exposure," 199). Mare poses this question in a surprising way: her video layers the soundtrack of a female voice repeating "I choose, I chose, I have chosen" and images that make us feel that we are "spectators to an apparent real-time [saline] abortion from what we are encouraged to view as the unmediated view of the victim" (202). The video's opening sequence sets the framework through which we read the rest of the video—a poetic meditation on loss, birth, and motherhood. That first image sequence, however, is a cinematic record not of the biospace of a saline abortion but of male ejaculation; learning this forces an interrogation of "what images 'are,' and what they 'mean'" (210). Hartouni explains: "What permits us to read ejaculation as a violent, traumatic, distinctly unnatural rupture of natural processes is not only our general illiteracy with respect to the functioning of bodies—this is to be expected. It is our illiteracy coupled with powerful, prior notions and anxieties themselves shaped by a larger public discourse and culture of abortion about what the practice is, means, and entails" (208).

Shvarts works in similar territory when she scrambles biopolitical narratives about the female body in a deliberate refusal of "the contemporary grammar and culture of abortion" (Hartouni, "Fetal Exposure," 209). Where Mare makes her critique of that grammar by underscoring "the conspicuous absence of . . . the gestating body in contemporary renderings" of abortion (209), Shvarts insists on placing the body back in the story in order to explore its disruptive effects. The attempt to stage this conversation about the artist's body proved controversial.

7 Shvarts, "Figuration and Failure, Pedagogy and Performance."

8 Charlie Finch does in his short article "Mission Aborted," *Artnet*, 18 May 2008.

9 Klasky's statement as well as my description of the administration's negotiations with Shvarts are taken from Zachary Abrahamson, Thomas Kaplan, and Martine Powers, "Shvarts, Yale, Clash over Project," *Yale Daily News*, 18 April 2008. There is ambiguity in the public record of the project over whether Shvarts actually went through the process she describes, in part because the project was interrupted, and so we do not even know how Shvarts might have presented documentation of the performance. We have perhaps a discursive version of Haley Newman's series of "Performance Photographs" which document performances that never happened (and indeed hide this fact from the viewer). But Newman's own statement anchors our understanding of those photographs as fictional. No such ground is given here. I choose to bypass the question of what really happened to focus on what *did* happen: the near universal condemnation of the whole enterprise.

10 Cited in Catherine Donaldson-Evans, "Yale to Cancel Controversial 'Abortion Art' Exhibit Unless Student Admits It's Fiction," 21 April 2008, http://www.foxnews.com/story/0,2933,351984,00.html.

11 Shvarts has since written a scholarly essay on the controversy: "Figuration and Failure, Pedagogy and Performance."

12 The performance compares nicely, for example, with Leslie Labowitz's *Menstruation Wait* (1971). She describes the performance as follows: "I wrote on a poster that I was waiting for my period, and if anyone wanted to come talk to me, I'd be in my studio." She was almost kicked out of the master's program at Otis for this piece. "They had a meeting with me—all men, of course—there was no woman on the faculty." Cited in Phelan, *Live Art in LA*, 84–85.

13 Cited in Samantha Broussard-Wilson, "Reaction to Shvarts: Outrage, Shock, Disgust," *Yale Daily News*, 18 April 2008. Nearly one in four pregnancies end in miscarriage; the obfuscation of this fact reproduces the affective protocols that require all interruptions of pregnancy to be emotional disasters.

14 Personal correspondence with Aliza Shvarts, December 2010.

15 Stevens, *Reproducing the State*, 210.

16 Deutschler, "The Inversions of Exceptionality," 63. See also Le Doeuff, *Hipparchia's Choice*.

17 Cited in Deutschler, "The Inversions of Exceptionality," 63.

18 For scholarship that steps outside the regulation of narratives of abortion to consider how women narrate their own experiences with abortion, see Alvaros, "Hindsight and the Abortion Experience." Expanding feminist sociological work on this topic, Alvaros explores the fluidity and complexity with which women narrate their experience of abortion and how those narratives shift for some women over time. Those narratives can be read as divided by the narrator's identification with what abortion makes possible or what it negates. Much feminist art about abortion navigates this narrative tension between past, present, and future.

19 Some of the details regarding this incident are taken from conversations with the instructor, Ron Athey, November 2006.

20 Kastner, "Gun Shy."

21 Blocker, *What the Body Cost*, 113, 108, 113.

22 Stabile, "Shooting the Mother," 172, 173.

23 Hartouni, "Fetal Exposures," 213.

24 Rose, "Mothers and Authors." See also Wiegman, "Intimate Publics," which discusses a similar case with important complications (the surrogacy was unintentional and cross-racial).

25 Poovey, "The Abortion Question and the Death of Man," 242.

26 Ibid., 249.

27 Ibid., 252.

28 Doyle, *Sex Objects* and "Sex, Scandal, and Thomas Eakins's *Gross Clinic*."

29 See Fried, *Realism, Writing, and Disfiguration* for a discussion of this woman's symbolic role as one figure for castration among many offered by this painting.

30 In the words of one *New York Tribune* critic, "It is a picture that even strong men find it difficult to look at long, if they can look at it at all; as for people with nerves and stomachs, the scene is so real that they might as well go to a dissecting

room and have done with it." Cited in Hendricks, *The Life and Work of Thomas Eakins*, 63.

31 See Adams, *Eakins Revealed*, for a thorough portrait of Eakins's personal and professional difficulties, as well as a comprehensive literature review on the subject. My own work on Eakins looks closely at the relationship between his complex attitudes about gender and the difficulty of this painting. See "Sex, Sodomy, and Scandal: Art and Undress in the Work of Thomas Eakins," in Doyle, *Sex Objects*, 14–44.

32 The scholarly field on Eakins is rapidly expanding. Major voices in the field include Elizabeth Johns, Daryl Sewell, Mark Simpson, Kathleen Foster, Cheryl Liebold, Michael Leja, Michael Fried, Martin Berger, Michael Hatt, Whitney Davis, Alan Braddock, and Sarah Burns.

33 One can imagine the editorial decisions that favored the rowers over the portrait of Samuel Gross. The museum wanted to sell copies of its book, and buyers would have been put off by such an aggressive image. Newspaper readers might not have enjoyed being met by this picture while drinking their morning coffee. The very dark and crowded image is also much harder to reproduce well in print—and who wants to have that image as a poster hanging on the wall? It would make for a very strange souvenir. For these reasons, it has always been something of a bête noire in terms of selling Eakins to the public.

34 Walton was on the hunt for major works in American art history to fill Crystal Bridges, a museum of American art in Arkansas. Some of her most significant purchases were made secretly in deals with cash-strapped public institutions (such as the New York Public Library). That secrecy allowed her to bypass competition from large institutions like the Smithsonian (and also other billionaire collectors), while avoiding the cooling effect of public opinion on the seller. The Eakins painting was too big, too important, however, to sell discreetly. So it was held hostage.

35 Before Walton made her offer to Jefferson Medical College, *The Gross Clinic* had only a handful of visitors a day. As it happens, within academic discourse, scholarly writing about *The Gross Clinic* enjoyed a similar life. American art history (American art from the colonial period until modernism) has long held a minor disciplinary status, in much the same way that American literature did in the early twentieth century. It is accorded much less importance in the field than European art from the same period. It is not uncommon, for example, for smaller art history departments to offer no courses in the field.

36 It was originally submitted for an art exhibit at Philadelphia's Centennial Exposition but was rejected and exiled to a medical display in the same fair.

37 For some insight into the sociology of early Eakins studies, see Adams's *Eakins Revealed*, which maps in great detail how early biographers actively suppressed the most disturbing stories about Eakins's behavior, in no small part because they were explicitly attempting to redeem him from the scandals that so shaped his career.

38 See Butt, *Between You and Me* for a discussion of the gendering of discourse on

the artist in the 1950s, and my review of his book for a comparison of the traditions he describes there and the discourse surrounding Eakins as a legendary figure: "Secrets and Lies: Gossip and Art's Queer Histories," *American Quarterly* 59.2 (2007), 511–21.

39 Perhaps in those cases we see what Steiner called a "strategic difficulty" (which was contemporary with the work's creation) evolve into a "modal difficulty" (where the work's importance grows from the scandal it generated in its immediate context, but which is no longer palpable).

40 Art historical narratives covering the nineteenth and twentieth centuries are structured by the singular break of modernism—by the movement toward what Clement Greenberg famously described as the "all over canvas" of painters like Mondrian and Pollock and by the refusal of narrative painting as an inherently bourgeois form. *The Gross Clinic* is clearly not part of modernism's party; no work of Eakins makes the challenges to representational logic that we associate with many of his contemporaries. His is a backward practice by many standards—very unglamorous.

41 For more on this point regarding Duchamp, see Jones, *Postmodernism and the En-Gendering of Marcel Duchamp*.

42 This is why Michael Fried argued in his work on the painting that it generates in us a sense of there being something "behind" or "before" the painting, which the artist recorded. Fried's intervention in critical writing about the painting was to assert that our desire to assess the painting's fidelity to an actual event seen and recorded by the artist was a formal effect of its realism. Realism gives us the impression of a recording of an original scene not because Eakins saw this surgery and decided to paint it, but by virtue of the *way* it is painted: certain elements (like the superabundance of detail) heighten the sense that there is something real there, which we gain access to by looking at the painting closely, reading it for signs of its accuracy. Attempts to identify the patient, to figure out who stands in for whom, and to assess the painting's accuracy as a depiction of the surgical theater of the 1860s might add something to our knowledge of Dr. Gross's circle, but it does not resolve the problems *The Gross Clinic* creates for the viewers. It doesn't make looking at the painting any easier. In fact it makes the act of looking part of the problem. And, more problematically, it masks what is actually there on the canvas. Fried draws our attention to the artist's obsession with techniques of representation. In the painting, we see a man record the surgery with his pen, students take notes, and the surgeon wield a scalpel as though it were a brush. The artist has signed the painting on the bottom of the surgical table so that it looks as though it were carved into the table's wood. Instruments of representation are aligned with the scalpel, and their use is aligned with a bloody violation of the boundary between the inside and the outside of the body.

43 Costello and Willsdon, introduction, 13.

44 Ibid.

45 Butler, *Precarious Life*, 20.

46 A number of people read this image, which he has produced in different ways

across several performances, as one of castration. One might also read it as an exaggeration of the antiphallic properties of the penis, its malleability, its flexibility and wetness.

47 See Jones, "Rupture," and also her discussion of Athey's work in *Self/Image*, 179–82; Richards, "Ron Athey, AIDS and the Politics of Pain." See also Johnson, "Ron Athey's Visions of Excess"; Lazare, "An Endless Insurrection."

48 Miglietti, *Extreme Bodies*, 46.

49 Butler, *Precarious Life*, 134. Butler takes the title of her book from Levinas's discussion of "the face of the other." She cites the philosopher as he imagines the face representing "the extreme precariousness of the other." She expands on this postulation: "To respond to the face, to understand its meaning, means to be awake to what is precarious in another life, or, rather, the precariousness of life itself. This cannot be an awakeness . . . to my own life . . . it has to be an understanding of the precariousness of the Other." Butler also teases out from Levinas the following distinction: "The human is not represented by the face. Rather, the human is indirectly affirmed in that very disjunction that makes representation impossible, and this disjunction is conveyed in the impossible representation. For representation to convey the human, then, representation must not only fail, but it must *show* its failure" (144).

50 For more on defacing and discourse on sex and power, see Merck, *In Your Face*.

51 Blocker, *What the Body Cost*.

52 Lunch, "The Violent Disbelief of Ron Athey," *Will Work for Drugs*, 142.

53 Richards, "Ron Athey, AIDS and the Politics of Pain." *Martyrs and Saints* also includes an enactment of St. Sebastian, in which a pierced, tattooed queer woman is pierced with arrows and then tended to by Athey, now costumed in a tight corset and white dress evocative of the evangelical leader Aimee Semple McPherson.

54 In the program notes for a performance of *Martyrs and Saints* in May 1993 at Randolph Street Gallery in Chicago, Athey writes, "I wrote 'Nurse's Penance' the day after David Wojnarowicz died of AIDS. It was in my grief and sense of loss over his passing—and over realizing that all of my role models are dead or dying—that many of the images in this work were born." See also Liesegang, "Perforating Saint," in which Athey explains, "For instance, when David Wojnarowicz died, I tried to imagine what it would be like for a nurse who truly loved their patient and was helpless to save them. What would their penance be?" John Edward McGrath writes about "A Nurse's Penance" in "Trusting in Rubber." McGrath's essay confronts the difficult of Athey's work directly and is an excellent introduction to his most challenging work. It also contains a brief but important acknowledgment of how Athey works with sound. Drawing from a club background, "Athey's music stimulates our bodies, acts on our emotions like a drug"; it "drives us to forget the past, to remember only the pulses of the moment, this moment in which we are both excessively stimulated and very aware that we are not getting everything we seem to want" (30–31).

55 A longer excerpt of this passage is worth reading:

There seemed to be an obsession among those close to him to be present at his death. In his hospital room a few weeks before, I witnessed a series of Cliff's temper tantrums. He was in a state of rage over meningitis, PCP, CMV, a surgery date to have his gall bladder removed and more. I was afraid he'd die bitter and hateful. But there was an intense healing experience. Cliff had the most special relationships with strong women, and they were present. Archetypal goddesses and wood nymphs, skinheads and punks, all expressed their love. They spoon-fed meals, massaged and shaved and talked and prayed and confirmed their love. . . . And to cap off his final days, a man Cliff had been interested in spent the night two days before the gall bladder surgery—and they sucked dick all night. (Ron Athey, "Cliff Diller, 1964–1992," *LA Weekly*, 30 October–5 November 1992, 45)

56 *Momento Mori* was also the last art exhibit David Wojnarowicz saw. Cynthia Carr recounts the artist's trip to the New Museum in *Fire in the Belly*, 557.

57 Stosh Fila ("Pigpen"), interview with Catherine Gund, director of *Hallelujah! Ron Athey: A Story of Deliverance* (1998), 1997. These remarks are from Gund's transcripts of interviews with Ron Athey's company, stored in the artist's personal archive.

58 Johnson, *"Perverse Martyrologies."* See also Athey, "Deliverance."

59 Mary Brennan, review of *Incorruptible Flesh (in progress)*, *The Herald* (Glasgow), 10 February 1996.

60 John McGrath writes, "Athey disrupts a theatricalization of the space of death itself, *disallows* an imagery of death which creates its space as special, over there, beyond the line" ("Trusting in Rubber," 32).

61 Cited in Lawrence Ferber, "Deliverance: Performance Artist Ron Athey on the Boundary Pushing Thing," *Frontiers*, 11 December 1998, 37.

62 Jonathan Coleman describes Opie's session with Athey and Moby C in "Taking Pictures in the Belly of the World's Largest Camera," *New Yorker*, 5 June 2000, 34. Their work anticipates more commercial applications of photography to performance art, such as Vanessa Beecroft's prints of her installations.

63 Richard Meyer explores Mapplethorpe's relationship to censorship and prohibition in *Outlaw Representation*; J. Jack Halberstam addresses Opie's work in *Female Masculinity*.

64 See Opie and Crimp, "Catherine Opie in Conversation with Douglas Crimp," 302. The photograph ought to be attributed to both artists; it was part of a series of photographs of Athey commissioned by The Estate Project to benefit people with HIV/AIDS. As Opie explains, she took the occasion of these photographs to extend earlier portraits she'd made of the artist, but here she could focus on "a series of moments from various performances Ron had done." Photographs from this series were included in the Tate Liverpool exhibition *Art, Lies, and Videotape* in 2004, where they were problematically exhibited as authored by Catherine Opie and listed as *Untitled*, an amazing error given the exhibition's theme of performance documentation. (The misattribution started with Opie's

gallery.) This was the worst example in the history of this work's circulation as art by Catherine Opie, and not as Opie's portrait of Athey's performance practice, or even more accurate, as a collaboration between the two artists, which is how Opie and Athey have represented the work. The problem is not unique to Athey and this work; the ownership of performance documentation is a problem for many live artists, especially those who made work in the 1970s and 1980s with few models for assuming ownership of such images (e.g., Carolee Schneeman, on whose early performances there is an extensive but inaccessible archive of documentation hoarded by an early audience member). It also poses problems for the photographer's work, as its market value is diminished by a shared authorship or the designation "documentation."

65 This invocation of the image of Athey's body as an emblem for risk is extended in the Getty Research Institute anthology inspired by the conference. *The Aesthetics of Risk* includes a conversation between Opie and Douglas Crimp that opens with a photograph of the two speakers dwarfed by a projection of Athey on all fours, with his asshole presented to the camera. The caption does not identify the subject that in fact dominates the image. See Opie and Crimp, "Catherine Opie in Conversation with Douglas Crimp," 298.

66 Blocker, *What the Body Cost*, 133.

67 Ironically, the fact that he had never benefited directly from federal support for his work kept his work off the radar for art historians writing about the censorship and the Supreme Court fight over the "NEA Four"—Karen Finley, Andreas Serrano, Robert Mapplethorpe, and Holly Hughes. For an in-depth discussion of how censored artists like Mapplethorpe, Hughes, and Wojnarowicz (whom I discuss in the last chapter) anticipate prohibition in their work, see Meyer, *Outlaw Representation*.

68 Blocker, *What the Body Cost*, 111.

69 Andrew Hultkrans, "May Pole," *Artforum.com*, 5 May 2006.

70 Blocker, *What the Body Cost*, 112.

71 In that year, I should note, Athey became a licensed massage therapist.

72 See Ann Cvetkovich's chapters on AIDS activism and the impact of the AIDS crisis on lesbian activists in *An Archive of Feelings*.

73 In an interview with Sarah Wilson, Athey explains, "Why are the women always tending the men, why are the men sick and the women strong. It's always this hard woman tending this broken down man. In pictures of women saints they are just left with their cut-off breasts or their poked out eyes. Men are collapsed, all over the place, being held up by women." See the unreleased documentary film that accompanied the South Bank's 1998 exhibition *Body Art*: Ron Athey and Sarah Wilson, "Contemporary Practitioners 3: Ron Athey: On Paintings and Photography," Youtube, 21 April 2008, accessed 30 August 2012.

74 Nelson, *The Art of Cruelty*, 76.

75 Stović, "The Art of Marina Abramović," 24.

76 Butler, *Precarious Life*, 27.

3. Thinking Feeling

1 Elkins, "On the Absence of Judgment in Art Criticism." Other overviews of the dominant paradigms in contemporary art history (and its relationship to the field of visual studies) influence my discussion here. These include Butt, "Introduction: The Paradoxes of Criticism"; Crimp, "Getting the Warhol We Deserve"; Jones, "The Baroness and Neurasthenic Art History," *Irrational Modernism*, 2–33; Murray and Murray, "Uneasy Bedfellows."

2 See Jones, "Art History / Art Criticism: Performing Meaning."

3 Cited in Newman in *Challenging Art*. I read this passage first as it was cited in Elkins, "On the Absence of Judgment in Art Criticism," 84.

4 Elkins, "On the Absence of Judgment in Art Criticism," 85.

5 Carter Radcliff, cited in Newman, *Challenging Art*. Elkins refers to these words from Radcliff ("On the Absence of Judgment in Art Criticism," 84).

6 Butt, "How I Died for Kiki and Herb," 89.

7 Ibid., 90.

8 Elkins, *Picture and Tears*, 92, 88.

9 Elkins, "On the Absence of Judgment in Art Criticism," 85.

10 A range of critics work successfully outside these circles—Carol Mavor, Christine Ross, Darby English, Jennifer González—though none is a regular contributor to either *Artforum* or *October*.

11 For discussions of the politicization of self-imaging, see Jones, *Self/Image*, especially "'No Movies' . . . (No) Bodies, (No) Cities," 80–86.

12 In 2008 Franko B asserted that he would no longer perform bleeding pieces, as his interactions with art institutions commissioning work had become increasingly complicated by a demand for blood. It is not always possible to tap into a vein safely, and many institutions were not prepared to deal with this uncertainty. One went so far as to require the artist to sign a contract in which he would be paid according to whether he bled from one arm or two.

13 Nyong'o, "Brown Punk," 75.

14 Burnham, "'High Performances,' Performance Art, and Me," 44–45.

15 Greenberg, "Avant-Garde and Kitsch," *The Collected Essays and Criticism*, 12.

16 Bishop, "The Social Turn." Bishop develops her reading of participator art practices in *Artificial Hells: Participatory Art and the Politics of Spectatorship*. This work is particularly useful for its explication and analysis of the discursive opposition of the aesthetic and the social, as it is presented and challenged by diverse artists.

17 Bishop, "Public Opinion."

18 Bishop, "The Social Turn."

19 Foster, *The Return of the Real*, 199.

20 Ibid., 202–3.

21 Baldwin, "Everybody's Protest Novel," 476. The essay was originally published in *Notes of a Native Son* (Boston: Beacon, 1955).

22 Baldwin's argument is less with sentimentality per se than with what Berlant calls

"compassionate liberalism"—a particular combination of sentiment and politics, aimed at (in Stowe's words) making the reader "feel right" through its presentation of social injustice and the personal suffering of (in this instance) racism's victims. Such work is ameliorative: it aims at making the world a better place, as readers bond over a shared sense of grief or outrage. Expanding on this side of sentimentality's emotional politics, Berlant writes, "Compassionate liberalism is, at best, a kind of sandpaper on the surface of the racist monument whose structural and economic solidity endures: in the intimate sphere of femininity a kind of soft supremacy rooted in compassion and coercive identification wants to dissolve all that structure through the work of good intentionality, while busily exoticizing and diminishing the inconvenient and the noncompliant" (*The Female Complaint*, 6). She spends some time with Baldwin's writing on Stowe and demonstrates that his own writing practices in fact mine the "politco-sentimental aesthetics," even if they do so ambivalently (57–60). Berlant names here the political dubiousness of one version of "politico-sentimental culture" that presents itself as a mistress whose benevolence is contingent upon her retention of power and privilege. While it may work to forward a public conversation about race and class (e.g., *Crash* [2004], Paul Haggis's popular film mapping racial conflict in Los Angeles), this kind of text can also provide the platform for a kind of emotional tourism, allowing its audience risk-free contact with the suffering of others. (For an incisive reading of liberal humanism and the politics of sentiment in Haggis's film, see Nunley, "*Crash.*" In *The Female Complaint* Berlant analyzes the relationship of affect to the politics of gender and race as they collect around the term *sentimentality*.

23 Berlant, *The Female Complaint*, 56–47. See also Lauren Berlant, ed., *Compassion: The Culture and Politics of an Emotion* (New York: Routledge, 2004). This is also Claire Bishop's concern, as she warns that the failure to think complexly about the interface of art and politics can produce art as "'edu-tainment' or 'pedagogical aesthetics'" (*Artificial Hells*, 274).

24 Sentimentality, Sedgwick writes, has had "a strange career," "from the later eighteenth century when it was a term of high ethical and aesthetic praise, to the twentieth when it can be used to connote, beyond pathetic weakness, an actual principle of evil" (*Epistemology of the Closet*, 150).

25 Sedgwick, *Epistemology of the Closet*, 152.

26 Sentimentality is explored explicitly as a dynamic and narrative problem by such canonical authors as Henry James, Gustave Flaubert, and Marcel Proust.

27 In the interest of full disclosure, Radway was the chair of my Ph.D. committee.

28 Berlant, *The Female Complaint*, 56.

29 For more on the dynamics of body art and masochism, see O'Dell, *Contract with the Skin*.

30 Nyong'o, "Do You Want Queer Theory (or Do You Want the Truth)?," 109. Take, for example, Nyong'o's description of a scene from the documentary *The Filth and Fury* (Julien Temple, 2000), in which the Sex Pistols host a benefit

concert for the families of striking firefighters. Archival footage shows the band members serving cake to children, playing with the kids by smearing cake over each other, and then launching into a performance of "Bodies," itself a disturbing song about pregnancy, babies, and abortion. The crowd—adults, adolescents, and children—dances to the song in obvious enjoyment. The band seems to belong to the whole scene, one of very straightforward politics and sociability. There is no mistaking, in fact, the quite happy relation of art and politics in this footage and the circulation of pleasure, desire, and outrage in and around their performance. As we watch a montage of these scenes, Johnny Rotten remembers this concert as one of the highlights of the band's life together. Their politics, music, and audience felt, for him, perfectly aligned. Nyong'o describes the scene as a "truly shocking conflation of the sentimental and the obscene, the perverse and the innocent." That moment in the film is a glimpse of punk's utopianism, the fading of which has made some fans of the music scene of that era deeply melancholic and sometimes intensely self-righteous.

31 See Freeman, *Wedding Complex*.

32 For a history of how we have understood crying (and representations of crying), see Lutz, *Crying*.

33 Cited in Žižek, *The Fright of Real Tears*, 72.

34 It has always struck me as ironic that so much of the work associated with relational aesthetics is so very dry. Howells's experiments in "accelerated intimacy" and its extimate shadow constitute an exploration of relational aesthetics, but works like *Held* and *Thirteen Stations*, so obviously grounded in the emotional poetics of relationships, have no place in the major texts surveying the art practices centered on the relationship between the artist and the spectator or participant. Most of that criticism centers on art staged in museums and galleries or in process-oriented work done in collaboration with community organizations, with an explicit social and political aim.

35 The term *outsourcing* has figured regularly in reviews of especially Sierra's performances. Bishop used the term more recently as a curatorial principle for her exhibit *Double Agent* (London ICA, 2008).

36 See Foster's attack on such turns in *The Return of the Real*. See also Crimp, "Getting the Warhol We Deserve."

37 Jeffrey Deitch, cited in Phoebe Hoban, "How Far Is Too Far," *ARTnews*, Summer 2008. Beecroft is more eager to ward off such a calamity: she pays her models far more than Sierra pays his workers. She also writes into their contract the following condition: if one of the women walks off the job, none will be paid. See Steinmentz, Cassils, and Leary, "Behind Enemy Lines." See also Jennifer González's discussion of Fred Wilson's performance *My Life as a Dog*, in which he offers a group of people a tour of a gallery, then appears in the gallery dressed as a security guard and is unrecognizable to the gallery patrons (*Subject to Display*, 1–2).

38 Hardt and Negri, *Multitude*, 111.

39 This way of thinking about work and emotion actually grows out of feminist

writing about "women's work"; feminists have long argued that women are caught up in the complex web of interpersonal labor, in which their desires are bound up with the needs and desires of those they care for. See, for example, Hochschild, *The Managed Heart*.

4. Feeling Overdetermined

1 Murray and Murray, "Uneasy Bedfellows," 39.

2 Kester, "Another Turn," 22.

3 English, *How to See a Work of Art in Total Darkness*, 1.

4 Ibid., 4, my emphasis.

5 Hammonds's negation of the visible may also be read as responding to the problematic place of the visual within African American cultural discourse regarding the arts, in that historically literature and music have been privileged over visual art. See Collins, "A Visual Paradox: Art and Aesthetics in African American Thought," *The Art of History*, 1–10.

6 English, *How to See a Work of Art in Total Darkness*, 45.

7 Ibid., 7. Kobena Mercer makes a similar intervention in "Tropes of the Grotesque in the Black Avant-Garde."

8 Murray and Murray, "Uneasy Bedfellows," 28.

9 Kobena Mercer has made similar interventions in art historical discourse, taking on both the tendencies English describes and reductive curatorial framing of art by black artists as case studies, each modeling competing definitions of "black art." He writes, "Once for example, 'black' is understood not as a category of identity given by nature, but as a subject-position historically created by discursive regimes of power and knowledge in the social domain of 'race,' then the goal is to explore how art produces a signifying difference in the cultural codes of collective consciousness and thus has the power to alter or modify prevailing consensus in the symbolic construction of reality" ("Tropes of the Grotesque in the Black Avant-Garde," 138). This essay also contains a valuable discussion of David Hammons's work.

10 McHugh, "Profane Illuminations," 436, 453. See also Julia Barnes Mandle and Deborah Rothschild's exhibition catalog *Sites of Recollection: Four Altars and a Rap Opera*, especially Philip Brookman's essay "The Politics of Hope," which includes discussion of Luna's work. On depression and disengagement in contemporary art, see Ross, *The Aesthetics of Disengagement*. This work was an important reference point in developing the archive for this project, insofar as most of the artists I work with are engaged even when their work takes on depressive aspects. Ross helps us to distinguish between modes of engagement and disengagement around affect and to access the politics in work even as it seems to withdraw from its environment.

11 Blocker, "Failures of Self-Seeing," 22.

12 I commissioned this performance as part of the exhibit *I Feel Different* (Los Angeles Contemporary Exhibitions, October 2009–January 2010).

13 Raheja, *Reservation Realism*, 108.

14 Lindsay Westbrook, cited in Muñoz, "Feeling Brown, Feeling Down," 686.

15 Muñoz, "Feeling Brown, Feeling Down," 687, 680. See also Ahmed, *The Promise of Happiness*; Eng, *Loss*; Muñoz, *Cruising Utopia*; Viejo, *Dead Subjects*.

16 Viejo, *Dead Subjects*, 4. See also Anne Anlin Cheng's examination of the paradoxes of racial identity as both resistance and oppression in *The Melancholy of Race*.

17 Signs are arbitrary, as Julia Kristeva explains, and one can't function "normally" within language unless one is able to "forget" the distance between a signifier and its signified (between the sound of the word, for example, and the concept it represents). "Depressed persons, on the contrary, *disavow the negation*" and cocoon with a powerful negativity. Alienated from language, indeed from all forms of expression, one is taken over by an overwhelming depressive affect (*Black Sun*, 43–44).

18 Viejo, *Dead Subjects*, 6.

19 These are just three significant interventions in the discipline of history that serve to denaturalize the narratives that organize the relationship of past to present: Scott, "Fantasy Echo"; Benjamin, "Thesis on the Philosophy of History"; Jameson, *The Political Unconscious*.

20 Jameson, *The Political Unconscious*, 102.

21 Murray, "Kehinde Wiley."

22 Terada, *Feeling in Theory*, 11.

23 Looking at Warhol's work, we can also see how feelings can be also moved down the line, as it were, to the people who, like Sierra's angry workers, can't afford *not* to have them. The art historian Richard Meyer tells a story about giving a talk in Kazakhstan in support of a U.S. State Department exhibit of Warhol's work, the first exhibition of American art staged in the region. A woman in the audience asked why the U.S. government would send such them such "soulless" work. She was, Meyer recalls, furious. Taken from its context and shipped across the world, Warhol's work looks like the indifferent face of U.S. imperialism. Which, in turn, provokes very strong feelings in those expected to swallow it. If the work itself appeared to be affectless for this audience, the affective field around the work in that context was supercharged with anger. Affect isn't eliminated by Pop Art so much as it is passed around or passed on.

24 Terada, *Feeling in Theory*, 8. Similar arguments have been made about cinematic melodrama, in which the spectator is moved at least in part by the scriptedness of the genre's affective flows. For such audience members, awareness of the genre's stylization of emotion makes these films *more* powerful, not less. See, for example, Williams, "'Something Else Besides a Mother.'" I discuss this dynamic in relation to Tracey Emin's work in Doyle, *Sex Objects*.

25 Ahmed, *The Cultural Politics of Emotion*, 10.

26 Nyong'o, "Brown Punk," 73.

27 Ahmed, *The Cultural Politics of Emotion*, 11.

28 Adorno, *Minima Moralia*, 110.

29 Nicholas Mirzoeff discusses the contradictory uses of antebellum portraits of free and enslaved African American subjects as portraits of accomplishment and dignity, emblems of resistance, but also as bills of sale and racist evidence (*Introduction to Visual Culture*, 77–84). He draws on Deborah Willis's discussion of photographers of this period in *Reflections in Black*.

30 The exoticism of these photographs is of a piece with the historical processes that minimize and obscure African American agency. Throughout his career, W. E. B. Du Bois intervened in popular and academic discourse that approached African American history in terms of black subordination, passivity, and abjection. In such narratives the end of slavery is structured as the accomplishment of white liberal humanism, as if African Americans had nothing to do with the end of the Civil War; and the end of the Civil War is celebrated, but the betrayal of the project of Reconstruction is forgotten. He writes, "The freedmen, far from being the inert recipients of freedom at the hands of philanthropists, furnished 200,000 soldiers in the Civil War who took part in nearly 200 battles and skirmishes, in addition perhaps 300,000 others as effective laborers and helpers. In proportion to population, more Negroes than whites fought in the Civil War. . . . Yet one would search current American histories almost in vain to find a clear statement or even faint recognition of these perfectly well-authenticated facts" (*Black Reconstruction in America*, 716–17).

31 When Alan Trachtenberg produced his overview of American photography, he included a lengthy discussion of these problematic images as (among other things) unavoidable evidence of racialist technologies of vision (*Reading American Photographs*, 53–60). For an overview of Agassiz and Zealy's collaboration, see Wallis, "Black Bodies, White Science." Molly Rogers blends history and fiction in her novelistic account of the production of these photographs, *Delia's Tears*, the most detailed writing on the subject.

32 Rodgers, *Delia's Tears*, 6.

33 Weems's *Ain't Joking* captions portraits of black men and women, pictured in ordinary settings, with racist rhymes and jokes. *And 22 Million Very Tired and Angry People* couples images with phrases lifted out of the movement for black liberation; a rolling pin, for instance, floats above the phrase "By any means necessary." Those works are deadpan in tone, as the joke is shifted from the racist context that allows it to be funny into an antiracist context that disarms the joke's mechanisms. *From Here I Saw* is similar to those projects in that it is overtly dialogic, triangulating the spectator in an exchange between text and image. Cherise Smith describes Weems's redeployment of these images within this critical project as an act of "repatriation" for precisely the way that the original photographs represent a form of psychic theft ("Fragmented Documents," 254). But the term suggests that a full recovery is possible. One can also say that the installation marks out the desire for that repatriation but leaves the viewer with the distinct feeling that such a gesture arrives too late.

34 Susan Muchnic, "Going for a Gut Reaction," *Los Angeles Times*, 26 February 1995.

35 For a good point of entry into the political landscape of Los Angeles during these years, see Smith, *Twilight: Los Angeles, 1992*. The year of Weems's exhibition at the Getty also saw the beginning of *The People v O. J. Simpson*, which would become the longest trial in California's history and one of the country's most infamous celebrity trials. Simpson's acquittal for the murder of his (white) wife ignited furious debates about celebrity culture, racism, and violence against women.

36 The period produced a series of influential articles on race and visual representation, most notably Elizabeth Alexander's "'Can You Be BLACK and Look at This?'"

37 The reactive and didactic tone of Weems's installation led to some of its harshest criticism. Writing for the contemporary art magazine *Frieze*, David Pagel complained, "The main difference between the exhibitions is that 'Hidden Witness' gave viewers something to look at and 'Carrie Mae Weems Reacts' downplayed the open-ended uncontrollability of the visible in favour of the determinism of the word." The nature of the commission itself posed a problem for Pagel, as it seemed "under the banner of multiculturalism [to] provide very limited roles for artists who supposedly fit into pre-determined categories." Worse, in his view, the commission "is a part of a nationwide institutional trend in which contemporary art is subjugated, with increasing frequency, to educational outreach under the rubric of community-building." He calls the pairing "racist" and concludes (rather shockingly), "Putting forth a monkey-see, monkey-do argument, the paired exhibits suggest that viewers need to be taught how to properly respond to the 150-year old photographs. This is noblesse oblige at its most arrogant and condescending; it has no place in any institution" ("Hidden Witness," n.p.).

38 Alexander, "'Can You Be BLACK and Look at This?,'" 108.

39 For more on this work, see Kimberly Lamm, "Portraits of the Past, Imagined Now: Reading Carrie Mae Weems and Lorna Simpson," *Unmaking Race/ Remaking Soul: Transformative Aesthetics and the Practice of Freedom*, ed. Christa Davis Acampora and Angela Cotton (Albany: State University of New York Press, 2007), 103–40; Smith, "Fragmented Documents."

40 Bernier, *African American Visual Arts*, 15.

41 Most critical discussions of *From Here I Saw* focus on these four images, as Weems's appropriation of the Zealy daguerreotypes represents an antiracist intervention in the history of photography. See, for example, Celeste-Marie Bernier's introduction to *African American Visual Arts*, especially 14–17. Brian Wallis also gestures toward Weems's use of the Zealy images in another project at the conclusion of his essay "Black Bodies, White Science."

42 Stuart Hall describes the "'absent' but imperializing 'white eye'" as "the unmarked position from which all these observations are made and from which, alone, they make sense. This is the history of slavery and conquest, written, seen, drawn, and photographed by The Winners. They cannot be *read* and made sense of from any other position. The 'white eye' is always outside the frame—but seeing and positioning everything within it" ("The Whites of Their Eyes," 38–39).

43 Collins, *The Art of History*, 31. In this passage Collins is writing about Weems's *Sea Island* installation (1991–92), which also repositions the Zealy daguerreotypes within an African American context.

44 Interview with the artist produced for Art21.org and available on its website.

45 Cherise Smith discusses this aspect of the photograph's history in "Fragmented Documents" and draws from Kathleen Collins's scholarship on the photograph as she does so. See Collins, "The Scourged Back."

46 As Nicholas Mirzoeff writes, even though this image was produced in an abolitionist context intent on documenting slavery's inhuman violence, from the pro-slavery position the image reads "simply [as] evidence of a crime committed and properly punished" and of "the irrepressible malfeasance of Africans who, therefore, could only be controlled by force" (*Introduction to Visual Culture*, 81).

47 See Davis, *Blues Legacies and Black Feminism*. Davis's discussion of Holiday's performances of "Strange Fruit" (an "unsellable" song) is particularly relevant to this project's discussion of difficulty and emotion in performance.

48 Morrison, *Playing in the Dark*, 6–7.

49 Ibid., 7.

50 Sharpe, *Monstrous Intimacies*, 154.

51 Benjamin, "Theses on the Philosophy of History," 254–56.

52 Golden, "Some Thoughts on Carrie Mae Weems," 32.

53 The controversy surrounding Kara Walker's violent and sexually explicit plantation dystopias, Ferguson observes, "takes place because she dares to target that invention and its machinery" ("A Special Place within the Order of Knowledge," 186).

54 Moten, "Black Mo'nin'," 62.

55 Not all viewers are able to recognize this. One of the challenges of Weems's installation is the viewer's familiarity with the history of debate regarding art and politics within African American art, as well as the rich stories behind the sources for and references made within each of the installation's chapters. Writing for *Frieze*, David Pagel thus takes the didactic and rhetorical dimension of the work literally, to conclude that the series "downplayed the open-ended uncontrollability of the visible in favour of the determinism of the word" ("Hidden Witness," n.p.). Reviewing the exhibit for the *Los Angeles Times*, Susan Kandel identified that didacticism as a strength: "Her work is indeed didactic; of that there is no question. It is also harsh, sarcastic and accusatory. This is what traps us; but it is not what moves us." Susan Kandel, "'Witness': Lives of Blacks Considered," *Los Angeles Times*, 4 March 1995.

56 "[The historical materialist] regards it as his task to brush history against the grain" (Benjamin, "Theses on the Philosophy of History," 257).

57 The installation's interrogation of the protocols of history and its documents recalls interventions of Du Bois's *Black Reconstruction in America* (1935), which countered dominant historical narratives regarding slavery, the Civil War, and the post–Civil War period known as Reconstruction. Such histories erased black

participation in abolition and resistance as well as the accomplishments of African American men and women in the social and political reorganization of life in the post–Civil War South. Du Bois analyzes the collaboration between racist and capitalist systems that not only unraveled that progress but obliterated it from the historical record. *Black Reconstruction in America* offers a history, but it is also a sustained critique of the ideological work of history as a discipline. In his polemical conclusion to the work, titled "The Propaganda of History," Du Bois asserts that all history is propaganda and that the most dangerous history is that which cloaks itself in a mantle of disinterest and objectivity. In a similar polemic on politics and African American art, Du Bois also asserted that he was not interested in art that was not propaganda. He writes, "All Art is propaganda and ever must be, despite the wailing of purists. I stand in utter shamelessness and say that whatever art I have for writing has been used always for propaganda for gaining the right of black folk to love and enjoy. I do not care a damn for any art that is not used for propaganda. But I do care when propaganda is confined to one side while the other is stripped and silent" ("Criteria of Negro Art," 296). This essay is discussed by Darby English in *How to See a Work of Art in Total Darkness*, 56.

58 Gould, *Moving Politics*, 3.

Conclusion

1 This untitled work is archived in the David Wojnarowicz Papers in the Fales Library at New York University. See Cynthia Carr's *Fire in the Belly* for a comprehensive discussion of Wojnarowicz's life and work.

2 Wojnarowicz's partner Tom Rauffenbart recalled Hujar and Wojnarowicz's relationship in an interview with Cynthia Carr: "'It became clear that these guys were cemented somewhere,' said Tom. 'They were like extensions of each other. They were so similar. Each had a kind of presence, a depth. It radiated from them.'" Carr, *Fire in the Belly*, 352.

3 The most frequently discussed works of Wojnarowicz's are those that have been the subject of controversy. His essay "Postcards from America: X Rays from Hell" provoked a fight over the use of federal arts dollars to fund an attack on the Catholic Church; he sued the American Family Association over its illegal appropriation of partial images from his work for use in a homophobic pamphlet mailed out as an attack on the National Endowment for the Arts; and, more recently, an unfinished film included in an exhibit at the National Portrait Gallery was pulled from the show after a Catholic fundamentalist group complained to the Smithsonian's leaders about, again, Wojnarowicz's attack on the Church. Carr reviews Wojnarowicz's struggles against censorship in *Fire in the Belly*, especially in the chapters "Witnesses" and "With a Target on His Back," 442–95. See also Richard Meyer's discussion of the first two incidents in *Outlaw Representation*, 244–75. *Untitled (Hujar Dead)* may be the most frequently discussed

of those works of his that never gained such notoriety; a number of critics responded to it in unusual depth in their reviews of shows in which it appeared in 1989 and 1990. Articles that discuss this work in detail include Deitcher, "Ideas and Emotions"; Durant, "Sustained Rage"; Lippard, "Out of the Safety Zone"; Saltz, "Not Going Gentle."

4 Wojnarowicz often sampled and remixed his work. Accordingly, this text appears in other places. It can be found in "Do Not Doubt the Dangerousness of the 12-Inch Politician," in *Close to the Knives*, 159. Marion Scemama filmed Wojnarowicz reading this text in 1989. An audio recording of Wojnarowicz's performance of the text is layered over a segment of *ITSOFOMO* (In the Shadow of Forward Motion), his multimedia collaboration with Ben Neill. This work was a series of live projections of Wojnarowicz's filmic montages, for which Neill mixed sound and Wojnarowicz read segments of his writings. These live performances were only partially choreographed, and each performance was slightly different. Neill speaks to their collaboration in Lotringer, "Ben Neill." I discuss other uses of this text later.

5 Carr, "Portrait of an Artist in the Age of AIDS," in *On Edge*, 254.

6 Allison and Curry, "'All Anger and Understanding,'" 157.

7 Lippard, "Out of the Safety Zone."

8 This conflict in our relationship with the "traumatic photograph" (in which an ethical and an aesthetic relation to the image are positioned as mutually exclusive) is examined and contested by Griselda Pollock in "Dying, Seeing, Feeling."

9 Speaking to the miscasting of art and politics as opposite forces, the poet James Scully asserts, "Political poetry is not a contradiction in terms but an instructive redundancy. It does not hold the mirror up to nature. It holds social reality up to the sheep, showing poetry its own face, its conditions, its grounds and horizons" (*Line Break*, 61). There is no poetry without politics—even the desire for an apolitical poetry is itself a political fantasy. But this is not to say that the politics of poetry—or art—is always knowable or translatable into social action. Political art, in other words, does not always cooperate with politics as a sphere of social action in open dialogue with institutional power. It can in fact mark the political turn to what lies on the other side of what is officially represented as politics, in zones marked as private, personal, or experiential.

10 Deborah Gould opens her discussion of AIDS activism emotion and politics with this text, which Wojnarowicz read at the Drawing Center in 1992 in a benefit for Needle Exchange, recorded for and broadcast on DIVA TV (*Moving Politics*, 1–2).

11 Wojnarowicz, "Postcards from America: X Rays from Hell," in *Close to the Knives*, 114.

12 The photograph of his mouth sewn shut is from *Silence=Death* (1990) and appeared on the cover of *High Performance* (Fall 1990); the photograph of his face buried in dirt, *Untitled* (1990, 1993), was staged on a road trip with Marion Scemama, who took the picture for Wojnarowicz (it was printed posthumously);

Untitled (Falling Buffalo) (1988–89) was taken at the Museum of Natural History in New York and is a series of photographic studies of displays there, depicting especially Native American culture. In this instance, that photograph is of a diorama in which Indian hunters on horseback drive a herd of American Buffalo over a cliff. *Silence=Death* is discussed briefly by Kathy O'Dell in *Contract with the Skin*, 78. Carr describes the production of *Untitled (Falling Buffalo)* and the collaboration with Scemama in *Fire in the Belly*, 404–6 and 542–44, respectively.

13 José Muñoz's *Cruising Utopia* addresses this directly, especially in his chapter "Ghosts of Public Sex: Utopian Longings, Queer Memories." For the concern with futurity in queer studies, see also the exchange between Muñoz, Robert L. Caserio, Tim Dean, Lee Edelman, and Judith Halberstam in "The Antisocial Thesis in Queer Theory" and Elizabeth Freeman's excellent analysis of the poetics of time and timing for queer artists and critics in *Time Binds*.

14 Smith continues this line of thought by observing that he explored the "cultivation of one's life as a practice" and names his lawsuit against the American Family Association as perhaps his greatest work of art. Lotringer, "Kiki Smith," 84. Robert Semper makes a similar point regarding the importance of experience as a critical category in Wojnarowicz's work when he observes that the artist explores "the invented quality of reality and the fact that convention disguises the mechanism of its production" ("Seeing Death," 33). Semper also describes a sensual turn in Wojnarowicz's work, in which vision and touch operate as vehicles for intimacy and as "excavations" of histories of the self and the body. That turn can't be fully appreciated, Semper observes, without understanding the impact of the artist's diagnosis, illness, and death on his practice; within a community that was structured by illness, death, grief, and activism, the anticipation of death yields a cyclical poetics of compression. Thus *ITSOFOMO* (In the Shadow of Forward Motion), the title of the multimedia performance collaboration with Ben Neill. See also Rizk, "Constructing Histories."

15 Cvetkovich, *An Archive of Feelings*.

16 In "The Weather in Proust," Eve Kosofsky Sedgwick explores the entanglement of desire and need in that author's writing. Looking for critical language attuned to the way that some desires can and must be met as the requirement for living, Sedgwick turns to the work of the Hungarian psychoanalyst Michael Balint. Balint posits "malignant" and "benign" forms of transference (our dynamic investment and attachment to people and things as necessary for happiness as well as a sense of self). For Balint, the Oedipal desire (always configured around what one wants but can't have) is "malignant" because it is insatiable. It is by definition frustrated and expanding. To this he opposes a "benign" set of desires that "presupposes an environment that accepts and consents to sustain and carry the patient like the earth or the water sustains and carries a man who entrusts his weight to them. In contrast to ordinary objects, especially to ordinary human objects, no action is expected from these primary objects or substances; yet they must be there and must—tacitly or explicitly—consent to be used, otherwise

the patient cannot achieve any change: without water it is impossible to swim, without earth impossible to move on" (11). The failure of the environment to support the subject induces panic: to not be cared for, in this most basic way, makes life impossible. We do not notice the air we breathe until we can't breathe, at which point nothing else matters. Sedgwick uses Balint's writing to explore the "Proustian reality"—the environment of the Proustian novel and its otherwise nearly unaccountable preoccupation with the weather. We might also use that distinction regarding the malignant and benign to name the very different values that orient Wojnarowicz's work, as well as that of other artists whose work taps into experiences with living and dying.

17 Text often appears in art works as a negation of the privilege assigned to visual knowledge and pleasure. It is not unusual to see words used in contemporary art, but Wojnarowicz's use of text is atypical. In an interesting parallel to the antiliterary turn in art criticism, artists of the late 1960s and 1970s dragged words into their work; these words were treated as things, as material objects. In such work, the literary function of writing is minimized, often quite radically. Liz Kotz considers, for example, Robert Smithson's description of an exhibition at the Dwan Gallery in Los Angeles in 1967. The show "consist[ed] of Language to be Looked at and/or Things to be Read." Kotz's work on the use of text in contemporary art helps make sense of the difficulty of Wojnarowicz's use of writing. She charts shifting approaches to the use of text in contemporary art in *Words to Be Looked At*. In much of that work, however, the expressive function of language is severely restricted as artists attempt to disarticulate language and meaning. At the very least, artists working in that vein sought to disassociate the words in their work from authorial intention. Kotz cites Douglas Huebler, for example, who asserted that his intention was "to empty [his work], to empty it of history, to empty it of mythology, to empty it of literature and allow it to speak of being empty" (254). This way of thinking about language and the visual echoes the general antipathy toward the literary in post-1960s art criticism. Wojnarowicz's text is meant to be read, on the other hand, and also to be looked *through*. The exhibit was one of four language art exhibits at the gallery, in which, Kotz writes, "words . . . were treated in some sense like objects—to be looked at, and also to be accumulated, built up, moved around, and broken apart" (2). Kotz's book charts visual experimentation with language throughout the 1960s, with especially language's indexical functions: to catalogue, number, graph, and plot. Suppressed in the work she analyzes is the narrative function of language—its novelistic and literary dimensions. In Ed Ruscha's paintings, for example, words hang in emptied landscapes. Torn from context, they are things that never quite manage to shake meaning.

18 Those events are recorded in *Close to the Knives*. The text covering *Untitled (Hujar Dead)* concludes the essay "Do Not Doubt the Dangerousness of the 12-Inch Politician."

19 Crimp, "Mourning and Militancy," *Melancholia and Moralism*, 133.

20 Ibid., 137.

21 Wojnarowicz, "Postcards from America," 122.

22 For more on the political funeral, see discussion of the display of Emmett Till's brutalized body at a public wake in Alexander, "'Can You Be BLACK and Look at This?'" and Harold and DeLuca, "Behold the Corpse."

23 Some of the artists who took on this subject did so very differently from each other. See, for example, Gregg Bordowitz, *Fast Trip / Long Drop*; General Idea's multimedia project *Imagevirus*; Derek Jarman's *Blue*; Isaac Julien's *Looking for Langston*; and much of Felix Gonzalez-Torres's work, such as his billboard of an empty bed, *Untitled* (1991), and his installation of a pile of candy that viewers were invited to take with them, *Untitled (Portrait of Ross in LA)* (1991). The latter installation starts at the weight of his dying lover (175 pounds) and slowly erodes to nothing.

24 Crimp, "Portraits of People with AIDS," *Melancholia and Moralism*, 86.

25 A range of scholars have addressed the shape and character of art produced within the AIDS crisis. A few of the titles that inform my writing here are Edelman, *Homographesis*, especially part II, "Equations, Identities, and 'AIDS,'"; Bordowitz, *The AIDS Crisis Is Ridiculous and Other Writings* and *General Idea*; Crimp, *Melancholia and Moralism*; White, *Loss within Loss*; Griffin, *Representations of HIV and AIDS*; Juhasz, *AIDS TV*; Rocchi, "Writing As I Lay Dying."

26 Barthes, *Camera Lucida*, 92. For a cogent and accessible overview of criticism on this subject, see Nicholas Mirzoeff's chapter "Photography and Death" in *Introduction to Visual Culture*, 119–26.

27 Sontag, introduction, n.p. Wojnarowicz was interested in the links between photography and death (more on this later), but he was also compelled by the historical association of the use of photography in documenting people to represent them as already gone. The Museum of Natural History in New York was a treasure trove of found images that he used in a range of works. Slides and postcards sold by the museum made their way into his collages, and his signature image of Buffalo tumbling over a cliff was a snapshot of one of the museum's dioramic re-creations of "extinct" tribal cultures.

28 Carr, "Portrait in Twenty-Three Rounds," 79. Carr offers a more detailed account of their initial meetings in *Fire in the Belly*, 170–73.

29 Thek was briefly infamous in the art world for *Tomb* (1967), a spooky installation centered on an effigy of himself, in which he was presented as a corpse dressed in a pink suit. *Tomb* toured though the late 1960s and early 1970s and is sometimes referred to as "Dead Hippie." See Falckenberg, *Paul Thek*; Sussman and Zelevansky, *Paul Thek*.

30 He also looks through a book of St. Sebastian images. Other segments in the film include the laying out of Hujar's panel within the AIDS Quilt (Central Park, 1988), film of Hujar making sweeping motions with his hands toward the camera, and a shot of Hujar lying on his back on the ground. He made repeated notes in his journals about how this film might be composed; some of those notes anticipate this film and *ITSOFOMO*.

31 Sussman, "Photography in Life and Death," 29.

32 As Drew Gilpin Faust notes, "As late as the first decade of the twentieth-century, as few as fifteen percent of people died away from home" (*This Republic of Suffering*, 9).

33 Nudelman, *John Brown's Body*, 104, 105, 131. Nudelman's writing also suggests a new way of approaching the affective intensity of *The Gross Clinic*: the vulnerability of the body under the knife is inextricably tied to *its* anonymity within the framework of the painting and within the structure of relationships that the painting describes. The cringing woman, so overcome by feeling that she can't look at what is happening to that body to which she is no doubt attached, so out of place in the painting in terms of mood and scale, begins to make some sense: to the men in this image, that body is a thing. To the lone woman in the surgical theater, that body is a person, it is "hers." To look at the body within Eakins's frame is to acquiesce to a depersonalizing, desensitizing visual logic: to look at the body in that painting is to cut into it. In painting that difference and in gendering that difference, Eakins draws a line between warring positions in late nineteenth-century affective culture: the world of reason, emotional restraint, and distance and the world of feeling, attachment, and sentimental proximity.

34 Faust, *This Republic of Suffering*, 10.

35 This resonates with Sontag's writing on trauma and photographs of violence, insofar as the trauma captured by the image is extended in the viewer's dismay at being helpless to prevent it. See Sontag, *Regarding the Pain of Others*.

36 Sontag, introduction.

37 Wojnarowicz would repeat this tradition in his own fascination with folkloric death culture in Mexico.

38 Bataille, *Eroticism*, 57.

39 Haggerty, "Love and Loss," 387.

40 When asked at a public lecture at Princeton University in 2010 why his work seemed so much less "angry" than other work about AIDS, Bronson speculated that this might reflect the Canadian's access to decent health care. Taking care of each other did not always involve the struggle for basic health care that it does for so many people in the United States.

41 Cited in Katz and Ward, *Hide/Seek*, 228.

42 Smithsonian's secretary G. Wayne Clough implicitly supported the Catholic League's description of *A Fire in My Belly* as "hate speech" when he pulled the video from the exhibit. See http://www.hideseek.org/print-news for a comprehensive archive of press regarding this controversy.

43 Molly McGarry and Fred Wasserman's *Becoming Visible* is *Hide/Seek*'s closest precedent.

44 The video displayed at the National Portrait Gallery was a four-minute excerpt from an unfinished film in Wojnarowicz's archive. The Fales Collection houses a thirteen-minute film with the title *A Fire in My Belly (Film in Progress)* as well as seven minutes of unfinished footage found after the artist's death, associated

with the same work. There are several excerpts from this sequence of footage in circulation. Wojnarowicz edited a segment of this film for Rosa von Praunheim's *Silence=Death*, which was scored with Diamanda Galás's *Plague Mass*. The segment displayed at the National Portrait Gallery was edited by Jonathan Katz and Bart Everly, a Fales archivist. This included an audio recording of an ACT-UP march, also in Wojnarowicz's archive. The resultant video is best approached as archival material, edited by the curators at the National Portrait Gallery with the support of the archivists at the Fales Collection at New York University and with the approval of PPOW, which administers Wojnarowicz's estate.

45 Diamanda Galás addresses the use of *Plague Mass* in one of the iterations of *A Fire in My Belly* in "Diamanda Galás Responds to the Smithsonian's Removal of David Wojnarowicz's Work," *Washington City Paper*, 3 December 2010. Holland Cotter offers a very detailed description of *Fire in My Belly (A Work in Progress)* in "As Ants Crawl over Crucifix, Dead Artist Is Assailed Again," *New York Times*, 10 December 2010.

46 Holland Cotter, "Sexuality in Modernism: The (Partial) History," *New York Times*, 10 December 2010.

47 These issues were discussed by David C. Ward and Jonathan Katz at a symposium at the National Portrait Gallery on 28 January 2010.

48 Romberger, "Wojnarowicz's Apostasy." Carr describes the versions archived in his papers as well as versions of *A Fire in My Belly* as recalled by friends and collaborators in *Fire in the Belly*, 357–60.

49 Several writers have made similar observations. See, for example, Kreiter, "Editing Wojnarowicz's *A Fire in My Belly* Distracts from Larger Themes."

50 AA Bronson, email to director of the National Portrait Gallery (Martin Sullivan), published on his Facebook page, and also in Blake Gopnik, "Artist Asks to Withdraw Work from 'Hide/Seek' Exhibit to Protest Video Removal," *Washington Post* blog *ArtsPost*, 16 December 2010. Also cited in Paddy Johnson, "AA Bronson Requests the Smithsonian Remove His Work from Hide/Seek," *Art Fag City*, 16 December 2010, http://artfagcity.com.

51 McGarry, *Ghosts of Futures Past*, 7, 176.

52 For AA Bronson's writing on surviving General Idea, see his *Negative Thoughts*; for more on General Idea's work around AIDS, see Bordowitz, *General Idea*. My repetition of the phrase *still here* in the conclusion of this book is an oblique gesture to the debates surrounding *Still/Here* (1994), a Bill T. Jones / Arnie Zane Dance Company performance that was developed in "survival workshops" with people who had lived through life-threatening illness. The work was famously attacked by the *New Yorker*'s dance critic Arlene Croce, who dismissed it as "victim art."

53 Unpublished poem reproduced with permission from the Estate of David Wojnarowicz. See the David Wojnarowicz Papers, Series 3, Subseries A, Box 5, Folder 137, Fales Library, New York University. Exact date unknown (ca. late 1980s).

54 Joan Scott observes, "It is not individuals who have experience but subjects who are constituted through experience" ("The Evidence of Experience," 780). She describes a critically engaged model of experience as taking the following shape: "Experience in this definition then becomes not the origin of our explanation, not the authoritative (because seen or felt) evidence that grounds what is known, but rather that which we seek to explain, that about which knowledge is produced. To think about experience in this way is to historicize it as well as to historicize the identities it produces. . . . It is a historicizing that implies critical scrutiny of all explanatory categories usually taken for granted, including the category of 'experience'" (780). In an otherwise valuable essay, Scott misreads Samuel Delany's *The Motion of Light in Water* to suggest that Delany produces in that memoir a naïve model for both experience and identification. Gavin Butt puts Delany's writing to very different use and recovers from that same text a critical methodology that is very close to that Scott calls for. See Butt, "Happenings in History."

BIBLIOGRAPHY

Adams, Henry. *Eakins Revealed: The Secret Life of an American Artist*. New York: Oxford University Press, 2006.

Adler, Amy M. "Post-modern Art and the Death of Obscenity Law." *Yale Law Journal* 99.6 (1990), 1359–78.

Adorno, Theodor. *Minima Moralia*. Trans. E. F. N. Jephcott. London: Verso, 1978.

Ahmed, Sarah. *The Cultural Politics of Emotion*. New York: Routledge, 2004.

———. *The Promise of Happiness*. Durham: Duke University Press, 2010.

Alexander, Elizabeth. "'Can You Be BLACK and Look at This?' Reading the Rodney King Video(s)." *Black Male: Representations of Masculinity in Contemporary American Art*. Ed. Thelma Golden. New York: Whitney Museum of Art, 1994. 91–110.

Allison, Terry L., and Renée R. Curry. "'All Anger and Understanding': Kureishi, Culture, and Contemporary Constrictions of Rage." *States of Rage: Emotional Eruption, Violence, and Social Change*. Ed. Renée Curry. New York: New York University Press, 1996. 146–66.

Alvaros, Lisa. "Hindsight and the Abortion Experience: What Abortion Means to Women Years Later." *Gender Issues* 17.2 (1999), 35–57.

Athey, Ron. "Deliverance." *Acting on AIDS: Sex, Drugs and Politics*. Ed. Joshua Oppenheimer and Helena Reckitt. New York: Serpent's Tail, 1997. 430–44.

Attali, Jacques. *Noise: The Political Economy of Music*. Trans. Brian Massumi. Minneapolis: University of Minnesota Press, 1985.

Baldwin, James. "Everybody's Protest Novel." *Uncle Tom's Cabin*. By Harriet Beecher Stowe. Ed. Elizabeth Ammons. New York: Norton, 1993. 475–501.

Barthes, Roland. *Camera Lucida: Reflections on Photography*. Trans. Richard Howard. New York: Hill and Wang, 1982.

———. *The Pleasure of the Text*. Trans. Richard Miller. New York: Hill and Wang, 1975.

Bataille, Georges. *Eroticism: Death and Sensuality*. Trans. Mary Dalwood. San Francisco: City Lights, 1986.

Beatty, Carrie Lambert. "Twelve Miles: Boundaries of the New Art / Activism." *Signs: Journal of Women in Culture and Society* 33.2 (2008), 309–27.

Benjamin, Walter. "Theses on the Philosophy of History." *Illuminations: Essays and Reflections*. Ed. Hannah Arendt. New York: Schocken, 1968. 253–64.

Berlant, Lauren. *The Female Complaint: The Unfinished Business of Sentimentality in American Culture*. Durham: Duke University Press, 2008.

———. *The Queen of America Goes to Washington City: Essays on Sex and Citizenship*. Durham: Duke University Press, 1997.

Bernier, Celeste-Marie. *African American Visual Arts: From Slavery to the Present*. Chapel Hill: University of North Carolina Press, 2009.

Bishop, Claire. *Artificial Hells: Participatory Art and the Politics of Spectatorship*. London: Verso, 2012.

———. "Public Opinion." *Artforum.com*, 29 October 2009.

———."The Social Turn: Collaboration and Its Discontents." *Artforum*, February 2006, 179–85.

Blocker, Jane. "Failures of Self-Seeing: James Luna Remembers Dino." *Performance Art Journal* 67 (2001), 18–32.

———. *What the Body Cost: Desire, History and Performance*. Minneapolis: University of Minnesota Press, 2004.

Bordowitz, Gregg. *The AIDS Crisis Is Ridiculous and Other Writings (1986–2003)*. Ed. James Meyer. Cambridge: MIT Press, 2006.

———. *General Idea: Imagevirus*. London: Afterall Books, 2010.

Bourriaud, Nicholas. *Relational Aesthetics*. Dijon: Les presses du Réelles, 2002.

Bronson, A. A. "AIDS and Art." Public lecture. Princeton University, 2010.

———. *Negative Thoughts*. Chicago: Museum of Contemporary Art, 2001.

Brookman, Philip. "The Politics of Hope: Sites and Sounds of Memory." *Sites of Recollection: Four Altars and a Rap Opera*. Ed. Julia Barnes Mandle and Deborah Rothschild. Williamstown, Mass.: Williams College Museum of Art, 1992. 14–42.

Burnham, Linda Frye. "'High Performances,' Performance Art, and Me." *TDR: Theater and Drama Review* 30.1 (1986), 15–51.

Butler, Judith. "The Force of Fantasy: Feminism, Mapplethorpe, and Discursive Excess." *Differences: A Journal of Feminist Cultural Studies* 2.2 (1990), 105–25.

———. *Precarious Life: The Powers of Mourning and Violence*. New York: Verso, 2004.

Butt, Gavin. *Between You and Me: Queer Disclosures in the New York Art World, 1948–1963*. Durham: Duke University Press, 2005.

———. "Happenings in History, or, The Epistemology of the Memoir." *Oxford Art Journal* 24.2 (2001), 113–26.

———. "How I Died for Kiki and Herb." *The Art of Queering Art*. Ed. Henry Rogers. Birmingham, U.K.: ARTicle, 2007. 85–94.

———. "Introduction: The Paradoxes of Criticism." *After Criticism: New Responses to Art and Performance*. Ed. Gavin Butt. London: Blackwell, 2005. 1–20.

Cairns, Jon. "Ambivalent Intimacies: Performance and Domestic Photography in the Work of Adrian Howells." *Contemporary Theater Review* 22.3 (2012), 355–71.

Carr, Cynthia. *Fire in the Belly: The Life and Times of David Wojnarowicz*. New York: Bloomsbury, 2012.

———. *On Edge: Performance at the End of the Twentieth Century*. Middletown, Conn.: Wesleyan University Press, 2008.

———. "Portrait in Twenty-Three Rounds." *Fever: The Art of David Wojnarowicz*. Ed. Dan Cameron. New York: The New Museum, 1999. 68–89.

Cheng, Anne. *The Melancholy of Race: Psychoanalysis, Assimilation, and Hidden Grief*. Oxford: Oxford University Press, 2001.

Collins, Kathleen. "The Scourged Black." *The History of Photography* 9.1 (1989), 43–45.

Collins, Lisa Gail. *The Art of History: African American Women Artists Engage the Past*. New Brunswick, N.J.: Rutgers University Press, 2002.

Costello, Diarmuid, and Dominic Willsdon. Introduction. *The Life and Death of Images: Ethics and Aesthetics*. Ed. Diarmuid Costello and Dominic Willsdon. London: Tate Modern, 2008. 7–36.

Crary, Jonathan. *Techniques of the Observer: On Vision and Modernity in the 19th Century*. Cambridge: MIT Press, 1992.

Crimp, Douglas. *AIDS Demo Graphics*. Seattle: Bay Press, 1990.

———. "Getting the Warhol We Deserve." *Social Text* 17.2 (1999), 49–66.

———. *Melancholia and Moralism: Essays on AIDS and Queer Politics*. Cambridge: MIT Press, 2002.

Cvetkovich, Ann. *An Archive of Feelings: Trauma, Sexuality, and Lesbian Public Cultures*. Durham: Duke University Press, 2003.

Davis, Angela. *Blues Legacies and Black Feminism: Gertrude "Ma" Rainey, Bessie Smith, and Billie Holiday*. New York: Vintage, 1999.

Deitcher, David. "Ideas and Emotion." *Artforum* 28.9 (1989), 122–27.

Deutschler, Penelope. "The Inversion of Exceptionality: Foucault, Agamben and 'Reproductive Rights.'" *South Atlantic Quarterly* 107.1 (2008), 55–70.

Devereux, Mary. "Oppressive Texts, Resisting Readers and the Gendered Spectator: The New Aesthetics." *Journal of Aesthetics and Culture* 48.4 (1990), 334–47.

Doyle, Jennifer. *Sex Objects: Art and the Dialectics of Desire*. Minneapolis: University of Minnesota Press, 2006.

———. "Sex, Scandal, and Thomas Eakins's *Gross Clinic*." *Representations* 68.1 (1999), 1–33.

Du Bois, W. E. B. *Black Reconstruction in America, 1860–1880*. New York: Free Press, 1999.

———. "Criteria of Negro Art." *The Crisis* 32 (1926), 290–97.

Durant, Mary Alice. "Sustained Rage." *New Art Examiner,* September 1990, 35–38.

Edelman, Lee. *Homographesis: Essays in Gay Literary and Cultural Theory.* New York: Routledge, 1994.

Elkins, James. "On the Absence of Judgment in Art Criticism." *The State of Art Criticism.* Ed. James Elkins and Michael Newman. New York: Routledge, 2008. 71–96.

———. *Pictures and Tears: A History of People Who Have Cried in Front of Paintings.* New York: Routledge, 2001.

Eng, David L., and David Kazanjian, eds. *Loss: The Politics of Mourning.* Berkeley: University of California Press, 2002.

English, Darby. *How to See a Work of Art in Total Darkness.* Cambridge: MIT Press, 2007.

Falckenberg, Harald. *Paul Thek: Artist's Artist.* Cambridge: MIT Press, 2009.

Faust, Drew Gilpin. *This Republic of Suffering: Death and the American Civil War.* New York: Alfred A. Knopf, 2008.

Ferguson, Roderick A. "A Special Place within the Order of Knowledge: The Art of Kara Walker and the Conventions of African American History." *American Quarterly* 61.1 (2009), 185–92.

Finch, Charlie. "Mission Aborted." *Artnet,* 18 May 2008. Online.

Fish, Stanley. *Is There a Text in This Class? The Authority of Interpretive Communities.* Cambridge: Harvard University Press, 1980.

Foster, Hal. *The Return of the Real: The Avant-Garde at the Turn of the Century.* Cambridge: MIT Press, 1996.

Freeman, Elizabeth. *Time Binds: Queer Temporalities, Queer Histories.* Durham: Duke University Press, 2010.

———. *Wedding Complex: Forms of Belonging in Modern American Culture.* Durham: Duke University Press, 2002.

Fried, Michael. *Realism, Writing, and Disfiguration: On Thomas Eakins and Stephen Crane.* Chicago: University of Chicago Press, 1987.

Fusco, Coco. "Captain Shit and Other Allegories of Black Stardom: The Work of Chris Ofili." *The Bodies That Were Not Ours and Other Writings.* New York: Routledge, 2001. 37–42.

Gamboa, Harry. *Urban Exile: The Collected Writings of Harry Gamboa.* Ed. Chon Noriega. Minneapolis: University of Minnesota Press, 1998.

Golden, Thelma. "Some Thoughts on Carrie Mae Weems." *Carrie Mae Weems: Recent Work, 1992–1998.* By Carrie Mae Weems. New York: George Braziller / Everson Museum of Art, 1998. 29–34.

Gómez-Peña, Guillermo. "Disclaimer." *Drama Review* 50.1 (2006), 149–58.

González, Jennifer. *Subject to Display: Reframing Race in Contemporary Installation Art.* Cambridge: MIT Press, 2008.

Gould, Deborah. *Moving Politics: Emotion and ACT UP's Fight against AIDS.* Chicago: University of Chicago Press, 2009.

Greenberg, Clement. *The Collected Essays and Criticism: Perceptions and Judgments, 1939–1944*. Chicago: University of Chicago Press, 1988.

Griffin, Gabrielle. *Representations of HIV and AIDS: Visibility Blues*. Manchester, U.K.: University of Manchester Press, 2001.

Haggerty, George. "Love and Loss: An Elegy." *GLQ: A Journal of Lesbian and Gay Studies* 10.3 (2004), 385–405.

Halberstam, Judith. *Female Masculinity*. Durham: Duke University Press, 1998.

Hall, Stuart. "The Whites of Their Eyes: Racist Ideologies and the Media." *Silver Linings: Some Strategies for the Eighties*. Ed. George Bridges and Rosalind Brunt. London: Lawrence and Wishart, 1981. 28–51.

Hardt, Michael, and Antonio Negri. *Multitude: War and Democracy in the Age of Empire*. New York: Penguin, 2004.

Harold, Christine, and Kevin Michael DeLuca. "Behold the Corpse: Violent Images and the Case of Emmett Till." *Rhetoric and Public Affairs* 8.2 (2005), 263–86.

Hartouni, Valerie. "Fetal Exposure: Abortion Politics and Optics of Allusion." *The Visible Woman: Imaging Technologies, Gender and Science*. Ed. Paula A. Treichler, Lisa Cartwright, and Constance Penley. New York: New York University Press, 1998. 198–216.

Hendricks, Gordon. *The Life and Work of Thomas Eakins*. New York: Grossman, 1974.

Hochschild, Arlie. *The Managed Heart: Commercialization of Human Feeling*. Berkeley: University of California Press, 1983.

Jameson, Fredric. *The Political Unconscious: Narrative as Socially Symbolic Act*. Ithaca: Cornell University Press, 1981.

Johnson, Dominic. "*Perverse Martyrologies:* An Interview with Ron Athey." *Contemporary Theatre Review* 18.4 (2008), 503–13.

———. "Ron Athey's Visions of Excess: Performance after Georges Bataille." *Papers of Surrealism* 8 (2010), 1–12. Online.

Jones, Amelia. "Art History / Art Criticism: Performing Meaning." *Performing the Body / Performing the Text*. Ed. Amelia Jones and Andrew Stephenson. New York: Routledge, 1999. 36–51.

———. *Irrational Modernism: A Neurasthenic History of New York Dada*. Cambridge: MIT Press, 2004.

———. *Postmodernism and the En-Gendering of Marcel Duchamp*. Cambridge: Cambridge University Press, 1995.

———. "Rupture." *Parachute* 123 (2006), 15–37.

———. *Self/Image: Technology, Representation and the Contemporary Subject*. New York: Routledge, 2006.

Juhasz, Alexandra. *AIDS TV: Identity, Community, and Alternative Video*. Durham: Duke University Press, 1995.

Kastner, Jeffrey. "Gun Shy." *Artforum*, 20 January 2005. Online.

Katz, Jonathan D., and David C. Ward. *Hide/Seek: Difference and Desire in American Portraiture*. Washington, DC: Smithsonian, 2010.

Kester, Grant. "Another Turn." *Artforum* 44.9 (2006), 22.

———. *Conversation Pieces: Community and Communication in Modern Art*. Berkeley: University of California Press, 2004.

Koch, Cynthia. "The Contest for American Culture: A Leadership Case Study on the NEA and NEH Funding Crisis." *Public Talk: The Online Journal of Discourse Leadership*. University of Pennsylvania, 1998.

Kotz, Liz. *Words to Be Looked At: Language in 1960s Art*. Cambridge: MIT Press, 2007.

Kreiter, Rachel P. "Editing Wojnarowicz's *A Fire in My Belly* Distracts from Larger Themes." *BurnAway*, 3 March 2011. Online.

Kristeva, Julia. *Black Sun: Depression and Melancholia*. New York: Columbia University Press, 1989.

Lazare, Gilles. "An Endless Insurrection: Gordon Matta-Clark, Ron Athey and Sacred Economy." *COIL* 9–10 (2000). Online.

Le Doeuff, Michèle. *Hipparchia's Choice: An Essay Concerning Women, Philosophy, Etc.* Trans. Trista Selous. New York: Columbia University Press, 2007.

Liesegang, Tom. "Perforating Saint." Interview with Ron Athey. *Fad Magazine* 30 (1993), 48–49.

Lippard, Lucy. "Out of the Safety Zone." *Art in America* 78 (1990), 130–39. Online.

Lotringer, Sylvère. "Ben Neill." Interview with Ben Neill. *David Wojnarowicz: A Definitive History of Five or Six Years on the Lower East Side*. Ed. Giancarlo Ambrosino. New York: Semiotext(e), 2007. 112–15.

———. "Kiki Smith." Interview with Kiki Smith. *David Wojnarowicz: A Definitive History of Five or Six Years on the Lower East Side*. Ed. Giancarlo Ambrosino. New York: Semiotext(e), 2007. 83–88.

Ludlow, Jeannie. "The Things We Cannot Say: Witnessing the Trauma-tization of Abortion in the United States." *WSQ: Women's Studies Quarterly* 36.1–2 (2008), 28–41.

Lunch, Lydia. *Will Work for Drugs*. New York: Akashic, 2009.

Lutz, Tom. *Crying: The Natural and Cultural History of Tears*. New York: W. W. Norton, 1999.

Mandle, Julia Barnes, and Deborah Rothschild, eds. *Sites of Recollection: Four Altars and a Rap Opera*. Williamstown, Mass.: Williams College Museum of Art, 1992.

Mavor, Carol. *Reading Boyishly: Roland Barthes, J. M. Barrie, Jacques Henri Lartigue, Marcel Proust, and D. W. Winnicott*. Durham: Duke University Press, 2008.

McClarey, Susan. "The Politics of Silence and Sound." *Noise: The Political Economy of Music*. By Jacques Attali. Minneapolis: University of Minnesota Press, 1985. 149–58.

McGarry, Molly. *Ghosts of Futures Past: Spiritualism and the Cultural Politics of Nineteenth-Century America*. Berkeley: University of California Press, 2008.

McGarry, Molly, and Fred Wasserman. *Becoming Visible: An Illustrated History of Lesbian and Gay Life in Twentieth-Century America*. New York: Penguin Studio, 1998.

McGrath, John Edward. "Trusting in Rubber: Performing Boundaries during the AIDS Epidemic." *Drama Review* 39.2 (1995), 21–38.

McHugh, Kathleen Anne. "Profane Illuminations: History and Collaboration in James Luna and Isaac Artenstein's *The History of the Luiseño People.*" *Biography* 31.3 (2008), 429–60.

Mercer, Kobena. "Tropes of the Grotesque in the Black Avant-Garde." *Pop Art and Vernacular Cultures.* Ed. Kobena Mercer. London: Iniva, 2008. 136–59.

Merck, Mandy. *In Your Face: Nine Sexual Studies.* New York: New York University Press, 2000.

Meyer, Richard. "The Jesse Helms Theory of Art." *October* 104 (2003), 131–48.

———. *Outlaw Representation: Censorship and Homosexuality in Twentieth-Century American Art.* New York: Oxford University Press, 2002.

Miglietti, Francesca Alfano. *Extreme Bodies: The Use of Abuse of the Body in Art.* Milan: Slira, 2003.

Mirzeoff, Nicholas. *Introduction to Visual Culture.* New York: Routledge, 2009.

Mitchell, W. J. T. *What Do Pictures Want? The Lives and Loves of Images.* Chicago: University of Chicago Press, 2006.

Montano, Linda M. *Letters from Linda M. Montano.* Ed. Jennie Klein. New York: Routledge, 2005.

Morrison, Toni. *Playing in the Dark: Whiteness and the Literary Imagination.* New York: Vintage, 1993.

Moten, Fred. "Black Mo'nin'." *Loss: The Politics of Mourning.* Ed. David L. Eng and David Kazanjian. Berkeley: University of California Press, 2002. 59–76.

Mulvey, Laura. "Visual Pleasure and Narrative Cinema." *Screen* 16.3 (1975), 6–18.

Muñoz, José. *Cruising Utopia: The Then and There of Queer Futurity.* New York: New York University Press, 2009.

———. "Feeling Brown, Feeling Down: Latina Affect, the Performativity of Race, and the Depressive Position." *Signs: Journal of Women in Culture and Society* 31.3 (2006), 675–88.

Muñoz, José, Robert L. Caserio, Tim Dean, Lee Edelman, and Judith Halberstam. "The Antisocial Thesis in Queer Theory." *PMLA* 121. 3 (2006), 819–36.

Murray, Derek. "Kehinde Wiley: Splendid Bodies." *NKA: Journal of Contemporary African Art* 21 (2007), 90–101.

Murray, Derek, and Soraya Murray. "Uneasy Bedfellows: Canonical Art Theory and the Politics of Identity." *Art Journal* 65.1 (2003), 22–39.

Nelson, Maggie. *The Art of Cruelty.* New York: W. W. Norton, 2011.

Newman, Amy. *Challenging Art: Artforum 1962–1974.* New York: Soho, 2000.

Noriega, Chon. "The Orphans of Modernism." *Phantom Sightings: Art after the Chicano Movement.* Ed. Rita Gonzalez, Howard N. Fox, and Chon Noriega. Berkeley: University of California Press and LACMA, 2008. 16–45.

Nudelman, Franny. *John Brown's Body: Slavery, Violence, and the Culture of War.* Chapel Hill: University of North Carolina Press, 2004.

Nunley, Vorris. "*Crash*: Rhetorically Wrecking Discourses of Race, Tolerance and White Privilege." *College English* 69.4 (2007), 335–46.

Nyong'o, Tavia. "Brown Punk: Kalup Linzy's Musical Anticipations." *TDR: Theater and Drama Review* 54.3 (2010), 71–86.

———. "Do You Want Queer Theory (or Do You Want the Truth)? Intersections of Punk and Queer in the 1970s." *Radical History Review* 100 (2008), 103–19.

O'Dell, Kathy. *Contract with the Skin: Masochism, Performance Art and the 1970s.* Minneapolis: University of Minnesota Press, 1998.

Opie, Catherine, and Douglas Crimp. "Catherine Opie in Conversation with Douglas Crimp." *The Aesthetics of Risk.* Ed. John C. Welchman. Zurich: JRP|Ringier, 2008. 298–313.

Pagel, David. "Hidden Witness: African Americans in Early Photography. Carrie Mae Weems Reacts to 'Hidden Witness.'" *Frieze* 24 (1995). Online.

Phelan, Peggy, ed. *Live Art in LA: Performance in Southern California, 1970–1983.* New York: Routledge, 2012.

———. *Unmarked: The Politics of Performance.* New York: Routledge, 1993.

Pollock, Griselda. "Dying, Seeing, Feeling: Transforming the Ethical Space of Feminist Aesthetics." *The Life and Death of Images: Ethics and Aesthetics.* Ed. Diarmuid Costello and Dominic Willsdon. London: Tate Modern, 2008. 213–35.

Poovey, Mary. "The Abortion Question and the Death of Man." *Feminists Theorize the Political.* Ed. Judith Butler and Joan Scott. New York: New York University Press, 1998. 239–56.

Radway, Janice. *Reading the Romance: Women, Patriarchy and Popular Literature.* Chapel Hill: University of North Carolina Press, 1984.

Raheja, Michelle. *Reservation Realism: Redfacing, Visual Sovereignty, and Representations of Native Americans in Film.* Lincoln: University of Nebraska Press, 2010.

Rancière, Jacques. *The Emancipated Spectator.* New York: Verso, 2009.

Richards, Mary. "Ron Athey, AIDS and the Politics of Pain." *Bodies, Space and Technology* 3.2 (2003), 163–80. Online.

Rizk, Mysoon. "Constructing Histories: David Wojnarowicz's *Arthur Rimbaud in New York.*" *Passionate Camera: Photography and Bodies of Desire.* Ed. Deborah Bright. New York: Routledge, 1998. 178–94.

Rocchi, Jean-Paul. "Writing As I Lay Dying—AIDS Literature and the Death of Identity." *Études Anglais* 61.3 (2008), 351–59.

Rogers, Molly. *Delia's Tears: Race, Science, and Photography in Nineteenth-Century America.* New Haven: Yale University Press, 2010.

Rogoff, Irit. "Looking Away: Participations in Visual Culture." *After Criticism: New Responses to Art and Performance* Ed. Gavin Butt. London: Blackwell, 2005. 117–34.

Romberger, James. "Wojnarowicz's Apostasy." *The Hooded Utilitarian,* 12 December 2010. Online.

Rose, Mark. "Mothers and Authors: *Johnson v. Calvert* and the New Children of Our Imaginations." *The Visible Woman: Imaging Technologies, Gender and Science.* Ed. Paula A. Treichler, Lisa Cartwright, and Constance Penley. New York: New York University Press, 1998. 217–39.

Ross, Christine. *The Aesthetics of Disengagement: Contemporary Art and Depression.* Minneapolis: University of Minnesota Press, 2006.

Saltz, Jerry. "Not Going Gentle." *Arts Magazine*, February 1989, 14.

Scott, Joan. "The Evidence of Experience." *Critical Inquiry* 17.4 (1991), 773–97.

———. "Fantasy Echo: History and the Construction of Identity." *Critical Inquiry* 27.2 (2001), 284–304.

Scully, James. *Line Break: Poetry as Social Practice*. Willimantic, Conn.: Curbstone, 2005.

Sedgwick, Eve Kosofsky. *Epistemology of the Closet*. Berkeley: University of California Press, 1990.

———. "The Weather in Proust." *The Weather in Proust*. Ed. Jonathan Goldberg. Durham: Duke University Press, 2011. 1–41.

Semper, Robert. "Seeing Death: The Photography of David Wojnarowicz." *The Ends of Performance*. Ed. Peggy Phelan and Jill Lane. New York: New York University Press, 1998. 31–51.

Sharpe, Christina. *Monstrous Intimacies: Making Post-slavery Subjects*. Durham: Duke University Press, 2010.

Shaw, Gwendolyn DuBois. *Seeing the Unspeakable: The Art of Kara Walker*. Durham: Duke University Press, 2005.

Shockley, Gordon, and Connie L. McNeely. "A Seismic Shift in U.S. Federal Arts Policy: A Tale of Organizational Challenge and Controversy in the 1990s." *Journal of Arts Management, Law, and Society* 39.1 (2009), 7–23.

Shvarts, Aliza. "Figuration and Failure, Pedagogy and Performance: Reflections Three Years Later." *Women and Performance: A Journal of Feminist Theory* 21.1 (2011), 155–62.

Sigman, Jill. "Self-Mutilation, Interpretation and Controversial Art." *Midwest Studies in Philosophy* 27 (2003), 88–114.

Sikes, Alan W. "The Performing Genome: Genetics and the Rearticulation of the Human." *Text and Performance Quarterly* 22.3 (2002), 163–80.

Smith, Anna Deavere. *Twilight: Los Angeles, 1992*. New York: Anchor, 1994.

Smith, Cherise. "Fragmented Documents: Works by Lorna Simpson, Carrie Mae Weems, and Willie Robert Middlebrook at the Art Institute of Chicago." *Museum Studies* 24.2 (1999), 244–61.

Sontag, Susan. Introduction. *Portraits in Life and Death*. By Peter Hujar. New York: De Capo, 1976.

———. *Regarding the Pain of Others*. New York: Farrar, Straus and Giroux, 2002.

Spurrier, Jeff. "Blood of a Poet." *Details*, February 1995, 106–11, 140.

Stabile, Carole. "Shooting the Mother: Fetal Photography and the Politics of Disappearance." *The Visible Woman: Imaging Technologies, Gender and Science*. Ed. Paula A. Treichler, Lisa Cartwright, and Constance Penley. New York: New York University Press, 1998. 171–97.

Steger, Larry. Interview with Ron Athey. *Dialogue*, September/October 1994, 8–9.

Steiner, George. "On Difficulty." *Journal of Aesthetics and Art Criticism* 36.3 (1978), 263–78.

Steiner, Wendy. *The Scandal of Pleasure: Art in the Age of Fundamentalism*. Chicago: University of Chicago Press, 1995.

Steinmetz, Julia, Heather Cassils, and Clover Leary. "Behind Enemy Lines: Toxic Titties Infiltrate Vanessa Beecroft." *Signs: Journal of Women in Culture and Society* 31.3 (2006), 753–83.

Stevens, Jacqueline. *Reproducing the State*. Princeton: Princeton University Press, 1999.

Stović, Jovana. "The Art of Marina Abramović: Leaving the Balkans, Entering the Other Side." *Marina Abramović: The Artist Is Present*. Ed. Klaus Biesenbach. New York: Museum of Modern Art, 2010. 23–27.

Suarez, Juan. *Pop Modernism: Noise and the Reinvention of the Everyday*. Chicago: University of Illinois Press, 2007.

Sussman, Elisabeth. "Photography in Life and Death: Paul Thek and Photography." *Paul Thek: Diver. A Retrospective*. Ed. Elisabeth Sussman and Lynn Zelevansky. New York: Whitney Museum of American Art, 2010. 28–41.

Sussman, Elisabeth, and Lynn Zelevansky. *Paul Thek: Diver. A Retrospective*. New York: Whitney Museum of American Art, 2010.

Terada, Rei. *Feeling in Theory: Emotion after the "Death of the Subject."* Cambridge: Harvard University Press, 2001.

Trachtenberg, Alan. *Reading American Photographs: Images as History, Mathew Brady to Walker Evans*. New York: Hill and Wang, 1989.

Tumlir, Jan. "Ron Athey, Bob Flanagan and the Practice of Secular Sacrifice." *X-TRA* 1.4 (1999). Online.

Viego, Antonio. *Dead Subjects: Toward a Politics of Loss in Latino Studies*. Durham: Duke University Press, 2007.

Vincent, John Emil. *Queer Lyrics: Difficulty and Closure in American Poetry*. New York: Palgrave Macmillan, 2002.

Wallis, Brian. "Black Bodies, White Science: Louis Agassiz's Slave Daguerreotypes." *American Art* 9.2 (1995), 38–61.

White, Edmund, ed. *Loss within Loss: Artists in the Age of AIDS*. Madison: University of Wisconsin Press, 2001.

Wiegman, Robyn. "Intimate Publics: Race, Property and Personhood." *American Literature* 74.4 (2002), 859–85.

Williams, Linda. "'Something Else besides a Mother': *Stella Dallas* and the Maternal Melodrama." *Cinema Journal* 24.1 (1984), 2–27.

Willis, Deborah. *Reflections in Black: A History of Black Photographers, 1840 to the Present*. New York: W. W. Norton, 2000.

Wojnarowicz, David. *Close to the Knives: A Memoir of Disintegration*. New York: Vintage, 1991.

Žižek, Slavoj. *The Fright of Real Tears: Krzysztof Kieslowski between Theory and Post-theory*. London: British Film Institute, 2001.

INDEX

ambiguity and uncertainty: abortion
art and, 29–30, 159–60n6; Shvarts's
Untitled and, 29, 160n9
American Family Association, 175n3
*And 22 Million Very Tired and Angry
People* (Weems), 172n33
archaeologies of feeling, 150n6
art criticism: controversy and, xiv–xvi,
13–14; difficulty and, xii; emotion,
place of, 69–73; expressive model
of emotion and, 107–9; focusing on
the work, xvi–xvii, 13, 20–21; limits
of critics, 1; racial identification, literalism, and identity politics, 94–98,
106–7; regulation of affect and, 8;
seriousness and, 71–72; style vs. politics, form vs. content and, 129
Artenstein, Isaac, 99
Artforum, 60, 62, 70–72
Artifact Piece, The, 1987–1990 (Luna), 101
Artificial Hells (Bishop), 167n16
Art in America, 120–21, 121f
Ashes Action (Wojnarowicz), 132
Athey, Ron, 18f, 26f; AIDS and, 56–57,
62, 64–65, 67–68; controversy and,
xiv, 156n26; countersentimental-
ity and, 82–83; Deutch and, 34;
Excerpted Rites of Transformation,
62; *Incorruptible Flesh (A Work in
Progress)* (with Lawrence Steger),
56–57; *Judas Cradle* (with Juliana
Snapper), 60–61; literalism and,
61–65; "Nurse's Penance" (from
Martyrs and Saints), 53–56, 54f, 55f,
164n54; obscenity or controversy
vs. difficulty and, 15–20; Opie's *Ron
Athey/Crown of Thorns wearing
Leigh Bowery's gown (from Martyrs
& Saints)*, 58–59, plate 2; Opie's
*Ron Athey/Suicide Bed (from 4
Scenes)*, plate 3; *Premature Ejacula-
tion* (with Rozz Williams), 157n30;
queer women and, 65–66; reception
history, 60–61; *Self Obliteration*

Solo, 156n27; "St. Sebastian" (from
Martyrs and Saints), 24, 63f, 164n53,
plate 4; *Torture Trilogy*, 57. See also
Four Scenes in a Harsh Life; *Incorruptible Flesh: Dissociative Sparkle*
Attali, Jacques, 22–23
Audience with Adrienne, An (Howells), 6
authenticity: antisentimental rhetoric
and, 80; expressive model of emotion and, 108; tears and, 85–89

Baldwin, James, 79, 110–11, 167–68n22
Balint, Michael, 177–78n16
Balka, Miroslaw, 96
b.a.n.g.lab collective: *Sustenance*, 10;
Transborder Immigrant Tool, xv–xvi,
xvf, 9–11, 23
Barney, Matthew, 61
Barthes, Roland, xiii, 133–34, 138, 151n7
Bataille, Georges, 138–39
Baudelaire, 47
Beatty, Carrie Lambert, 159n1
Beck, Glenn, 9–10
Beecroft, Vanessa, 15, 36, 165n62, 169n37
Behind the Mask (Alcott), 82
Benjamin, Walter, 121–22
Berlant, Lauren, 6, 79, 82, 167–68n22
Bishop, Claire: *Artificial Hells:
Participatory Art and the Politics of
Spectatorship*, 167n16, 168n23; Bour-
riaud and, 93; *Double Agent*, 169n35;
Sierra and, 90; "The Social Turn,"
77–78
Black Reconstruction in America
(Du Bois), 174–75n57
Blocker, Jane, 35, 52, 61, 62, 65, 101
blood: Athey and fear of contamination
by, 19–20, 62; demand for, 167n12;
Franko B's bleeding performances,
73–74, 167n12; sports and, 19
bodies. *See specific works and artists*
Bonheur, Rosa, 149n6
Bourriaud, Nicholas, 89, 93
Bowery, Leigh, 58, plate 2

difficulty: across genres, 7; contingency of, 6–7; emotional and identificatory geometries and, 21; noise and, 22–23; shifting from controversy to, 15–21; Steiner's categories of poetic difficulty, xii–xiv, 96–97, 148–51n6, 163n39; Vincent on, xii

Difunta Correa, La, 10

Diller, Cliff, 54–56, 165n55

disengagement, Ross on, 170n10

Dissociative Sparkle. See Incorruptible Flesh: Dissociative Sparkle

Divinity Fudge (a.k.a. Darryl Carlton), 17, 18f, 24–25, 62

domestic space, 6

Dominguez, Ricardo, xv–xvi, 9–11

Double Agent (Bishop), 169n35

Du Bois, W. E. B., 123, 172n30, 174–75n57

Duchamp, Marcel, 45

Duchess deSade, 27

Eakins, Susan, 44

Eakins, Thomas: character, life, and myth of, 41–42, 44; *The Gross Clinic*, 23, 39–49, 40f, 51–52, 80, 180n33; modernism and, 47–48; *Starting Out after the Rail*, 42

Electronic Disturbance Theater. *See* b.a.n.g.lab collective

Elkins, James, 70–72

emotion and feeling: *affect, feeling,* and *emotion* as terms, xiv, 147n3; archaeologies of feeling, 150n6; in art criticism, place of, 69–73; artist's emotionality, romance with, 69–70; expressive model of emotion, 107–9, 111–12; fetishization of, 111; ideology and, xi; intersubjectivity of, 109–10; mastery over, 41, 46; relational aesthetics, affective labor, and, 89–93. *See also* sentimentality

English, Darby, 95–98, 104

ethnicity. *See* race, ethnicity, and racialization

ethnographer envy, 21

Everly, Bart, 181n44

"Everybody's Protest Novel" (Baldwin), 79

Excerpted Rites of Transformation (Athey), 62

experience, 130, 177n14

expressive model of emotion, 107–9, 111–12

fainting, 27, 158n39

Faust, Drew Gilpin, 137, 180n32

feeling. *See* emotion and feeling

Felix, June 5 1994 (Bronson), 139–40, 142–44, plate 17

feminist theory and art: on abortion, 29, 158–59n1; on affective labor, 91–93; literalism and, 35; on sadistic dynamics of power, 66–67; on spectatorship, 152n7; on "women's work," 169–70n39

Ferguson, Roderick, 122, 174n53

Fila, Stosh "Pigpen," 24–26, 25f, 54–56, 63f, 65–66

"film for Peter Hujar" (unfinished) (Wojnarowicz), 126, 134, 136f

Filth and Fury, The (Temple), 168–69n30

Finley, Karen, 9, 17, 54, 158n1, 166n67

Fire in My Belly (Film in Progress) (Wojnarowicz), 7–8, 140–44, 153n6

Fish, Stanley, 151n7

Fletcher, Harrell, 78

Foster, Hal, 21, 78, 81, 124, 151n7

Four Months, Three Weeks, and Two Days (Mungiu), 159n3

Four Scenes in a Harsh Life (Athey), 18f; conventional narratives and, 7–8; critical defense of, xv, xvi; Minneapolis controversy, 17–19, 61–62, 154n13, 158n36; Sin-a-matic audience, Los Angeles, 26f, 27; "Suicide/Tattoo Salvation," 58

14 Stations in the Life and History of

155n22; Weems's *From Here I Saw and*, 112–24

Radcliffe, Ann, 149–50n6

Radway, Janice, 81, 151n7

Raheja, Michelle, 103

Ramírez-Cancio, Marlène, 10

Rauffenbart, Tom, 133, 175n2

reader: centrality of, xiii, 151n7; Vincent on refusal of closure and, 152n9

Reading the Romance (Radway), 81

realism, 44–45, 46, 163n42

relational aesthetics, 89–93, 97

reproductive body. *See* abortion

Rhythm O (Abramović), 66

Richards, Mary, 49

risk, 19–20, 57–60

risk management, 156n27

Road, The (McCarthy), 7

Rogers, Molly, 114, 172n31

Rogof, Irit, 14

Romberger, James, 141–42

Ron Athey/Crown of Thorns wearing Leigh Bowery's gown (from Martyrs & Saints) (Opie), 58–59, plate 2

Ron Athey/Suicide Bed (from 4 Scenes) (Opie), plate 3

Rosaldo, Renato, 103

Ross, Christine, 170n10

Ruscha, Ed, 178n17

sadomasochism. *See* masochism and sadomasochism

S'Aline's Solution (Mare), 160n6

Sargent, John Singer, 58

Scemama, Marion, 176n4, 176–77n12

Schneeman, Carolee, 166n65

"Scourged Back, The," 117, plate 14

Scully, James, 176n9

Sea Island (Weems), 174n43

Sedgwick, Eve Kosofsky, 80, 168n24, 177–78n16

Self Obliteration Solo (Athey), 156n27

Semper, Robert, 177n14

sentimentality: antisentimentality in art

criticism, 77–81; Baldwin on, 79, 110–11; countersentimental works, 82; Franko B and, 73–77, 82–83; Howells's *Held* and, 6; literary criticism and, 81–82; Sedgwick on, 80, 168n24; tears, theatricality of, 83–89; Temple's *The Filth and Fury* and, 168–69n30

seriousness, 71–72

Serrano, Andreas, 9, 17, 36, 166n67

Sex Pistols, 168–69n30

sexual entitlement and Shvarts's *Untitled*, 32

Sharpe, Christina, 120

Shaw, Gwendolyn DuBois, 155n22

Shockley, Gordon, 154n14

Shvarts, Aliza: *ARTnews* review of, 12–13; Athey compared to, 67; controversy and, xiv, xv; stigmatization of abortion, dependence on, xvi; *Untitled* (2008), 12–13, 23–24, 28–35, 39

Sierra, Santiago, 15, 36, 89–91, 93

Sigman, Jill, 154n13

Silence=Death (von Praunheim), 141, 176–77n12, 181n44

Simpson, O.J., 173n35

Sin-a-matic, Los Angeles, 26f, 27

Smith, Barbara Herrnstein, 151n7

Smith, Cherise, 172n33

Smith, Kiki, 130, 146, 177n14

Smithson, Robert, 178n17

Smithsonian, 140–44

Snapper, Juliana, 60–61

social spaces, 5, 6

"Social Turn, The" (Bishop), 77–78

Sontag, Susan, 134, 138, 180n35

spectatorship: Eakins's *The Gross Clinic* and, 49, 163n42; feminist film theory on, 152n7; Mulvey on politicized spectatorship, 151–52n7; text and privileging of the gaze, 131; the unmarked viewer, 116, 173n42

Spicer, Jack, xiii

173n37, plates 7–14; Getty Museum's *Hidden Witness* and, 112–15; *Sea Island*, 174n43

White, Richard, 27

Williams, Rozz, 157n30

Willsdon, Dominic, 48

Wilson, Fred: *Mining the Museum*, 72; *My Life as a Dog*, 169n37

Wilson, Jackie Napolean, 112–13, 119

Wojnarowicz, David: *Ashes Action*, 132; *Close to the Knives: A Memoir of Disintegration*, 126, 176n4; controversy and, xiv, xv, xvi–xvii, 140–44, 175n3; death from AIDS, 53, 164n54; *Eleventh Hour* television appearance, 126; "film for Peter Hujar" (unfinished), 126, 134, 136f; Finley's *Memento Mori* and, 165n56; *Fire in My Belly (Film in Progress)*, 7–8, 140–44, 153n6; "History keeps me awake some nights," 145; "If I had a dollar," 131; *ITSOFOMO* (with Ben Neill), 126, 141, 176n4, 177n14; *Memories That Smell Like Gasoline*, 54; *Peter Hujar Dreaming/Yokio Mishima; St. Sebastian*, 134, plate 16; "Postcards from America: X Rays from Hell," 132, 175n3; *Untitled* (1990, 1993), 176n12; *Untitled (Falling Buffalo)*, 176–77n12; *Untitled (Peter Hujar)*, 127f, 134, 135f. See also *Untitled (Hujar Dead)*

Woman on the Waves, 158–59n1

Wright, Richard, 79

Yale University, 28–29, 30, 32, 35

Zealy, J. T., 114, 115–17, 119, 173n41, 174n43

Zhang Huan, 36

Zontal, Jorge, 140